A *LIMP*
OF FAITH

A *LIMP* OF FAITH

Memoir of a Disabled Disciple

SUZANNE ROOD

credo
house publishers

For my faithful Lord Jesus
and for my husband, who continually reflects Him.

CONTENTS

Foreword   *1*

1. Diagnosis   *7*

2. Therapy   *16*

3. Miami   *27*

4. Discipline   *33*

5. Barbies and Broken Bones   *38*

6. Lisa   *46*

7. New York   *51*

8. Weeds   *56*

9. Cheryl   *63*

10. Choir   *70*

11. Seattle   *77*

12. Yakking   *83*

13. Spiders and Teeth   *88*

14. Dexterity   *93*

15. Jill   *97*

16. Ligia   *102*

17. Stephen   *106*

18. Runaway Breakfast   *115*

19. Springfield   *122*

20. Duct Tape   *129*

21. Grief   *144*

22. Coffee Shop *150*

23. Rescued by Music *157*

24. Mephibosheth *162*

25. Kevin *171*

26. Taking a Walk *181*

27. Kevin Again *186*

28. Pity Party *197*

29. James *202*

30. The Empathy of Christ *216*

31. Mizzou *219*

32. Crossing the Street *228*

33. Johnston Hall *231*

34. Piano Lessons *236*

35. Fishing *245*

36. December *262*

37. Senior Year *268*

38. Christmas Gifts *271*

39. Job Hunt *277*

40. Groceries *284*

41. Teaching *288*

42. Public Restrooms *293*

43. The Funny Bone *298*

44. Access *310*

45. "You're Pretty Interesting" *314*

46. Team Dinner *321*

47. Arches *333*

48. Falling *337*

49. Second Tee *342*

50. Leading Worship *345*

Afterword *362*

Acknowledgments *364*

FOREWORD

My husband and I recently took a nostalgia trip back to the Seattle area. While he has traveled there occasionally on business, I had not been there in thirty-five years, and I asked him to come back with me. We drove past my old house, where I had lived from the age of ten to the age of sixteen. We paused at the end of the driveway, and I could imagine my dog running out to greet me as I got off the school bus. Then we drove through the neighborhood where I had often walked to my best friend's home. I took a photo of her old house and texted it to her.

On Sunday morning we visited the church where decades ago I had made a decision to truly follow Christ and had sat under the teaching of excellent youth leaders. We walked into the foyer, and I stood in the exact spot where on countless Sundays I had laughed in a circle of teens before the service started. We wandered into the sanctuary, and I looked around at the rows of chairs where I had once worshiped alongside the dearest of friends, none of whom were there any longer.

At the edge of the platform, I expected to see the grand piano, where, encouraged by the minister of music, at the age of fifteen I had played my first offertory, watching the ushers nervously so I could end the song as they came forward. But the grand piano had been replaced by an electric keyboard that complemented the contemporary set-up of guitar, bass, and drums. Still, as the worship team began to play, it was a moving experience to lift my voice in song in that familiar room. I could close my eyes and imagine I was a teenager once again.

The next day my husband and I drove north toward Bellingham and followed Google Maps to a camp where I had spent a week each summer with the youth from our church. We wound our way along the edge of a lake and over a bridge until finally, driving in through the gate, I spied the familiar chapel, the mess hall, and the docks along the shore. There was no one around except a young woman in an office. There were no campers this late August week, so she said we could walk around as we pleased. I was anxious to peek into the chapel where guest speakers had encouraged my faith, and I wanted to stand along the lakeshore where friends and I had paddled out in a canoe on hot, lazy summer afternoons. Then I took my husband's arm as we started down the dirt trail that led to the place I wanted to find most of all.

Each morning at camp we had been given assignments for devotions, and after breakfast in the mess hall we were told to find a spot somewhere by ourselves to read the Bible passage for the day and pray. Some teens would go back to their cabin or sit out on a dock in the sun. But I would walk down a path along the lakeshore, past the campfire where we held evening vespers, past blackberry vines and pine trees, to my special rock. This rock was as big as a car and stuck out into the water from the shore, providing the perfect place for a conversation with God.

I would climb onto it, spread open my Bible, and look out into the water as I prayed.

Now, with my cane in one hand and my husband's elbow in the other, my heart yearned to find that rock. The trail to it was longer than I had remembered, and the tree roots grew thick across the path.

"Are you sure it's this way?" my husband asked when we stopped to take a breath.

"Pretty sure."

And then, after a few more steps, I saw it. A cedar tree hugged one side of it closely (perhaps it had been just a sapling before), and a wild rosebush had spread long canes between the trail and my rock. My husband led me over to the tree, where I braced myself with one hand leaning on the prickly bark while he bent over and gently pulled away the rose branches, clearing an entrance, like Sleeping Beauty's prince.

But we still had a challenge ahead of us: how to get me up onto the rock. From where I stood at the protruding roots of the cedar tree, the rock was at my waist. About halfway up its side was a notch where I had a vague memory of hooking the toe of my sneaker in my younger days. Lifting my knee with the help of my hand, I tried to get my toe into the notch. But the angle was wrong, and I didn't have the strength in my thigh to push myself up. My husband tried lifting me straight up, hugging me around the waist, but there was nothing for me to grab to pull myself over and onto the rock. After several failed attempts, and my constant tripping over tree roots, he finally climbed onto the rock himself and sat facing me. With my back to him, he hooked his arms under mine and pulled me up onto the rock with him. I felt like a rag doll, with legs dangling freely as he dragged me up, the back of my jeans scraping against the stone.

"We did it!" He scrambled around me and climbed down. "Want me to leave you here for a while?"

I sighed. "Yeah, give me a few minutes." I spun around to face the lake, lifting my legs with my hands to help them slide over the top of that great rock.

"Okay, I'll take a little walk and come back in five or ten minutes."

He walked back down the trail, and I looked out at the water. It was a familiar view. The opposite shore was a mass of evergreens, and a bridge spanned a narrow place in the lake about a mile away. It occurred to me that this was the bridge we had crossed on our way in, a realization I had never made as a teenager arriving on a church bus.

I took a deep breath and started to pray. *"Oh, Lord, here I am."*

But that was all I could say. I didn't have any more words. I didn't know what to pray. The tears began to flow. I simply sat on that rock and wept.

> *The Spirit also helps our weakness; for we do not know how to pray as we should, but the Spirit Himself intercedes for us with groanings too deep for words. (Romans 8:26 NASB)*

I thought of that verse and held onto the promise that God understood what I didn't know how to say. He knew the jumbled mixture of emotions that were tangled together in my heart.

I wept all the more.

I looked over at the shore and caught the color of my husband's shirt moving among the trees. He was on his way back to me, and when he reached the rock he climbed up beside me. "Are you okay?"

I nodded, with tears dripping off my chin.

"Are you crying because you're sad, or because you're happy?"

I shook my head. "I don't know."

Was I crying over all of the hardships, all of the painful challenges God had put me through during the past thirty-five years? Or was I crying in gratitude for the way He had provided for me and blessed me over and over again?

I think it was both.

When I had sat on this rock and prayed as a teenager with big dreams and strong muscles, did I have any idea what I was agreeing to by telling God I would live my life for Him?

Before I climbed down from the rock (with my husband's assistance), I wanted to leave something behind. Like a cairn or a monument, I wanted to leave something there to mark this moment in my spiritual journey, much as Samuel had done, as recorded in 1 Samuel 7:12. When the Lord thundered against the Philistines and protected the Israelites, "*Samuel took a stone and set it up between Mizpah and Shen. He named it Ebenezer, saying, 'Thus far the LORD has helped us.'*"

I looked around for something to erect in testament to my visit, but the best I could do was pull some cedar fronds from a branch that was hanging over my head. Still seated, I reached up, tore off four green pieces, and laid them on the rock, arranging them in the shape of a cross. It was a poor excuse for a monument.

In the months since that event, as I have typed out the remaining chapters of my story, I have come to realize that this book is my Ebenezer. It is the story of my journey this far. The joy together with the pain. The sorrow along with the blessings.

Thus far the Lord has helped me.

CHAPTER I

DIAGNOSIS

In April of 1981 I was just about to finish my sophomore year at Bothell High School in the growing suburbs of Seattle, . . . and my life was about to change. That spring and summer three significant, life-altering events occurred. Some would say that one of them brought about the others. Certainly, one of them prepared me for the others. However you want to look at it, I've always thought it curious that these events all transpired within a few months.

I was a skinny, uncoordinated teenager with shoulder-length, mousy brown hair, cut in the style we all wore then: parted in the middle and curled back on the sides. My favorite outfit was bell-bottom jeans and a flannel shirt, finished off by a bandana under the collar, with a knot tied in front so the point came down in the back.

My life basically revolved around the youth group at our church. All of my closest friends were there, including my older sister, Serena. We had pizza parties and crazy skit nights, a teen choir that rehearsed once a week, and our own Sunday night worship services in a large room separate from the adults, who were meeting in the sanctuary. Our youth pastor would strum his guitar as we called out requests for our favorite praise songs.

This could go on and on and cut into his time for teaching us from the Bible. But oh, how he did teach us. We learned the beautiful truths about God's great love for us, His never-ending grace to forgive us of any sin, and His desire to have a real relationship with each of us.

The youth pastor also organized a discipleship program for those of us who wanted to study the Bible more seriously. I eagerly signed up. We were paired up and expected to check in with our discipleship partner once a week to hold each other accountable to study assigned chapters of the Bible and memorize key verses. Standing in the foyer before church on Sunday morning as people milled around us, my friend Jill would quiz me: "Romans 10:9–10?"

I would comply. *"If you confess with your mouth Jesus as Lord, and believe in your heart that He raised Him from the dead, you will be saved . . ."* (NASB).

She stopped me. "That WHO raised him from the dead?"

I corrected myself: *"If you believe in your heart that GOD raised him from the dead . . ."*

"Okay. How about 1 John 1:9?"

"If we confess our sins, He is faithful and righteous to forgive us our sins and to cleanse us from all unrighteousness" (NASB).

Having quoted this to her satisfaction, I went to go find Stephen, who always sat with me during the service. My mother referred to him as my boyfriend, even though he had never kissed me, and we held hands only when we prayed together.

But he did hug me every morning in front of our locker at school. Technically it was his locker, but I stashed all of my books in there, and together we decorated the inside of it, scotch taping words and phrases we had cut out of magazines: "Bananas!"; "He is my inspiration"; "It won't be long now!"; "Xanadu" (his nickname for me); and my personal favorite, "KLUJICS," which stood for "Keep Looking Up, Jesus Is Coming Soon."

I had met Stephen in my art class. Although he was a senior, he was helping out in the sophomore art class while working on his capstone project. While we learned about one-point perspective and vanishing points, Stephen was in the back, laboring over a huge painting of the sky, using gesso and bright acrylics. My friends told me he was a Christian; in fact, some of his friends teasingly called him "Reverend."

Before long we were eating lunch together every day, walking the halls of the school together, laughing and talking. I don't remember what church he had been attending, but by spring semester he was meeting me at my church on Sunday mornings and was just as involved in the youth group as I was.

Our youth pastor approached Stephen one day about teaching the junior high Sunday school class. I could help, he said, and gave us each a copy of the teacher's guide to the curriculum. So Stephen began coming over to my house on Saturdays to study for it. We would sit on the floor of my living room, Bibles spread open and pages of notes between us. I'll have to admit that sometimes I would catch myself staring at him instead of studying my notes. His sandy brown hair was combed back over his ears, and his deep-set, pale blue eyes would be smiling down at his notebook as he composed a thought.

On Sunday mornings we would meet in the junior high classroom and arrange the chairs in a big, wide circle. The students would wander in and chat with us, and then I would listen admiringly as Stephen taught and laughed with those young teens.

Occasionally on a Sunday morning the minister of music, who was also my piano teacher, would ask me to play for the prelude or the offering. I had a book of modern praise songs I was pretty good at sight-reading, but he was also teaching me to improvise from the hymnal, looking at the key signature and chord structure of the hymn instead of just playing the written notes. He had also given me a book of more elaborate hymn arrangements that I was supposed to be practicing.

Once a week my mom would drive me over to his house for my piano lesson. A beautiful, shiny black grand piano engulfed what would otherwise have been his dining room. As my mom sat in his living room doing needlework, he would sit in a chair next to the piano bench while I attempted to play all the right notes. He would lean forward in his chair and scribble on the sheet music, "Slow down! Take this part again and make it majestic! Bring out those bass notes here. Start softly here, and let's add a big crescendo coming into this last chorus." When at last I could play all of the timing and dynamics and articulation and tempo changes to his liking, he would fold his arms across his chest and sigh, "All right, let's have you play that on Sunday."

That spring our church hosted a weeklong revival. The Cruse Family came. This was a group of musicians and preachers who toured around the country in a big bus, bringing a whole set-up of drums, electric guitars, keyboards, and powerful new worship songs. They were all related, either as brothers and sisters or as in-laws, and my mom, who loves to practice hospitality, signed up our family to host a husband and wife from the group, along with their toddler.

They stayed in our guest room that week. As I brushed my teeth before bed I could hear the young mother singing to her little son before tucking him in to a portable crib. And when I came home from school they would be hanging out in our kitchen, chatting with my mom as she prepared dinner.

I invited some friends from school to come and listen to this group, and each night that week I sat captivated by their music and the compelling words from the preachers. The last night of the revival I was sitting up in the balcony with Stephen and some other friends. The young husband who was staying at our house was preaching. I don't remember exactly what he said, but I do recall that I wanted to make a fresh commitment to follow Jesus. At the end of his sermon he invited people to come and pray at the altar. There were carpeted steps at the front of the sanctuary near the podium, and as I made my way down they began to fill with kneeling people. I couldn't even get to the front but knelt as closely as I could, in the aisle. *"Lord Jesus, take my life. I give it all to you."* I began listing off areas of my life and mentally handing each one over to God: my homework, my musical ability, my relationship with Stephen, my friends, my parents.

Now, you might argue that I was already a Christian, but I look back on the prayer that particular night as a pivotal point in my walk of faith. I count it as one of the most significant moments in my life. I was going deeper. I wanted to go all out for God. No holding back. Whatever God had in store for me, I was all in. Undoubtedly, God was preparing my heart for two upcoming challenges that were about to put this renewed devotion to the test.

While all of this was going on, my dad had been having some concerns about his health. Specifically, his lower legs seemed to be losing muscle tone, and he was often losing his balance. In all the traveling he did for his job, rushing through airports was becoming more difficult. He had always walked heavily, as long as I could remember, but now he thought his gait was getting worse. Sometimes friends would ask me whether my dad was limping, or if he had been in the war.

"No. Why?"

"I thought . . . just from the way he walks, maybe he had an injury."

That was ridiculous. He just walked that way. I didn't really think anything about it.

My dad's primary doctor referred him to a neurologist, who took one look at my father's feet and announced, "You have CMT." Further tests proved that he did indeed have Charcot-Marie-Tooth Disease, or CMT, for short.

It isn't a tooth disease. It's an inherited form of neuropathy that affects peripheral nerves and muscles—mostly hands and feet but sometimes more. The strange name comes from the three European doctors who identified it in 1886—Jean-Martin Charcot, Pierre Marie, and Howard Henry Tooth. It is fairly common, affecting 1 in every 2,500 people in the United States. According to the National Institute of Neurological Disorders,

A typical feature includes weakness of the foot and lower leg muscles, which may result in foot drop and a high-stepped gait with frequent tripping or falls. Foot deformities, such as high arches and hammertoes (a condition in which the middle joint of a toe bends upwards) are also characteristic due to weakness of the small muscles in the feet. Later in the disease, weakness and muscle atrophy may occur in the hands, resulting in difficulty with carrying out fine motor skills.

This described my dad's condition perfectly. But knowing the name of the disease was little comfort. There really wasn't anything doctors could do. There was no drug, no treatment. Later, as the disease progressed, he might need shoe inserts or leg braces, they said. And it was important for him to stay active, to keep stretching all of those joints that would otherwise get stiff: Achilles tendons, toes, fingers, and wrists.

To be completely honest, as I heard about CMT the thing that disturbed me most was that it was hereditary. We were told that my sister and I each had a fifty/fifty chance of having inherited the gene for this disease. So the doctors wanted to test us both.

At the University of Washington Neurology Clinic, Serena and I each sat on a table and took off our shoes and socks. The doctor examined our feet closely, noting our high arches. He took a straight pin from his pocket and began to tap my toes with its sharp point. "Tell me when you feel a difference." He tapped my big toe, then the top of my foot, and then my ankle. Suddenly, I could feel the sharp prick of the pin.

"Right there."

"It feels sharp?"

"Yes."

"But down here, it isn't sharp?" He tapped it against my toes again.

"No, it feels dull."

He scribbled some notes in a file folder.

Next he had me roll up my pant legs and lie down on the table. Then he taped one wire to my big toe and another further up my calf. "This is going to be a little uncomfortable. You're going to feel a little shock, but we are going to measure how fast the electrical impulse will travel through your nerves."

Zap. Yes, that was very uncomfortable.

Zap. He was watching a screen.

Zap. I was relieved when it was Serena's turn.

A lot of big words were being used that I didn't understand, and he kept making notes in his manila folder, but I understood one thing. Yes, he concluded. We both had CMT.

"It's no big deal," my mom tried to console me the next day as she cut up vegetables for supper. "Some people inherit blue eyes or brown eyes. You just inherited your dad's walk." She shrugged, and I went on with my homework at the kitchen table. We didn't say much more about it.

A few weeks later God had one more bend in my road. The four of us were seated around the dinner table in our usual fashion when my dad cleared his throat. "There's something we have to tell you girls."

It was never good when my dad began a conversation like that. My heart began to pound.

"We have to move."

I set down my fork.

"I'm starting a new position at work. The company wants me to move to Missouri."

My mind began to swim as I stared down at my plate. *I can't move away. What about Stephen? What about youth group? What about my friends? What about piano? Where was Missouri?*

CHAPTER 2

THERAPY

I wake to the sound of our front door closing softly and turn over to look at the clock. It's 7:12. He's right on schedule. My sweet husband will be walking the mile and a quarter to work, as he does every day, praying. He has confided in me that one of his regular prayers is that he will outlive me. Truthfully, that he will always be able to take care of me.

I roll over in bed and savor the warmth of the quilt wrapped around me. The sunlight peeks around the edges of the window shade next to our bed, and my eyes fall to the baby photos on the wall. My two darling, chubby babies are all grown up now and fledged. Baby John smiles at me from underneath the blanket that my grandmother crocheted for him, and Baby Lois models her elastic pink bow around her nearly bald head. I think of where they might be this morning: John walking along a sidewalk in downtown Chicago on his way to work, Lois getting fashionably dressed in her dorm room and sipping coffee. I say a short prayer for each of them, asking God to keep them safe today.

The glass box on my dresser catches a ray of sunlight, illuminating our wedding photo next to it. There I am, in the long, lacy sleeves of my mother's wedding gown, and my husband with thick dark hair and a well-groomed beard bending over to kiss me. Standing proudly beside the photo is the elegant French doll my sister brought back for me from one of her mission trips around the globe. Still hidden in the morning shadows next to my jewelry box are two other treasures: a bottle of perfume that my husband gave to me just before our honeymoon, and a small, heart-shaped box—a farewell gift from my fifth-grade classmates—which now holds my grandmother's thimble.

Next to my dresser my blue armchair is draped with yesterday's jeans and sweater, where I changed into my nightclothes eight hours ago. The slipcover on the chair is beginning to wear thin. Years ago I shopped for that blue upholstery fabric to cover the ugly brown chair my husband had brought into our marriage. He had acquired it during his single days, when he was living alone and didn't care about decorating. The slipcover had been quite a sewing project for me. I had measured every side and angle of the chair and even made my own piping with a ruffle around the bottom. Now, propped against the chair, my leg braces await me.

I'd better get into the shower. I have an appointment this morning.

I swing my legs over the edge of the bed and reach for the dresser to steady myself before putting weight on my feet. With one hand on the dresser and the other grasping the brass ball on our footboard, I take a few small steps, dragging my feet until I have to let go of the bed. Then my hand finds the doorframe that leads into the hallway. With each step I have to make sure that at least one of my hands is holding onto something firm: the doorknob, the bathroom counter, the towel rack, the windowsill.

In the shower I am clinging to the grab bar my husband installed a few years ago. I can hold onto it with one hand while I soap up with the other, but shampoo is a little trickier. That requires two hands. I lean into the corner of the tiled walls so that I can pour shampoo from the bottle into the palm of my hand. As I do this I am so thankful that Lisa, my cleaning lady, has scrubbed the slippery soap scum away where my shoulder meets the cold tile. Washing my head with one hand and grasping the bar with the other, I find myself praying, *"Lord, keep me steady."*

After my shower I manage my way back to my blue chair and plop down. The process of putting on my leg braces must be done in the right order. The first step is to don knee-high nylons. I have a whole basketful of them next to my chair. The braces are next. They are white plastic, with Velcro straps, technically called ankle-foot orthotics. I've been wearing them since I was about thirty years old. They are form-fitted to my legs, from just below the knee all the way down to my toes, and hold my foot at a ninety-degree flexed angle. Without them my foot dangles from my ankle like a damp rag. A couple of years ago I started to pull knee-highs over the braces themselves before putting them on, so that the white plastic would not be so stark against my pink skin. At least this camouflages them somewhat. I like to think that people don't notice them. Next I usually pull on my jeans, but today it is sweat pants. Finally, my sneakers go on over my braces. As I finish tying them I chuckle to myself, "You are now free to move about the cabin."

I push myself out of the chair, using both hands on the armrests, and go to my dresser to finish getting ready. I pull a brush through my wet hair and pick up my hair dryer. I want to look as well kept as possible. Today I am meeting the physical therapist who will be working with me for the next year.

I haven't tried physical therapy for a few years now, and I'm not sure it will help this time. But I want to give it a shot. Twelve years ago my doctor recommended that I work with a therapist on strengthening my quads and improving my balance. I went two evenings a week to a big open room with lots of people exercising on different equipment. There were lots of familiar faces from our small town: people I saw every week in the grocery store, parents of my piano students, folks with whom I had served on committees at school. There, in front of everyone, I had to pull up the legs of my sweat pants and take off my braces in order to work at the leg press. I tried to find an inconspicuous place to lay them while I stretched out on the mat and did the leg lifts the therapist assigned. People chatted with me from across the room. "How are your kids?" "Are you still teaching piano?"

I humbly stayed with it for a couple of years. But I felt as though I was always recovering from the workouts. I would be shaky the next day, and vacuuming or weeding the garden would be such a challenge. And I wasn't really improving. But I did always wonder whether it was helping me maintain strength. I went less and less frequently and finally stopped altogether.

Then, a few years ago, I tripped over a blanket while making the bed and twisted my knee. My doctor recommended PT and sent me to a therapist outside of town. She had a more private office; most of the time I was the only patient in the room. My knee got better, and we began to work on strength. But my insurance had only approved six weeks of treatment. When that ran out I was on my own. She offered to let me come and use the equipment for a small monthly fee, which I tried to do for a few weeks. But when winter came the thought of walking across the icy parking lot was daunting.

This spring, however, I have decided that I would like to try physical therapy one more time. As I've ventured outside to clean out my flower gardens, I'll have to admit that this winter was hard not only on my perennials but also on my muscles. I find myself tiring out quickly. My balance as I walk through the yard is deplorable. Not only do I need my walking stick, but I need my husband's arm as well. I heard from a friend that there is a new physical therapy business about twenty minutes from my house, and when I asked my doctor if I could try again she was all too happy to write a referral. This time she left it open-ended, with no limitations on the number of sessions.

I walk down the ramp in our garage and check my reflection in the car window. My dark brown eyes stare back at me as I practice a smile. "Hello, I'm Suzanne." I toss my cane across the passenger seat and climb into the car.

"Lord, I'm so nervous about this. I don't want to look like an idiot. I hope she's nice. I hope we can be in a private room. I hope I can walk into the facility without help. I hope this works."

As I pull onto the main road, I begin reciting the chapter from the Bible I've been trying to memorize. It's from Psalm 139:1–24:

> *You have searched me, LORD,*
> *and you know me.*

You know when I sit and when I rise;
    you perceive my thoughts from afar.
You discern my going out and my lying down;
    you are familiar with all my ways.
Before a word is on my tongue
    you, LORD, know it completely.
You hem me in behind and before,
    and you lay your hand upon me.
Such knowledge is too wonderful for me,
    too lofty for me to attain.
Where can I go from your Spirit?
    Where can I flee from your presence?
If I go up to the heavens, you are there;
    if I make my bed in the depths, you are there.
If I rise on the wings of the dawn,
    if I settle on the far side of the sea,
even there your hand will guide me,
    your right hand will hold me fast.
If I say, "Surely the darkness will hide me
    and the light become night around me,"
even the darkness will not be dark to you;
    the night will shine like the day,
    for darkness is as light to you.
For you created my inmost being;
    you knit me together in my mother's womb.
I praise you because I am fearfully and wonderfully made;
    your works are wonderful,
    I know that full well.

My frame was not hidden from you
> *when I was made in the secret place,*
> *when I was woven together in the depths of the earth.*

Your eyes saw my unformed body;
> *all the days ordained for me were written in your book*
> *before one of them came to be.*

How precious to me are your thoughts, God!
> *How vast is the sum of them!*

Were I to count them,
> *they would outnumber the grains of sand—*
> *when I awake, I am still with you.*

This drive up Route 7 in Vermont is one of the most scenic I've ever driven. To my left the Adirondacks form a majestic backdrop with Lake Champlain sparkling at their feet. To my right Camel's Hump and Mt. Mansfield rise above the farms and foothills. Homes and trees often block the view, but then a field will open up, and I glance over for an awe-inspiring glimpse of God's glory.

"Lord, walk beside me today. Hold me fast with your right hand."

I turn on the radio and immediately recognize the intro to Kari Jobe's song "I Am Not Alone." I know all the words; this is one I help lead at our church, so I sing along. By the time I pull into the handicap parking space in the unfamiliar parking lot, I am choking back tears.

"Okay, we can do this," I reassure myself out loud. I hang my orange handicap placard in the window, grab my cane, and step out.

There is a long, sloping sidewalk up to the door, and as I begin to walk I realize that it might be a challenge for me to get back to my car after my appointment. Going uphill is always easier for me than going down. Because the leg braces hold my foot at that ninety-degree angle, my ankles are not able to make the normal adjustments to compensate for the slope of the ground. There is a little give in them when walking uphill, but downhill is another story. Then I am forced to balance on my heels.

There is a big blue square button outside the door with the wheelchair icon on it, and I happily push it and wait like Queen Victoria for the door to open before me. As I enter the office I look around at the big, open gym with large, healthy-looking plants in the corners. A couple of people are working on equipment. There is a long glass wall on the far side of the gym, overlooking a pool. The receptionist greets me with a huge smile. "Hi, I'm Lauren! How can I help you?"

"I'm Suzanne Rood. I have an appointment with Becky. . . . Um, I may need help walking out to my car afterward."

"No problem at all!" she says, as though this happens every day. "Becky will be right with you."

I sit down next to a philodendron and look around. I watch as a therapist works with another patient over in the far corner.

A cute young lady with a blonde braid walks up to me. "Suzanne? Hi, I'm Becky!" She puts out a hand to shake mine. "Let's go in this private room over here." She points toward a doorway. "*Thank you, Lord.*"

She watches as I push myself up from the chair. It takes me a minute to steady myself with my cane before I can take a step forward. She leads me into a small room with an exercise table, a desk, and a couple of chairs. We both sit. "So. tell me what's going on."

Where do I start? "I have Charcot-Marie-Tooth Disease." I can feel my throat begin to tighten. "Have you heard of it?"

"I've heard of it." She opens up a laptop on the desk and starts to type. "But I can read up on it, too."

"It's a hereditary neuromuscular disease. It was named after the three doctors who identified it, Dr. Charcot, Dr. Marie, and Dr. Tooth. People get it confused with a tooth disease." I force a smile, but I can feel the tears right behind my eyes. "I've been getting worse . . ." And now the tears start flowing. "I'm sorry."

For a few moments I am unable to speak. Becky hands me a tissue. I hold it to my eyes and try to catch my breath. "I'm sorry. I'm not usually like this. I'm usually very put together." Becky waits quietly. "I'd like to see if we can strengthen my legs and improve my gait and work on my balance. . . . There's no guarantee . . . I've tried PT before, and I'm not sure if it really helped." I tell her about my past experiences, and my relief at being in a private space today.

Becky nods. "Well, as long as this room is available we can meet in here." She thinks for a minute. "How would you feel about getting in the pool sometimes?"

"Well . . ." I refold the tissue in my hands. "It might be tricky getting me in and out."

"We have a lift."

I sigh. "But walking without my leg braces from the locker room to the edge of the pool could be difficult. Especially if it's wet and slippery."

"Hmmm. We could use a wheelchair if we need to."

I feel a knot in my stomach. Picturing myself being wheeled into the pool makes me feel suddenly feeble.

"Let's take some measurements. Can you come over to the table?"

I push myself up out of the chair and move to the table. Sliding onto it, I hand my cane to Becky, and she leans it into the corner of the room. "Do you want me to take the braces off?" I offer.

"If you don't mind."

I untie my shoes and unstrap the braces. She lays them down, one by one, on the carpet next to the table.

"Now, can you push against my hand?" She puts a hand on the bottom of my foot. I push as hard as I can. She pushes back, gently.

"Okay, and can you lift your knee up?" She pushes down on the top of my knee. We go through several of these strength tests. She pauses now and then to type notes on her laptop. Then she pulls a long red elastic band from a box. She shows me some exercises she wants me to do at home, holding the band in both hands and pushing against it with the soles of my feet. As I try them, she asks me about my family, and when I tell her that my son is twenty-four and my daughter is twenty she looks shocked. "No way! You can't be that old."

"It's true. I'm turning fifty this year."

I learn that she earned her doctorate in Boston but grew up in this town and now coaches a high school girls' hockey team. I tell her about directing the community gospel choir and teaching piano. She laughs about not having practiced her clarinet in high school.

As I strap the braces back onto my legs and tie my shoes, I think again about that downhill sidewalk. "I'm going to need an elbow out to my car, especially now that I'm a little shaky."

She smiles. "I would be delighted."

CHAPTER 3

MIAMI

"Well, I'm not moving with you." Serena's reaction to my dad's announcement at the dinner table surprised me. "I'm going to college as planned," she shrugged.

Oh. I hadn't even thought of that. But of course it was true. We had just recently watched as Serena (and Stephen) had walked across the stage to receive their diplomas. She had already made plans to room with her best friend at Western Washington University. There was no reason why that should change. It suddenly struck me that we would be moving to Missouri without her.

This was not the first time our family had moved across the country.

We had started in Florida.

My dad has told this story so many times that I'm not sure whether I am remembering the actual event or just the story. I was three years old, and our family was moving from Ocala, Florida, to Miami, where my father had taken a job with French's Mustard as a sales representative. We were traveling in two separate cars, both piled high with books, dishes, clothes, toys, lamps, etc. Daddy would have said we were packed up "tighter than Dick's hatband." (I never knew who Dick was, but apparently his hatband was tight.) Mommy was driving one car, with five-year-old Serena beside her in the front seat. Daddy drove the other car, as I knelt on the backseat, staring out the back window at my mother and sister following us. Traffic on the highway got thick, and before long I lost sight of them as other cars got between us.

"Daddy, I can't see them."

"It's okay; they're back there."

"Daddy, I can't see Mommy. We've lost her."

"It's all right. I'm sure she knows how to get there."

"Daddy, pull over. Pull over and wait for them."

"I can't pull over—we're on the highway. They'll be fine."

By now I was in tears. "Daddy, if you don't pull over and wait for them I'm not going to love you anymore!"

He pulled over on the shoulder and we waited. Car after car passed, and soon I saw Mommy's car. She zoomed right past us without even seeing us.

Our new home in Miami was not far from aunts, uncles, cousins, and grandparents who lived in Fort Lauderdale, where my parents had both finished high school. Holidays brought the entire extended family together, with nine or ten little cousins looking for Easter eggs in my grandmother's backyard, avoiding fire ants and lizards. There were big family Sunday dinners, crowded around my little grandmother's dining room table, spread with fried chicken, butter beans, homemade pickles, and melt-in-your-mouth biscuits.

Serena taught me to draw hopscotch squares on the sidewalk in front of our new concrete block, three-bedroom house. There were several young families in our neighborhood, and on those hot afternoons bicycles, jump ropes, and hula-hoops came out to the sidewalks, where all the kids from our street gathered. One day a neighbor boy picked up a large palm branch that had fallen from one of the tall trees along the street. He waved it at me, and I stepped back, afraid of getting stuck by the prickly ends of the leaves. As I backed away he came toward me and began to chase me down the sidewalk. I screamed in panic. Serena ran after him, grabbed him, and punched him right in the nose.

Three doors down from us lived a girl my sister's age named Sheri. They were in the same class at school and often played together at our house or hers. I was allowed to play with them as long as I didn't bother them too much. Sheri had a record player and a vinyl album of someone telling Bible stories. We would dress up in whatever costumes we could muster and act them out as the voice on the record narrated. I would always have to be the lion in Daniel and the lions' den, because I had a tiger costume that I had worn for Halloween that still fit. My mother had probably purchased the cheap, one-piece, full-body polyester costume at the Five and Dime. It had a plastic mask with an elastic band that constantly got caught in my ponytail. My role was to hide under the table wearing the tiger/lion suit through the long story until finally King Darius threw Daniel under the table with me. Then, of course, I wasn't allowed to attack Daniel. I just had to sit there looking scary.

When I didn't have Serena and Sheri to play with, I was content to play school by myself. Daddy would often bring home extra paper from his office, with the French's red flag and letterhead across the top. I would scribble numbers and letters on the sheets and pass them out to my stuffed animals and dolls that were arranged in rows in the living room. The end table and footstool served as my desk, as I graded their papers with a red marker.

We attended a Baptist church, where I was expected to sit very still between my parents in the big sanctuary. I survived the long sermons by tracing the veins on the back of my daddy's hands or pulling my lace gloves on and off. When we opened the hymnals to sing, I joined in proudly on the songs I knew: *"Love lifted me, Love lifted me, When nothing else could help,"*— the pianist dragged out the last line—*"Love . . . lifted . . . me!"*

Our church held a vacation Bible school every summer, which meant hearing Bible stories every morning that week told by someone different from my usual Sunday school teacher. We said the Pledge of Allegiance to the American flag, the Christian flag, and the Bible. We made puppets out of paper bags, practiced saying Bible verses, and ate vanilla sandwich cookies. At one point they brought us outside in the blazing sunshine, and one of the teenage helpers asked if anyone would like to ask Jesus into their heart. I raised my hand. It sounded like a nice idea to have Jesus in my heart.

"Come with me." Several of us filed into the associate pastor's office and sat on the couch and chairs around the room. He talked for a bit and then said we were all going to pray. We would go around the room, and he wanted each of us to say *"Jesus, come into my heart."* When my turn came, I said it as clearly as I could. He told us that the following Sunday we would walk down the aisle at the end of the service and tell the head pastor that we had prayed those words. This I directly reported to my mother as soon as I got home.

On Sunday I waited nervously through the singing, the announcements, the offering, more singing, and the sermon. My mother had promised that she would walk with me. So as soon as the closing song began, I grabbed her hand and we started down the aisle. This "invitation hymn," as we called it, was always part of the weekly service. The pastor stepped down from the podium and stood at the head of the aisle, waiting for people to come forward. Sometimes we sang extra verses, as he encouraged more folks to come. I think there were six verses of "Just as I Am" in the hymnal, and we knew them all. At any rate, I knew the routine, and I was ready to go. As soon as we got close he reached down and grabbed me by the shoulders. "Why have you come?" he asked.

"I asked Jesus into my heart." Simple as that.

As a six year old, I had not understood that this meant I was to be baptized. But I was okay with that. On a Sunday soon afterward I was in a line of people in a little hallway behind the platform, waiting for my turn to walk down the steps into the cold water of the glass tank in front of the church. I was wearing a white robe, which floated on the surface of the water as I stepped in, and I was worried that everyone could see my underwear. I had watched people get baptized many times, from my usual vantage point in a padded pew of the sanctuary. From there I knew you could see about two feet of water through the glass, from the preacher's knees to his waist. He took my hands and helped me walk to the middle of that huge glass bathtub. "I baptize you, my sister, in the name of the Father, and of the

Son, and of the Holy Spirit." He pinched my nostrils closed and dunked me backward into the water. My feet flew out from under me, and when I came up out of the water I could hear the audience chuckling.

CHAPTER 4

DISCIPLINE

I have bought myself a cute box at T.J. Maxx. It matches the décor of my den. It is classy enough to display on the floor beside the couch and tall enough to set my mug on while I am watching *Masterpiece Theater*. But more importantly, it is large enough to house all of my equipment for the exercises Becky has assigned me.

I have a rolled-up hand towel with a rubber band wrapped around each end. Then there are various colors of stretchy bands. And for one of the exercises I had to buy myself a rubber ball at the drugstore. It's about the size of a volleyball, and plain black—nothing exciting like the rainbow striped one I had as a kid. All of that fits nicely into my box, and with the lid closed it looks as though it belongs there next to the couch.

This morning I have finished my breakfast, checked the messages on my phone, made myself a second cup of tea, read some Scripture, started a load of laundry, and answered a couple of emails. Enough procrastination. It's time to make myself do my exercises.

Standing in the kitchen, I find a playlist on my phone of some of my favorite worship songs. I set down my phone and grab the edge of the counter as the music starts. I'll begin with the simple leg lifts Becky showed me. Facing the counter, I lift my heel up, bending my knee. Ten reps. Then the other leg. Ten reps. Then back to the right leg. Then the left again. The drum pattern from my phone provides a pretty good beat for this.

Now I turn to the side, still holding onto the edge of the counter, and raise my knee as though I am marching. Ten reps. Then turn to the other side and raise the other knee. Ten reps. Now back to my right knee. Then the left again.

Now it's time to go to the box. I get out a yellow band. This one is tied into a loop just big enough to fit loosely around my ankles. I bring it back to the kitchen and hold onto the counter with one hand while I bend over to step into the loop. Facing the counter again, I lift one leg to the side. The band offers some resistance. Ten reps. Then the other leg. Then the right leg again. Then the left.

Finally, it is time to go and sit on the couch. I reach into the box for the blue band. This one is also tied into a loop, and I step into it with both feet, wrapping it around my knees. Still seated on the edge of the couch, I pull my knees apart to the rhythm of the song playing on my phone. This exercise is easier. Ten reps go quickly. I keep going and make it twenty without stopping.

Then I pull the band back over my feet and grab the rubber ball out of the box. I squeeze it between my knees. Hold for ten seconds, then relax. Squeeze and count to ten. Relax. A different song comes on now. I start singing along. Now I've lost count. Was that five or six? Ugh. I'd better say five. Squeeze and count to ten. Relax.

When I finally finish squeezing, I hold the ball in my lap and lean back on the couch, listening. Chris Tomlin's "Whom

Shall I Fear?" is playing now. This song is one of my favorites, and I can hardly sing it without getting choked up.

I look out the sliding glass door at the empty clay pots on my back porch. Oh, how I would love to plant pansies in them today. I wonder if I will have time to go and buy flowers before my piano students come this afternoon.

I take a deep breath and sit up. Time to take off my leg braces for this part of the routine. I untie my shoes and slip them off, setting them over to the side of the couch. Then I pull up my pant legs, peel back the Velcro straps of my braces, just below my knees, and wriggle out of them. I lay them on top of my shoes.

Hanging onto the front edge of the couch, I lower myself down to the carpet. I reach around to the box and pull out the rolled hand towel. It goes under my right knee. With my feet straight out in front of me and my hands leaning back on the carpet behind me, I pull my right foot toward myself, sliding my heel on the carpet. This takes a lot of concentration. After just two reps, I have to close my eyes and focus all my strength on bending my knee and dragging my heel toward me. Becky wants ten of these, too. It's going to take a lot of determination to get through ten. I hear myself grunting as I finish. Then I place the rolled-up towel under my left leg and pull that heel toward me. I didn't even notice that a new song had started.

"Whatever my lot, Thou hast taught me to say . . ." Though I'd like to sing along, I can't. I have to think about moving my foot. Eight . . . ugh! Nine . . . grr! Ten!

When I finish these, I lie back on the carpet and close my eyes. *"It is well . . . with my soul. . . . It is well, it is well with my soul."* The depth of these lyrics is a little more than what I can actually pray from my heart this morning. I open my eyes and stare up at the ceiling, listening for a few more minutes until the song is fading out, not knowing whether I can honestly, really trust God that much, not sure all is really well with my soul. I take a deep breath and sit up.

"Clams" are next. That's what Becky calls this exercise. I reach back to my box and fish out the blue band again. I put both feet through the loop and pull it up to my knees. Then I lie on my side with my knees bent and lift one knee, keeping my feet together. One. Back together. Two. These are much easier.

I look outside through the sliding glass door. My eyes are at a level with the gray painted floor of our back porch, and the sun is gleaming on the glossy paint, inviting me to come outside. I turn my body over and get into position to lift the other knee. One. Back together. Two. Now I am staring under the couch and wondering how many cobwebs are under there. I count to ten and turn over, gazing out onto the porch for ten more in that direction. Then it's over once again toward the dark unknown of the couch's underworld.

Okay, one more exercise. I reach into the box for my red band. It is a couple of feet long, with a knot tied at either end. I hold an end in each hand, with the middle of the band around my right foot. I straighten my leg against the resistance of the band. One. I let the band pull my foot back toward me. Then straighten my leg again. Two. Becky wants ten of these as well. Then the other foot. I am in a rhythm now, singing along to "Good, Good, Father" by Housefires.

I am finally finished, but I am exhausted. I lie back down on the floor and glance at my watch. That took me about forty-five minutes. I roll over and reach for my braces. Sitting up, I use my hands to pick up my foot and place it into the brace. Then I pull the Velcro strap around my leg and reach for my shoe. It is more difficult to get my foot and brace into my shoe at this angle on the floor, so it takes me a little longer. Then, of course, my other brace and my other shoe are waiting.

I tie up the laces and scoot myself over to the couch, where I roll over onto my knees. I put both hands up on the couch cushion, but before I hoist myself up it seems appropriate to pray in this position. I say a quick prayer for my kids. *"Lord, watch over them today. Keep them safe; keep them following You."* Still kneeling, I gather up the bands, the ball, and the towel and close them back up inside the box. There. The ugly elastic bands are out of sight, and I can forget about them for the rest of the day.

I push myself up until I get both my feet under me. It takes me a second to get my balance. I hold onto the arm of the couch until I am ready to take a step toward the kitchen. I'm a little unsteady.

I hear the dryer buzz. My clothes are dry. I should fold the laundry.

But first I think I'll sit and have another cup of tea.

CHAPTER 5

BARBIES AND BROKEN BONES

"These scissors are only to be used for fabric. Do you hear me?" Mommy was holding her heavy, stainless steel sewing scissors, her beautiful auburn hair clasped with a long barrette at the nape of her neck. "Don't ever use them for paper, or they will not be sharp anymore, and they won't cut the fabric."

The cardboard cutting mat was unfolded on the dining room table, and a layer of green calico fabric was spread over it. Mommy helped Serena and me place the thin paper pattern pieces so that the least amount of fabric would be used. Cautiously we pinned them into place, trying not to rip the delicate paper. Then she let us cut them out. They were small pieces. Most were no bigger than my hand. We were making Barbie doll clothes.

In the kitchen, taking up the space where a kitchen table would normally be, my mother's sewing cabinet was open and ready for little fingers to learn how to guide the fabric through the machine. My grandfather—"Papa," as we called him—had designed and built this grand piece of furniture. It had a bank of large drawers on the left side that were filled with envelopes of dress patterns and remnants of fabric. On the right, a swinging overhead door lifted up to reveal the steel blue sewing machine nestled inside a desk. The desk part was on wheels, with one corner attached to the cabinet with hinges, so that when my mother pulled it out it swung into the room and took up most of the free space in the kitchen.

We learned to thread the machine and wind the bobbin, and how to push down gently on the electric pedal so that the machine would gradually take the fabric and not jump. We made skirts and pants and blouses for our dolls, with tiny snaps that had to be sewn on by hand. But the big cardboard mat and all the fabric scraps, pattern pieces, and sewing pins had to be cleaned up before suppertime so we could eat at the table.

We heard Daddy's car in the driveway and ran to the door to greet him. "Daddy, Daddy, guess what's for supper?" This was a game we often played.

He swung me up to his shoulder. "Fish heads and rice?"

"No, no—yuck!"

"Spaghetti and chocolate cake?"

"No . . . Can you smell it?"

"Mmmm. Boy, howdy! I smell Purlow!"

I think my mother got this recipe from my dad's grandmother. It was an old family favorite. Smoked sausage, onion, green pepper, tomatoes, and rice all thrown together in one big pot. She always served it with cornbread, coleslaw, and black-eyed peas. Cube steak and onion gravy was another favorite. Or ham and rice casserole, always served with green peas. On occasion we would have fried shrimp with French fries and hush puppies, which Serena got to help with. It was her job to drop the spoonsful of cornbread batter into the hot grease and then turn them over with the slotted spoon as soon as the underside got brown. I would be in charge of the cocktail sauce. Mixing ketchup, Worcestershire sauce, mustard, and relish, this was never done by measuring but by tasting a finger that caught a drip on the side of the bowl.

Not surprisingly, my favorite meal was Thanksgiving. Daddy would make the ambrosia that morning, and if I were up early enough I could help. Waking and finding Daddy alone at the table, I would pad up next to him in my pajamas. He would pull me onto his lap. First we would have coffee together and read the newspaper. He would pour milk into a coffee cup for me, stirring in a spoonful of sugar with just a splash of coffee. "Want to read the funny papers?" He would pull that page loose from the serious stuff he'd been reading and place it before me. I couldn't read all the words, but I could look at the silly pictures.

When he was finished reading the paper, he would spread it out over the table and gather his supplies: two oranges and two apples from the refrigerator, a can of pineapple, a jar of maraschino cherries, a very large plastic bowl, a wooden spoon, the cutting board, and a sharp knife. We would sit at the table together, soaking the newspaper with juice as we created the best fruit salad in the world.

This would be served as a first course in our fancy meal that afternoon. It would be ladled into stemware and placed on a doily in the center of each china plate. My mother would prepare the perfect roast turkey, stuffing, green beans, and a sweet potato casserole with brown sugar and pecan topping. The same decadent meal would be repeated on Christmas Day, complete with pumpkin and pecan pies with crusts artistically crimped all around.

Grandma and Papa (my mother's parents) came on Christmas Eve to spend the night with us. That was exciting enough, but I could hardly stand still when Santa came to our neighborhood. Mr. Joe, who lived down the street, built a big stage for Santa out in his front yard. There were lights and music and decorations, and all the neighborhood children lined up on the sidewalk to greet Santa. He walked right out of Mr. Joe's front door and onto the stage in his big red suit. Santa! Right there in our neighborhood! When it was my turn to sit in his lap, I politely asked for Malibu Barbie. I had seen her on TV. She had long, straight blonde hair and came wearing a pink and orange swimsuit.

That night Serena slept in my room because Grandma and Papa would be sleeping in hers. We chattered and giggled in the dark until Daddy knocked on the door. "You'd better go to sleep, or Sanny Clause won't come! I don't want to hear another peep out of you. Not one more peep!" As soon as he walked away, we both whispered, "Peep!"

Christmas morning Serena and I ran out to the living room, my mission to find Malibu Barbie. There she was, in her clear plastic box, lying under the tree. But behind the tree, against the wall, was another wonderful surprise. Papa had built a toy stove for me. Just the right height, it was painted a beautiful white, with black knobs that turned and four black burners that had once been coffee can lids. It was lined with toy cups and dishes, and I went right to work, serving each family member a delicious pretend breakfast.

As Mommy went into the kitchen to prepare real food for us, Grandma motioned for me to come to the sliding glass door. "Did you see what Santa left in your backyard?" Serena and I ran to look. A swing set! (No doubt Daddy and Papa had been up late with a flashlight and screwdriver in the backyard.)

For the next few weeks the new swing set attracted lots of neighborhood children, including an annoying little boy named Mikey. He lived next door to Sheri but didn't have many friends, so my mother would encourage me to play with him. Once when all the kids were playing outside he came out of his house with a rubber band stretched around the top of his head. His forehead was turning purple, and we all laughed. Later when we told my mother about it she shook her head. "He doesn't know any better."

Mikey showed up on our back porch one day when I was playing with my Barbies. My mother, being gracious, invited him to stay and play. She went into the kitchen, cut an orange in half, and brought the sections out to us. I set down my Barbie on the cement floor, and we took our orange halves to the porch swing. We bit into them, slurping and laughing while the juice dripped down our chins. Everything was going well until Mikey spotted a spider in the corner of the porch. He hopped off the swing and caught it, then held it out to show me. I leaned away and whined, "Ewww!" Then he reached down and tore a wriggling leg from the spider and threw it at me. I shrieked. He threw another.

Curled up with my orange in the corner of the swing, I yelled what I had heard so many other kids in our neighborhood yell: "Go home, Mikey! Go home!"

And then Mikey did the unthinkable. He grabbed Malibu Barbie and twisted her leg. He bent her knee so far backward that it popped. The skin behind her knee split open, and the white plastic joint was hideously exposed. I gasped and stood up. Stamping my foot, I screamed through my tears, "GO HOME, MIKEY! GET OUT OF HERE!" He threw the disfigured doll at my feet and ran off.

Mommy came to the door. "What on earth?"

I picked up the Barbie and held it out to her, unable to speak. I began to sob.

"Oh, we can fix that." My mother's nursing skills kicked in. She found some white medical tape and sat down at the table, wrapping Barbie's leg firmly until it was in the right position. "Here, we'll make her a cast for her broken leg. And we'll make a crutch for her, too." She found a couple of popsicle sticks in the kitchen drawer and cut one in half. Like magic, she fashioned a Y shaped crutch, wrapping it in gauze and medical tape to make it soft under Barbie's arm.

Before having her babies, my smart mother had been a registered nurse in the operating room at Orange Memorial Hospital. For this reason we had various strange medical items in the kitchen drawers: syringes, surgical clamps, operating scissors, and all sizes of bandages. But more importantly, my mother was cool-headed and knowledgeable about what to do in a crisis.

Like the time the doorbell rang, and I opened it to find the lady who lived next door standing there crying, her hand dripping with blood. "Is your mother home? I was doing the dishes and I broke a glass . . ." Mommy quickly wrapped the woman's hand in a dishtowel and drove her to the emergency room.

Or the time I broke my arm.

After supper one evening my daddy had a surprise for us. Our cousin Scott, who lived in Tallahassee, was coming for a visit that night. I was so excited I got up onto a living room chair and jumped off, shouting, "Hooray!" As I came down, my foot hit the corner of the footstool, and I tumbled over. My forearm struck the carpet with a thud, and I looked down in bewilderment. My right arm was bent strangely, as though I had an extra elbow. Mommy grabbed a magazine from the nearby coffee table and wrapped it around my arm like a makeshift cast. She kept holding it tightly while we walked out to the car. And as Daddy drove us to the hospital she sat in the car right next to me, holding my arm in that magazine.

They sat me on a gurney in the hallway of the hospital, and a doctor pulled on my arm to make it straight again. I howled in pain, but Mommy was right by my side. And then, just like Malibu Barbie's leg, they wrapped it round and round in white gauze with plaster of Paris.

For the next six weeks Mommy had to help me do a lot of things. When it was bath time, she would wrap my cast in a bread bag and help me hold it up out of the water. As I stepped out of the tub, she would wrap me in a towel and lift me to stand on the lid of the toilet while she hugged me dry. She helped me get dressed for school, brushed and braided my hair, and tied my sling around my neck.

At school I tried holding a pencil in my right hand, but I couldn't quite grip it, with that bulky cast wrapped between my thumb and the rest of my fingers. So I did my best to write left-handed. The result was pretty sloppy, but I accomplished it. My normal recess activities were also thwarted. My favorite thing to play on was the jungle gym—that dome-shaped apparatus of metal bars. I would usually climb to the top and hang by my knees, but this would have to wait until I got my cast off. Swings were also impossible; I couldn't hang onto both chains.

But I could still chase boys. And this I did with fervor. The other girls and I would huddle together under the shade of the live oak tree and decide who would chase which boy. Then someone would yell "Go!" and we would run after them. I'm not sure what I would have done if I had ever caught the sleeve of Christopher or Matthew, but they ran from me all around the playground, circling the jungle gym and avoiding the flying feet of the kids on swings. And when the bell rang we filed back into the classroom sweaty and breathless, with beggar lice seeds stuck in our shoelaces.

CHAPTER 6

LISA

It's Wednesday morning, and I am trying to swallow down my oatmeal before Lisa comes. She will be here at 8:30 to clean my house. I am usually just finishing my breakfast when she arrives. She will be all smiles and spunk, while I am still yawning. The front door is unlocked, so she can come right in when she gets here.

I am rinsing my bowl in the sink when I hear the front door open. "Good morning, Suzanne! How are ya?"

"Hi, Lisa! I'm well. How 'bout you?"

"I'm good."

This is our usual routine. I stand in the kitchen doorway while she hangs up her jacket and gets her water bottle out of her bag.

"My kitchen floor is glad to see you," I remark, looking down at the crumbs and sticky spots near the stove and sink.

She walks into the kitchen. "Oh, it's waving hello!" She laughs and waves at the floor. I can't help but giggle.

"How has your week been?" I ask.

"Oh, pretty good. My daughter had her ultrasound, and she invited me to go with her so I got to see the baby." Her face lights up, and she claps her hands. "It's amazing what you can see now! That sweet little thing . . ." She tells me all about the appointment as she goes right to the cabinet above my washing machine and pulls out the cleaning supplies. We chat while she pulls on her gloves. I tell her Lois is coming home this weekend and ask if she wouldn't mind vacuuming her bedroom.

"Sure," she responds. "And I'll give it a good dusting, too. I'll make sure it's ship shape!" She snaps her glove at the wrist, giggling.

She carries a few things into my downstairs bathroom and starts scrubbing while I sit back down at the table and finish my cup of tea, feeling a bit like Lady Grantham while Baxter is tidying up the loo.

I originally met Lisa at the hair salon about six years ago. She was getting her hair trimmed in the chair next to me while I was getting my roots done. We started chatting, and I found out she cleaned houses. I had been really struggling with vacuuming, often losing my balance and lacking the stamina to do a decent job. God knew I needed her.

Taking a final sip, I set my teacup in the sink and go into the living room to straighten up the books on the piano. Practice sheets are folded up and stuck behind the music rack from yesterday's students. A few loose paper clips are strewn about. I put them back into their container next to my pencil holder, my pad of sticky notes, and the metronome. I'm sure all of that will get messed up later today when I am teaching, but at least now, while Lisa cleans, it will look good.

I go over to my husband's desk and get out the checkbook. I can hear Lisa rinsing out the bathroom sink as I write her name on a check. I tear it out and push myself back up out of the chair to hobble back through the living room. I set the check on the hall table, next to Lisa's keys.

I wait until I hear the water turn off before calling to her, "I'm heading upstairs, Lisa."

"Okay!" she answers.

It takes me awhile to get up the stairs, pulling hard on the railing and raising one foot at a time. Halfway up I notice a baby spider dangling in a tiny web that it has built in the corner of a step. *Lisa's going to get you!*

Once I'm up in my bedroom, I go to work making our bed. I fluff the pillows and pull up the sheets and quilt. I walk to the other side and do the same, then stand at the footboard and eye the spread to see whether it is even. I pull down on one corner to get it straight. *Who is going to see it?* Just me, my husband, and Lisa.

Then there's always the odd chance that one of my piano students will wander up the stairs while waiting for me to finish with the person before them. Oh, it has happened. I didn't know it until the little girl sat down on the piano bench for her lesson and proudly confessed, "I went exploring in your house. I looked upstairs in your bedrooms." I'm sure her mother would have been mortified.

"Well!" I answered her. "You know there are always books in the basket by the couch."

I gather up the dirty laundry that is scattered around my blue chair. There are several pair of knee-high nylons lying on the floor, and a pair of jeans that needs to be washed, and the shirt I slept in last night. I make a pile in my arms. One nylon escapes and floats silently to the carpet. I bend over to get it, bracing one knee against the chair. From here I have to make it to the laundry chute without dropping anything else. I am deathly afraid that I will drop something and trip over it, so I squeeze the pile against my chest. I have to do this one-handed, because I need the other to steady myself against the doorframe of my bedroom, and then the doorframe of the bathroom where the laundry chute is. I open the cabinet door and stuff the clothes down the chute.

With that task completed, I go to the pile of clean laundry that is stacked on the window seat in my bedroom. I did all the laundry on Monday, as my mother always did, even though I didn't finish folding the last load until yesterday. Then my husband carried the stacks of shirts and socks and underwear up the stairs for me. And now it is time to put them all away. I make piles. Things that should be hung up in my closet, things that go in my dresser, things that go in my husband's dresser, things that go in the linen closet. I hold a pile against my chest, leaving one hand free again in case I need to catch myself against the dresser or the footboard. I make a trip across the room to my dresser, then to his dresser, then out to the closet in the hall. By the time I have put all the clothes away, I need to sit down. My knees are tired, and I'm afraid one of them will give way if I try to walk around much more.

I can hear Lisa vacuuming downstairs. I sit down to rest in my blue chair. But I have nothing to do. I could check emails and messages on my phone, but I left it downstairs.

From this vantage point I can see down the hall into John's room, where the ironing board is set up. There's a pile of my husband's shirts lying on the bed in there that need to be pressed. I sigh. I can't do that now. My knees couldn't take it. Even if I pull the ironing board over next to the bed and sit on the edge while I iron, I would be shaky. It can wait.

I can hear Lisa coming toward the stairs with the vacuum, and I know she will be changing the attachment soon to clean each step as she comes up the staircase. (That spider doesn't have a chance.) I don't want her to catch me sitting here doing nothing while she is working up a sweat, so I hoist myself up out of the chair and walk to the computer desk in our little spare bedroom. The old office chair squeaks as I plop down. I check our email and take a glance at Facebook. But I also don't want to be hanging out on the internet while Lisa dusts around me. So I open up a new document and start typing this chapter. At least I can look as though I am doing something productive.

In the time I have been typing, she has come upstairs and cleaned the bathroom, as well as my daughter's room. I look up at the clock on the wall, knowing she must be nearly done. She comes into this room now to tell me goodbye and bends down to hug me while I remain seated.

"I'll see you next week," she says. "Oh, and your houseplants said to tell you they need water."

"Okay, thanks," I chuckle. "I'll take care of that."

"They said they would shed tears, but they are too dry." We both laugh out loud as she turns to leave.

"Thank you, Lisa."

"Have a great week!"

"You too!"

CHAPTER 7

NEW YORK

The summer after second grade I had to have my tonsils out. I don't remember much about it, except for waking up in a hospital bed with a horribly sore throat. Mommy was sitting in a chair next to my bed, knitting. She fed me ice chips until I went back to sleep.

I had been told that we would soon be moving to New York. At first all my seven-year-old mind could picture was skyscrapers and violent inner-city scenes from TV shows of which I had caught only a glimpse before the channel was abruptly changed. I was relieved when Daddy explained to me that we would not be living anywhere near the city but somewhere that people called "up-state."

"It snows in Rochester." Mommy tried to make this sound exciting. I convalesced in front of the TV at home, eating ice cream spoonful by painful spoonful while I thought of living in a place where it snowed. I had never seen snow.

We moved in August, just before I was about to start third grade. A moving van pulled up to our house in Miami, and strange men wrapped all our dishes in paper and packed them into boxes. When we arrived at the beautiful two-story house in the suburbs of Rochester, we unwrapped those same dishes one by one and stacked them into new cabinets.

My eighth birthday was just a few days after we moved in. Somehow my mother rounded up girls from the new neighborhood for a birthday party and baked me a doll cake. This was a cake baked in a bowl, and when you inverted it and stuck a Barbie doll into it up to her waist it looked just like the doll was wearing a big hoop skirt. Of course, Mommy was an expert at decorating it to look like a beautiful ball gown. In a photograph from that birthday, I am standing at the kitchen table with that resplendent cake and several girls I hardly knew.

I loved our new house. Serena and I could ride our bikes up and down our street for hours, and there was a tree in our backyard that I could climb. There was a finished basement where we had a pool table. I crawled underneath it to play with my Barbies. And there was a laundry chute that went all the way from the upstairs hallway on the second floor down to the laundry room in the basement. Serena and I sent many stuffed animals up and down that chute on long strands of yarn from Mommy's knitting basket.

And then my parents brought something into the house that would change my life forever. The woman who lived in the house across the street from us decided to sell her piano, and my parents agreed to buy it. Together they wheeled it out of her front door, down her driveway, across the street, and into our living room. It was probably thirty years old then, an Ivers and Pond spinet with a beautiful maple finish. My Mother asked around and found a piano teacher just a few blocks away from us. Serena and I began taking lessons, riding our bikes to her house with our piano books in the front baskets attached to our handlebars.

As winter came and we experienced our first snow, I was terribly disappointed. It wasn't at all what I had expected. I thought the snowflakes would come down as big as your hand, all lacy and sparkly like the cartoon Christmas specials. Instead I woke one morning to little specks of white dust coming down. Mommy assured me that it would be fun to play in the blanket of white that covered our front lawn. She had knitted hats and scarves for us, and she had saved empty bread bags for us to pull over our socks before we put on our snow boots. Serena and I spent hours in the front yard building a snowman and making a whole system of deep pathways in the snow.

We joined a little country church, where Serena and I became good friends with the pastor's girls, who were our ages. We often got together with other church families for Sunday dinners, sledding, and watching football games. On Wednesday nights Serena and I would play Crazy Eights with the other kids in the basement of our pastor's house while the grown-ups had a prayer meeting upstairs. And on Sunday nights at the church, the kids had our own class to sing about Jesus, practice Bible verses, and learn about famous missionaries.

One evening, driving home in the dark, I asked my mother if I could "go forward" in church again. From the back seat I explained to her that I hadn't really known what I was doing when I was "little." Now I understood that Jesus had died on the cross to pay for my sins. She suggested I tell the pastor that I wanted to "rededicate my life to Christ."

The next Sunday, as soon as the pianist began playing the closing hymn, I walked down the aisle and told the pastor just what my mother had suggested. Smiling warmly, he invited me to sit down with him in the front row. He asked whether I would like to be baptized again. Yes, I thought, I would like to do it all over again. The following Sunday found me in another white robe, stepping down into the water at the front of the church. This time, when the pastor tipped me backward, my feet stayed on the floor of the baptistery.

In the spring my parents began outdoor projects. They built a patio just outside our sliding glass back door. This involved hours of raking sand until it was perfectly level and fitting together irregular-shaped patio stones like a jigsaw puzzle. But the product of their shared labor was a utopian place for our porch swing within a lovely perennial garden. I remember being awestruck by a particular row of flowers. Lying on the sun-warmed patio stones, I propped my chin on my elbows to stare at them. They were bright pink, with white lacy edges, and when I asked Mommy what they were called she told me, "Sweet William." I decided I had never seen anything so beautiful.

We planted a vegetable garden in the backyard next to the patio, with rows of bush beans, tomatoes, cucumbers, yellow squash, and zucchini. The growing leaves of the squash plants spread out enormously, covering the pathway through the rows like the fort of blankets Serena and I sometimes built in our family room, leaving just enough room to crawl underneath it with a favorite volume of the *Childcraft Encyclopedia*.

One day while Mommy was picking zucchini, knee deep in squash leaves, we heard a shriek. A nest of baby bunnies was crouching at her feet. They were all snuggled together, a mass of trembling brown fur. Serena and I begged to keep them: "Oh, they are SO cute! Pleeeeease, can we keep just one?" But Daddy said they would eat up everything and chased them away.

"Scat!" he yelled, stomping toward them and clapping his hands. He picked up a little rock and threw it at them as they scampered out of our garden, striking one of the baby bunnies right in its eye.

"Oh, Daddy! How could you be so mean?" Serena and I were mad at him for the rest of the day.

Bunnies or no bunnies, there was plenty of produce. Our kitchen smelled of fresh tomatoes as Mommy lifted them out of a boiling pot on the stove with a wire basket. She lowered them right into the sink, which was filled with cold water, and I watched as their skins split open. Then she slid their skins off one by one and stuffed them down into canning jars, their juices seeping out around them.

Daddy said we were "broke out in cucumbers." He loaded up our little red wagon with them and sent me door-to-door in our neighborhood, selling them for ten cents each. Considering my long brown braids and freckles, he must have known this was a pretty good marketing scheme. Most people gave me a quarter.

CHAPTER 8

WEEDS

I love to pull weeds. There is something very therapeutic about being on my hands and knees in my flower garden and pulling out anything that doesn't belong. In the early spring I crave the feeling of getting my hands into the dirt and pulling out a long dandelion root or following the rhizome of grass as it snakes its way underneath my daylilies. Sometimes I find a sprout of daisies or black-eyed Susans coming up between my irises or in the middle of a patch of primrose. "I'm sorry, but you're not allowed to grow here. Your spot is over there." I am heartless.

Most of my flower garden is along both sides of a split rail fence. Our house sits on a corner lot, facing one of the main streets of our small town, while the fence and flower garden run along the side street. I can sit on the curb on the street side of the fence as I pick over the new spring growth. The few cars that come by are driven by my neighbors, who give me a hearty wave. And on the yard side of the fence, I can kneel in the grass and crawl along the garden with my weed bucket by my side.

This five-gallon white plastic bucket is my ticket for getting down on the ground, and also for getting up. I keep it right at the end of the ramp in my garage so that when I head out to the garden I can throw my hand shovel into it, grab my walking stick, and go. I usually stroll down the driveway and then take the sidewalk along the main road out to the fence, rather than cutting through the yard, because my balance is so much better on the smooth cement. Even though our yard is fairly flat, the small undulations are enough to throw me off, and I have fallen to my knees more than once.

When I reach the fence I set the bucket down. Leaning over, I grab the bucket rim with both hands, tossing my walking stick to the ground beside it. Then I can lower myself down slowly, still leaning on the bucket and taking small steps backward until I can bend my knees to meet the earth.

Getting up is a similar process. I have to start by kneeling next to the bucket and propping my walking stick against it. Then I grab the rim and push up until I can get a foot under myself. I take small steps toward the bucket, holding onto it for balance. Then, using the walking stick, I can prop myself up to a standing position.

Occasionally I have gotten caught in the middle of the yard with a bucket full of weeds. I have pushed myself up and found myself leaning on my walking stick twenty feet or more from the sidewalk. My legs are shaky from kneeling and pulling and crawling, and I don't know if I can make it back to the house without falling in the yard. This isn't a problem if I am on the street side of the fence, where walking on the pavement is easy. But if I am on the yard side I have resigned myself to crawling to the sidewalk, lugging the bucket a few feet at a time, and dragging my walking stick through the grass.

Of course, people are always walking by. The sidewalk in front of our house is a regular thoroughfare for joggers, strollers, and dog walkers. I pause and look around.

"Good morning!" A group of women jog by. I know their faces from seeing them at high school concerts. They all had kids similar in age to mine.

"Beautiful day!" I reply. I pretend to be looking for a few more weeds among the Sweet William until the coast is clear. Then I can hoist myself up from the ground without anyone watching me.

Today, Saturday, I have brought my faithful weed bucket out into the glorious sunshine on the street side of the fence to a long row of sunflowers that have sprouted from last year's seeds. When my son, John, graduated from kindergarten, he brought home a packet of sunflower seeds. We chose a spot along this fence, and he planted three. They grew and bloomed beautifully. There is an adorable photograph of him on his bicycle, wearing a superman cape, on the street in front of those three towering sunflowers. The next year ten sunflowers grew from seeds that fell, and the following year the row extended further down the fence line. Seeds have sprouted for almost twenty years now, and I have to thin them out today, pulling out the ones that are too near the road or too close together.

I park my bucket next to the curb and lean my walking stick along the fence. There is a hole in the knee of my grass-stained jeans that tears open a tiny bit more as I lower myself down onto the curb. "I'm sorry, little sprout, but you won't survive here." I pull it straight upward and toss it into the bucket.

I hear the mower start up and look through the fence at my husband, who gives me a cheerful wave. He is wearing ragged shorts and an old Detroit Tigers T-shirt. He starts pushing the mower back and forth across the lawn, and I go back to my seedlings.

As I scoot along the curb, a song is stuck in my head. One I was practicing earlier this morning to lead at church tomorrow. I am humming as my fingers dig in the cool dirt around the roots of some unwanted grass when suddenly I am reminded that after church last Sunday a woman had said something really unkind. At least, it had seemed unkind toward me. She told my husband that she actually comes late every week because she doesn't like the singing. *What? How can she say that? I thought most people really enjoyed the music. Didn't our pastor just tell me last week how much he had loved the songs we sang? Did she realize she was talking to the husband of the worship leader? "Yes, Lord, I know I'm bitter."*

This patch of grass has really taken root between the baby sunflowers, and I start digging with my hand shovel. I can get only little bits of it at a time. I've got to go down pretty deep to get the whole root system.

My mind wanders to a parable Jesus told about weeds. It's in Matthew 13:24–29:

> *Jesus told them another parable: "The kingdom of heaven is like a man who sowed good seed in his field. But while everyone was sleeping, his enemy came and sowed weeds among the wheat, and went away. When the wheat sprouted and formed heads, then the weeds also appeared.*

"The owner's servants came to him and said, 'Sir, didn't you sow good seed in your field? Where then did the weeds come from?'

"'An enemy did this,' he replied.

"The servants asked him, 'Do you want us to go and pull them up?'

"'No,' he answered, 'because while you are pulling the weeds, you may uproot the wheat with them.'"

Well, I'm uprooting the sunflowers with the grass. I sigh as I realize that I've unearthed a good sunflower seedling. I do my best to pat it back into its place in the soil, but from experience I know that it will probably not survive.

It occurs to me that I have a weed growing within my heart. Sigh. *"Yes, okay, Lord, that was pretty obvious. I won't let the bitterness destroy this good work that you have assigned me. She was probably just having a bad morning."*

A neighbor's car drives slowly past me and pulls into the driveway across the street. I hear car doors and footsteps and soon realize they are walking toward me. I look up to see three women. One I recognize as my neighbor, but the other two are not familiar to me, and they are wearing head coverings with long silky dresses. Evidently they are from a different culture.

"Hi, Suzanne! I want you to meet my house guests." My neighbor and her friends are coming closer.

I should get up. Would it be impolite for me to remain seated here on the curb? I don't know whether that would be considered rude to them. I look around for my walking stick and panic as I realize I have left it leaning against the fence where I first sat down on the curb, some ten feet away. I can't get up.

I suddenly notice that the lawn mower has been turned off, and my husband is hurrying toward me. He grabs my stick from the fence and is at my side in a flash.

"Hello!" I try to sound calm as my husband reaches under my arms from behind and pulls me to my feet. He quickly hands me my stick.

"This is my choir director." My neighbor politely introduces me to her friends. She tells me their names, as I smile and nod. I would put out a hand to them, but my free hand is filthy. I try to repeat the names, and they giggle. I'm sure I didn't pronounce them correctly.

They smile at me, and I apologize for my appearance. "I'm sorry. I'm a mess. I've just been weeding . . ."

"They don't speak much English," my neighbor explains, "but I wanted them to meet you. I enjoy singing in your choir so much."

"Thank you," I stammer. "Nice to meet you."

They start to walk back toward my neighbor's house, and I turn to thank my husband. "How did you get here so fast?"

He smiles. "Want me to empty your bucket?"

"Sure," I sigh. "I think I'd better stop for today."

Together we look down at the fence row. "Wow. You've done a lot," he says. "How many sunflowers do you think you'll have?"

"Well, I think there are at least fifteen in this section, and more further down." I point to a patch of frilly greens at the base of a fencepost. "And these are daisies that came up from last year. I think I'll end up with a clump at each post along here."

"Nice." He grabs the handle of my bucket in one hand and my grubby hand in the other. "I'll walk you back."

CHAPTER 9

CHERYL

My best friend at school was Cheryl Hayes. She was taller than me, with long, red hair that was often pulled back into a single ponytail, or parted in the middle, like mine, and fastened into twin ponytails behind her ears. We had been in the same third grade class, where our beloved teacher, Mrs. Waters, had taught us to write in cursive.

Mrs. Waters had a three-pronged chalk holder that she would pull across the blackboard to make three parallel lines, perfectly suited for demonstrating her elegant capital letters. "The little curl at the top of the T should just touch the top line, then swoop down slightly as we go to the right and end our swoosh at the top line." We all practiced on our lined paper at our desks, scrawling rows and rows of capital Ts.

Mrs. Waters also loved to sing patriotic songs, and every morning, after standing and reciting the Pledge of Allegiance with our hands over our hearts, we sang one of the songs she had taught us. Some mornings it would be Irving Berlin's "God Bless America." Or Katharine Lee Bates's "America the Beautiful." Or Samuel Francis Smith's "My Country 'Tis of Thee." And, of course, we often sang Frances Scott Key's "Star Spangled Banner." But Mrs. Waters' personal favorite was "This

Land Is Your Land" by Woody Guthrie. She loved the line that included her name: "*From the redwood forest to the gulf stream waters . . .*" Belting out these songs was the highlight of my morning.

But my absolute favorite hour of the week was when the big piano on wheels came through our classroom door, pushed by our music teacher, Mrs. Cornelia Foster. Graceful and refined, Mrs. Foster was the most beautiful person in the world to me. She introduced us to Dukas's symphonic poem "The Sorcerer's Apprentice." We would listen to the recording as she played it on the vinyl record player, and if we were well behaved she would choose actors for the different roles and allow us to act it out. "Who would like to be the broom?" Several hands shot straight up from our desks.

The sorcerer would command his apprentice to fetch water. The apprentice would cast a spell on the broom. The broom would bounce down the pathway to the brook, carrying the water bucket, and the music would give us the cues for bouncing and spilling the water. But then the broom would keep going for water, and the apprentice couldn't stop it. The apprentice would break the broom in half, and then both halves would go for water. The music got louder and faster. The house began to fill with water. The apprentice was furious. The music was frantic. Finally, the sorcerer returned and angrily banished the broomstick to the corner.

Mrs. Foster also taught us the songs that we would be singing for the holiday concert, where we would stand in rows at the front of the gymnasium to sing for our families. Since I was fairly short, I stood in the front row, while Cheryl stood in the back. Mrs. Foster said we should dress up, so I proudly wore my "cherry suit," a matching blouse and pants that Grandmother Butler had sewn and mailed to me from Florida. The thick white fabric had red cherries printed on it, and Grandmother had finished it off with red rickrack trim and cherry-shaped buttons down the front. I thought I looked very Christmassy, standing in the front row confidently singing "The First Noel" and "Dreidel, Dreidel, Dreidel."

But Mrs. Foster's crowning achievement each spring was the fifth-grade play. And when it was announced that this year the fifth-grade classes would be doing a production of *The Wizard of Oz*, the whole school was abuzz. Serena, who was lucky enough to be in the fifth grade, was cast as a munchkin. There were countless after school rehearsals, and my mother volunteered to sew costumes.

I would go with Mommy to pick up Serena at the end of a rehearsal, and if she had to find one of the other moms to ask about a costume detail I would catch a few peeks at the stage. I got to watch as Mrs. Foster directed the munchkins how to pop out of their giant bird nest to greet Glinda, the good witch. Serena taught me all the songs, and we would sing them loudly in the car on the drive home. *"Ding dong, the witch is dead. Which old witch? The wicked witch!"* The final production, with all its music and dancing, costumes and make-up, was spellbinding to my eight-year old eyes, and I couldn't wait until I was in the fifth grade.

Near the end of the school year, we all had to take a standardized test. Mrs. Waters was very specific about the rules. We all had to pick up our pencils at the same time and open the test booklets together. She watched the clock on the wall very carefully and warned us when we had only one minute left. Then, when she said "Time," we all had to lay our pencils down, whether or not we were finished filling in the ovals on our answer sheet. The rigidity made me sick to my stomach. I would read some of the questions over and over again while the clock ticked away. Sometimes I simply did not know the answer. I had to fill in one of the ovals. What if I filled in the wrong one? What if I got lost in the rows of my answer sheet and filled in all the wrong ovals?

This testing took us a few days to complete, and one morning while I was getting ready for school Mommy found me in the bathroom in tears. As she braided my hair in front of the mirror, she asked me, "Have you prayed about it?"

"Yes," I sniffled.

"Well then, you're not allowed to worry about it anymore."

I thought about that as I carried my books out to the bus stop.

"You can't give something to God," she had said, "and then take it back again."

In fourth grade Cheryl and I sat across from each other in Mrs. Clicquennoi's classroom, where the desks were arranged in "pods." On the first day of school, our teacher had us spell her name out loud together and practice pronouncing it (click-win-oy), even though I accidently called her Grandma more than once. She looked like my grandma, was of comparable age, and wore similar home-sewn calico dresses. I was delighted when she assigned Cheryl and me to the same math group. We often consulted each other as we tried to work out the long division problems on our blue-lined notebook paper.

Mrs. Clicquennoi announced one morning that the other fourth grade classroom would be joining us for "Pioneer Day" that Friday. We could dress in the style of the pioneers; girls were encouraged to wear dresses and bonnets, and boys could wear jeans and button-up shirts. Even Mrs. Clicquennoi wore a white bonnet to school that day. Cheryl and I stood next to each other with our matching braids as we dipped long strings into hot wax, over and over again, making homemade candles. We strung buttons on strings to make old-fashioned toys, and Mrs. Clicquennoi read several chapters aloud from Laura Ingalls Wilder's *Little House in the Big Woods*.

Cheryl and I would always sit together at lunchtime in the cafeteria. Swinging my feet from the bench of the lunch table, I would regularly read the Snoopy comic strips printed on all sides of my tin lunch box while I took a bite of the bologna sandwich my mother had packed. As soon as Cheryl and I were both finished, we would run outside with the other girls to play Red Rover. Two lines of girls faced each other, hand in hand. Our team would call out "Red Rover, Red Rover, send [name of a child] right over!" Then Cheryl and I would hold our hands as tightly together as we could, while a runner from the other side tried to break through our line of defense.

But at some point during our fourth-grade year, Cheryl and I discovered the joy of just walking and talking together during recess. We would walk along the white lines of the soccer field and chat about our families; what we wanted to be when we grew up; and, of course, which boys we liked. We talked about books we were reading, TV shows we enjoyed watching, and which girls in our class we thought were already wearing bras.

Mrs. Foster and the fifth-grade class performed *Fiddler On the Roof* that year. My mother wasn't involved this time, since Serena was now in sixth grade at the middle school, but my family went to see it, and once again I was mesmerized by the magic of a musical stage production. For weeks afterward I was singing "Tradition!"

When fifth grade finally came for us, Cheryl and I were happily both placed in Mr. Turner's class, where a giant map of the United States covered one wall. We worked on memorizing the states and all their capitals. We wrote letters to chambers of commerce and asked them to send our class brochures or maps of their state. I was assigned to write to Jefferson City, Missouri. Every few days a package or a large envelope would be delivered to our class, and Mr. Turner would pass around whatever that state had sent to us. Sometimes it would be stickers, post cards, or political race paraphernalia. We would hang one of the items on the giant map on the wall, on that state. I was so proud when my day came to pin up a brochure of Missouri. The picture on the front showed a sunset over the Missouri River.

In December Mr. Turner asked Cheryl and me to decorate the bulletin board in the hallway outside our classroom. We could do whatever we wanted, he said. We decided to make a winter scene with snowflakes cut out of paper. Cheryl and I sat on the tile floor in the hallway, folding white paper and cutting snowflakes, with a million tiny paper pieces sprinkled over our laps like confetti. This remains a vivid memory in my mind because I knew there was something I had to tell her.

The previous evening at the dinner table my father had broken the news that we would be moving to Seattle. His job was changing, he said, and we would have to leave during the holiday school break. I would have to finish fifth grade in a different state, in a different school, without Cheryl. "Well, I guess we can write letters," she responded when I told her, looking up from the snowflake she was cutting. We promised each other to do that.

On my last day at Baird Road Elementary School, Mr. Turner and the class threw a party for me. Someone brought cupcakes, and there were handwritten farewell cards made from construction paper and markers. All the students crowded around my desk as I read them. And then Cheryl placed on my desk a little gift, wrapped in Christmas paper. As I opened it she explained that they had all pooled their spare change for her to purchase this. It was a delicate, heart-shaped ceramic box, with a pink rose painted on the lid. It was beautiful.

Mr. Turner hugged me goodbye when the bell rang, and as I walked down the hallway, carrying my cards and my precious gift in my book bag, I happened to see Mrs. Foster walking out of the school office. I ran over to hug her.

She smiled down at me. "I'm so sorry you are moving away," she said. "I was really looking forward to having you in the fifth-grade play this spring. We're going to do *The King and I*, and I was so hoping you would have an important role."

I swallowed the disappointment as best I could. "I will write to you," I promised. "You are my favorite teacher."

CHAPTER 10

CHOIR

"Maw, Meh, Mee, Moh, Moo . . ." My twenty year-old daughter, Lois, is standing at the front of the church, facing thirty or more choir members. "Do the hand motions with me." She demonstrates as we try to make our vowels sound as pure as hers.

People tell me she looks just like me, but I would have to say that she is way more glamorous than I ever was. Certainly more graceful. She skips up the steps at the front of the sanctuary like a ballerina. "Loosen your knees and put your hands on your sides like this. You should feel your ribs expand as you breathe. Now hiss. Ready? *Ssssss . . .*"

I am so fortunate to have her assisting me with the choir this summer. I have learned so much from her. After two years at Wheaton College Music Conservatory, with formal training in choral conducting, she knows far more about the technical side of directing a choir than I do. I often remind the choir (especially when I make an obvious blunder) that my degree was in elementary education, even though I took a few college courses in music, just because I loved it.

This is my tenth summer of directing the Addison County Gospel Choir, a group that originally started some thirty odd years ago when singers from several local churches got together to sing hymns at the county fair. Since then it has morphed into a full-blown gospel choir and band, pulling participants from over a dozen local congregations and performing not only at the fair but at several area churches as well. Even the building in which we are gathered tonight is not my own home church but one that opens its doors for us each week for our rehearsals. Part of my job as director is making all of those arrangements.

I inherited the job when the former director retired, and I opened my big mouth to admit that I'd like to try it. She pulled up in my driveway with a box full of sheet music in her backseat and happily plopped it onto my dining room table. Ten years later I have an entire four-drawer filing cabinet in my basement bursting with folders of sheet music.

With our voices warmed up, we are ready to begin learning a song. I sit down at the piano, leaning my cane against it. "All right, have a seat." I raise my voice to address the group. "Let's start tonight with 'Just A Closer Walk.' You should have that in your packet." I play through the chorus as the papers shuffle. "Sopranos, sing the melody with me."

> *Just a closer walk with Thee*
> *Grant it, Jesus, is my plea*
> *Daily walking close to Thee*
> *Let it be, dear Lord, let it be.*

"That's lovely! Now tenors, here's your part." I plunk out the notes as they attempt the harmony line.

Most of my work with the choir can be done from the piano bench. But at some point I have to stand in front of the choir to direct. That's why I have my tall wooden stool. It is sitting there waiting for me in front of the choir, next to my sturdy wooden music stand.

A few years ago one of the gentlemen in the choir who loves to do woodworking designed and built this wonderful music stand for me. It has four feet for secured balance and a solid post holding a tilted tray for my music binder. It is beautifully finished, highlighting various colors of the wood. Then, a couple of years ago, my husband added one final touch—a place for my cane. It's actually a metal clip for hanging a broom handle, but, screwed to the edge of the tray, it works perfectly for ensuring that my cane doesn't fall to the ground while I'm waving my arms around to the beat of the music.

When we arrived at the church for our rehearsal this evening, Lois carried in all of my directing gear like my own personal Sherpa. She threw my heavy bag over her shoulder. It contains my binder, a tambourine, and all the extra packets of music for the choir. Then she grabbed my stool in one hand and my wooden music stand in the other, while I walked beside her into the church with only my cane.

Typically, someone else arriving in the parking lot greets us warmly with "Can I carry something?" or "Do you have anything else to bring in? Let me get the door for you." I humbly accept the chivalry, feeling helpless to carry anything myself.

Those same gentlemen are serenading me now. I listen as the basses sing their rich, low part. "Let's go over that third phrase again." I play the notes on the piano, emphasizing the difference between the E flat and the E natural. *"Daily walking close to Thee-ee."*

The altos are next. Their part seems intuitive. Then we try all four parts together. I play a short introduction, and the full choir sings out strongly.

"Let's stand and sing it a cappella," I suggest. I've got to stand, too, or they won't all be able to see me. I plunk out our starting notes, push myself up off the piano bench, and grab my cane. I hobble over to my stool and settle onto it. "All right. One, two, three, four."

I make the pattern of beats in the air with my hand, and the voices join in. I'm aware that my hands don't look right. I've seen myself on videos talking with my hands, and I know that there is something about them that looks weird. But right now everyone is watching my hands (hopefully) for cut offs and cues to come in singing. The harmonies resound as we resolve the last chord and hold it. "Beautiful!"

We traditionally end every rehearsal in the same way: "Circle up!" We form one large circle, filing out from between the pews to make a link across the front so we can all see and hear each other more clearly. I leave the stool and find a place to join the circle between the altos and the sopranos. Balancing with my cane in one hand, I direct our customary closing song with the other.

The Lord bless you and keep you
The Lord lift His countenance upon you
And give you peace, and give you peace
The Lord make His face to shine upon you
And be gracious unto you
The Lord be gracious, gracious unto you
Amen, Amen, Amen.

The "Amens" fill the sanctuary and soar to the rafters. It is always a holy moment when we hum the final *nnnnn* in magnificent harmony. I sustain it for an extra glorious second before cutting us off, and we stand in silence for a brief instant.

"Will you pray with me?" My mind searches for the right words. *"Heavenly Father, thank You for this choir and for all the voices You have brought to it. Lord, we give You all the glory. It's all for You. In Jesus' name."*

People start chatting with each other as I go back to the piano to gather up my music. This is where the real ministry of the choir begins. Folks from various churches are all socializing together. "How are your kids?" "Hey, did you take that job?" "Did you get all your corn planted?" The chatter continues as a couple of people come up and give me a hug. "Thank you, Suzanne."

"My pleasure. I'm glad you're here!"

Lois is packing up my bag as she laughs with a couple of sopranos. She throws the bag over her shoulder. "Ready, Mama?"

"I think so."

She grabs my stool and we walk up the aisle while I look into each pew to make sure nobody has left anything behind.

At the door I realize that it has gotten dark outside while we were practicing. I hesitate. There is a sloping cement walkway from the door of the church to the gravel parking lot. This was easy enough for me to negotiate when we were walking into the church in the daylight, but now I can't see clearly where I am planting my foot. I freeze, leaning hard on my cane.

I would grab Lois's elbow, but her arms are full. I look around and I am relieved to see that Jessica is right behind us.

One of my soprano soloists, Jess has been singing with me for years. "Jess, would you mind if I take your elbow?"

"Oh, sure!" she smiles. We walk together out into the darkness. There is something about the way Jessica treats me that God understands. I think that is why he put her in my path just now. I wouldn't feel comfortable asking just anybody for an arm, but I am perfectly okay with Jess. I don't sense that she feels sorry for me. I feel as though she almost looks up to me. Even now, as she is walking with me, her tone of voice makes me feel as though we are old chums. "How's your summer going?"

Sometimes I have had people speak to me as though I were a small child. Once, when I walked into the local hardware store, a woman behind the counter commented in a high, condescending voice, "Aww, you got a sore foot?"

I cleared my throat and answered in the most dignified voice I could muster, "I'm looking for a pair of pliers."

But Jessica isn't like that. "Where is your car?"

"Oh, it's right here."

We stroll over to the passenger door.

"Thank you so much."

"You ladies have a great night!"

Lois loads the cargo into the back and climbs into the driver's seat as I close my own door. "McRun?" she asks.

"You bet." We have a tradition of going through the McDonald's drive through on the way home from choir practice.

She drives slowly through the church parking lot and pulls out onto the road, leaving a few choir members still conversing next to their cars.

I sigh, "Well, that went pretty well."

She nods. "Yeah, the sopranos are a little nasally on those high notes, but we'll work on that."

"Hmm," I agree. "I think it will all come together."

We ride for a while in silence. She flicks on the blinker and turns in at the glowing drive through sign. "What do you want?"

"Oh, I'll have a smoothie."

"Strawberry banana?"

"Yep. Small."

We pull around to the speaker and she orders for both of us. I fumble with the zipper of my purse. It takes me an extra minute to get it open. She drives up to the window, and I am frustrated at myself for how long it takes me to pull out my credit card.

Lois hands it to the cashier, then hands it back to me along with my smoothie. I slip the card back into my purse as she sets her drink on top of the spare change in the cup holder between us.

"How was your PT appointment today?" she asks as she pulls forward.

"Oh, it went great! Becky graduated me up to blue bands for most of my exercises. Maybe that's why my legs feel a little tired tonight."

She turns back out onto the road toward home. "Do you feel like it's helping?"

I take a long sip of my smoothie. "Mmmmm . . . I don't know. It's hard to tell."

CHAPTER II

SEATTLE

The house my parents had bought in the booming Seattle area was in a new development, winding up the side of a hill, with tall Douglas firs towering over our roof. The constant sound of hammering and loud machinery had become the everyday background noise as roads were paved, trees were cut down, and other new houses were built in the lots near our home. As I got ready for school in the mornings, this droning racket would be drowned out only by the radio in the kitchen, typically playing John Denver or Ronnie Milsap.

A school bus picked me up at the end of our gravel driveway and took me to the new elementary school. Coming into a fifth-grade classroom in the middle of the school year, I found it hard to make new friends. There was one girl named Sasha who said she would be my friend, but only if I promised not to play with certain other girls. My mother said that was absolutely ridiculous and that I should look for other friends. So the next day at school, in the girls' bathroom, while wiping our hands on paper towels, I told Sasha that my mother said I shouldn't play with her anymore. (This was not exactly what my mother had said, but it was my ten-year-old translation.) To this, Sasha replied that if I wouldn't be her friend she would beat me up.

I got off the bus that afternoon in tears. I ran past my mom, who was in the front yard pulling weeds, and went straight upstairs to my room, where I plopped down on my bed, sobbing. I was terrified that Sasha would punch me the first chance she got. My mother followed quickly behind me, and once she heard my story she went right to the phone. I don't know who she called, or what she said, but the next day at school Sasha acted as though nothing had happened and simply ignored me at recess time.

At home, Mom and Dad enlisted Serena and me to help with yard work, which included clearing away underbrush, stacking wood for our fireplace, and building a little campfire area in our woodsy backyard. My dad would teach me the names of the plants we were pulling up: Oregon grape, alder saplings, wild blackberries, huckleberries, ferns, and skunk cabbage (that one was easy to remember). We cleared a place to start a small fire and burned the weeds as we pulled them up.

Standing back from this brush fire after poking it with his hoe, Dad would look up into the treetops and spy a Douglas fir that had lost its needles. He became proficient at taking down trees. Tying a rock to a long string, he would throw the rock up into the top of the tree. This might take several attempts, until the rock would go over a branch and fall back to the ground, with the string draped and caught up high. Then he would tie a thick rope to the string and pulley the rope up into the treetop. It was Serena's job to stand at a distance and pull on the rope to guide the direction that the tree would fall, while Dad used his chainsaw to cut the trunk. "Here it goes!" he would yell, and then we would hear the loud *CRACK* and watch its slow-motion fall, as its limbs brushed against brother trees, crashing to the ground.

For the next few days my dad would come home from work and change from his business suit into a flannel shirt and jeans to tackle the fallen tree with his chainsaw. He would cut off the small limbs to burn in our brush pile, but the trunk would be sliced into sections a couple of feet long, then split with my dad's ax into firewood. Serena and I would haul them with the wheelbarrow to the woodpile near our backdoor and stack them neatly until the supply for our evening fires in the fireplace was as tall as we were.

My mother got a reference for a piano teacher from one of the neighbors. It was a twenty-minute drive to this new teacher's house, on the top of a steep, wooded hill, in a secluded neighborhood of grand homes. Nancy Downhour was beautiful and soft spoken. She was the young wife of a physician, and when I walked into the foyer of her house I imagined I was walking into a magazine. A curved, sweeping staircase graced the front hallway, and the dark walnut baby grand piano filled the bay window of her formal living room. A sky blue carpet and lush twin loveseats faced each other from either side of a polished mahogany coffee table. As I sat on the black leather cushioned piano bench, she invited me to adjust the height by turning the knob on the side. Her long dark hair fell over her shoulder as she leaned forward to watch my fingers play. Occasionally her toddler daughter would interrupt our lesson to ask her mommy for something; then she would go back to watching *Sesame Street* in the other room.

Mrs. Downhour was the first person to use the term *dynamics* with me. I soon learned that she would not settle for my simply playing the notes and rhythm correctly. She wanted feeling. My former teacher in New York had usually given me a new song to work on each week, but Mrs. Downhour would assign the same song a second, third, and sometimes a fourth week until I met her demand for emotion and sensation in a piece. Granted, we were also working on longer, more complicated pieces like sonatinas and Bach's Prelude in C. She also introduced me to Hanon. These classic finger-strengthening exercises were boring to me, but she made me repeat them until I could play them at a quick tempo with proper technique. Of course, I didn't complain. I wanted to play well for her. On the weeks that had gone by without much practice on my part, my lesson would be heartbreaking, as I sat at her piano and realized I was not any better than I had been the week before. She would set her pencil in her lap and in her quiet voice remind me that if I didn't put in the practice time I couldn't expect to improve.

It wasn't so much that I wasn't spending time at the piano. I just wasn't practicing what I had been assigned. I loved fiddling around at the keys, making up tunes, and then playing my old favorites from songbooks that my mother had bought for me. John Denver's "Sunshine on My Shoulders" might be followed by Evie's "Oh, How He Loves You and Me" and then polished off with Will Hudson's "Moonglow" from the *Reader's Digest Treasury of Best Loved Songs*.

Winding down after school for me entailed either goofing off at the piano or taking a walk with our dog, Shag. Soon after we had settled into this new home, my mom started checking the classified ads for a dog. One evening after dinner, the four of us went to check out a dog that was listed in the paper. The owner was moving out of state and needed to find a home for a three year-old purebred collie. We sat in her living room as she introduced us to her kind companion, Shag. He was big, even for a collie, with dark fur on most of his body, except for a white mane around his neck and a long brown nose. He sat compliantly as we stroked his long back, and he obeyed perfectly when the woman asked him to lie down by the front door. When we agreed to take him home with us that night, she knelt in front of him and cried as she hugged him good-bye. She gave us his dish and the heavy bag of dry dog food, as she explained to my mother how he liked to have his dinner prepared. Then we squeezed him into our back seat between Serena and me and petted him all the way home.

Shag loved to greet me when I came home from school, with his tail going crazy and his breath puffing. He loved to play tug-of-war with a stick from the yard or an empty moving box from the garage. And we would take long walks in the woods behind our house. He would lap up a drink from the little streams we crossed, water dripping from his long snout onto the thick white fur under his chin. If we walked too far and I found myself confused about the way home, I could defer to his instincts. "Shag, let's go home!" I would announce, and he would show me the way. My dad hung a tire swing from one of the tall trees in our backyard, and if I climbed onto it Shag would grab the edge of the tire in his teeth to pull me back and forth, teasing me with growls while his tail wagged elatedly.

On school mornings Shag would walk with Serena and me to the bus stop, just a short distance down the street from our house. Serena's bus to the middle school came first, and after she got on Shag waited with me until my bus came. I climbed aboard and sat in the first row, in a dark green seat by the window, clutching my lunch box and watching as Shag trotted back home, waving his white tail flag like a sentinel on guard duty.

CHAPTER 12

YAKKING

"We're all loaded up!" My husband sticks his head in the kitchen door to tell me he has put the kayaks in the back of the Subaru.

"Okay, I'll be right out!" I make one final stop in the restroom before heading outside to join him in the driveway. I am wearing my old sneakers, because they will probably get wet, and an old pair of cargo pants that has a hole in the knee. They will cover my leg braces, for modesty's sake, but I don't care if they get muddy. My old, faded tank top won't even be seen underneath the life jacket. I pause in front of the bathroom mirror to gather my brown hair into a ponytail and pull it through the back of my baseball cap. Now I'm ready.

I walk down the ramp in our garage and grab my walking stick from its corner.

"Ready?" My husband is wearing his water shoes, swim trunks, and a Wheaton College T-shirt.

"Yeah!" I climb into the front seat of our old Subaru. "Did you get the paddles?"

"Yes, of course."

"And both life jackets?"

"Yes, yes, yes." He double-checks the street in both directions before backing out of our driveway. It's hard to see around the kayaks.

Our little corner of Vermont has so many great places to go "yakking." Otter Creek runs right through our small town, with a gorgeous thirty-five foot waterfall. You can put in above the falls and paddle upstream, or you can put in below the falls and float easily with the current. Dead Creek flows into the Otter a few miles from our house, slow moving, wide and shallow, and if you like to look for turtles and herons that is the place to go. But today we are heading over to Button Bay, a beautiful little part of Lake Champlain.

We pull onto the gravel road that leads down to the boat access, and my husband maneuvers the car around so he can back up as close as he can to the water. He will have to carry both kayaks, one at a time, to the water's edge.

He stops the car, and I wait as he pulls my kayak out of the back. I step out of the car with my walking stick, but I have to wait for him to come and get me. The incline down to the water is too steep for me, and it is mostly covered in small, loose stones. I don't dare attempt it on my own. He lays my yellow kayak down at the shore so that the front end is sticking into the shallow water, then comes back up the bank and grabs my life jacket out of the back of the car. "Ah! It's such a perfect day," he smiles as he helps me strap it on.

My walking stick sinks into the loose stones as I plant it for balance and hook my free hand around my husband's elbow. We walk slowly down the embankment, one careful step at a time until finally we reach the side of the kayak. The water is right at my feet. Cautiously, I put one foot into the kayak, worried that it will move, but it only shifts slightly. My hubby supports me with both arms underneath mine and lowers me down into the seat. "Got it?"

"Yeah." I have to use my hands to lift my other foot over the side of the boat, and then I have to get both feet out in front of me inside it.

He runs back up the hill to get my paddle. Down the shore a short distance some people are fishing at the water's edge, and I wonder if they have been watching that whole production.

I take this moment to finally look out at the blue-gray water in front of me. There are some small waves, but the sunlight dancing on the little ripples welcomes me. Across the lake the mountains loom, as though challenging me to come near. A lonely duck bobs in the swells out in the middle of the bay, beckoning me.

My hubby is back and hands me the paddle. "Ready?"

I grasp it tightly and look forward. "Yes."

He pushes me off. The bottom of my plastic kayak scrapes slightly against the rocks, but in a half-second I am afloat and free. I paddle out into the middle of the bay and swing my kayak around to watch my husband carry his own boat down to the water, wade in a little, and hop in.

"Race you to the island!" he calls as he paddles up next to me.

Without even answering, I take off. This is one situation in which we can actually compete. My leg muscles may be weak, but I do have some upper body strength that can carry me across the water. About three quarters of a mile out there is a small island off a point. I have to stop paddling and catch my breath occasionally, but so does my hubby. There are plenty of other boaters out here today, enjoying the sun, and I know enough to aim my kayak into their wakes crosswise. Our flat-bottom kayaks won't tip all the way over, but a big wake will certainly shake me up.

When we get near the island we both slow our paddling. We are tired, and there are big rocks just under the water to watch out for.

"Let's go around to the left," my husband calls. There are fewer rocks on that side, away from the point.

I paddle up close to the island to get a look at some pink flowers blooming along the edge. My hubby floats up beside me. "What are you looking at?"

"Those pink flowers growing between the rocks. I wonder what they are."

He steers his kayak over to them and reaches way out to pluck a stem for me. The swells knock his boat gently against the rocks. Then he places the bloom in his lap as he glides his way back to my side.

"It looks vaguely like something you have in your garden." He hands it to me from across the water.

"Oh, I think it must be some kind of phlox," I decide, inspecting the dainty petals.

He paddles back out away from the island. "Want to go up the shore a ways?"

"Let's go out into the middle," I suggest.

Together we ride across the dark blue waters, out into the open expanse of the lake, out past the pathways of the speedboats, scaring up lazy seagulls and watching the trees on the shoreline behind us get smaller and smaller.

"How far do you want to go?" he calls, after we have paddled out into quiet waters.

"Oh, this is probably good."

There is something absolutely worshipful about being out this far. I feel tiny. I don't know how deep the water is underneath my little yellow plastic boat, but it's best not to think about that. And the water spreads out on every side so far that if I yelled I don't know whether anyone would hear me. But God is here.

I lean back and slink down inside my kayak so that my head can rest against my seat cushion, and I gaze up into the sky. It is a perfect blue, with white puffy clouds. God sees me, way out here in the middle of His grand creation. And suddenly, I cannot help but praise Him. Lying here in the middle of the waters, I raise my voice toward the sky and sing:

> *Praise God from whom all blessings flow.*
> *Praise Him all creatures here below.*
> *Praise Him above, ye heavenly hosts.*
> *Praise Father, Son, and Holy Ghost.*

CHAPTER 13

SPIDERS AND TEETH

I have always hated spiders. Loathed them. Even before Mikey taunted me. There is something creepy about the way their legs move—gingerly, simultaneously, and—God forbid—quickly.

Maybe it was the location of this new home in the woods, or maybe it was because their habitat was being disturbed by all the new roads and homes going in, but spiders were prevalent, especially in the bathroom.

If I beat Serena to the shower on a school morning, I would have to kill a spider. Inevitably, one would be waiting somewhere in the tub. I couldn't bring myself to get near enough to squash it, even with a tissue in hand. And they didn't drown easily. Oh, they could swim. I would turn on the shower and use a little paper Dixie cup to throw water in the spider's direction, hopefully washing him down toward the drain where he might get caught in the swirl of the whirlpool and finally go down, down, down, into the oblivion of the plumbing, where the constant flow of my shower water would keep him from climbing back out of the drain, gasping for breath.

But as much as I despised these repulsive creatures, I could not stop staring at the tarantula in the glass tank in the waiting room at the orthodontist. Mostly it sat still, its furry legs hiding behind a fake leaf, trying to blend in with the dark brown rocks and sand in its phony ecosystem. I did not want to know how or what it ate. Occasionally it would move, raising a woolly foot, sending a shiver through my whole being.

"Suzanne?" the technician, with her clipboard and white shoes, saved me from its allure by beckoning me to follow her to her chair.

"How have you been this month?" she asked as she tied a paper bib around my neck.

"Oh, pretty good," I answered, as I lay back in the blue vinyl chair.

"I'm going to be tightening you up a little today."

I opened my mouth wide as she began poking around the metal trappings that connected my teeth together. I could see the reflection of my gaping mouth in her glasses as she bent over me. Tink, tap, chink, I watched as her wrench made small tweaks to the metal bands around my back molars. She reached up to adjust the bright light over my head so that it shone more directly into the back of my mouth, and I looked past the reflection in her glasses to her hazel eyes, intent and focused, framed by thick, dark eyelashes that were coated in excessive mascara, like spiders' legs.

The next day at Leota Junior High School my teeth hurt. The sound of locker doors slamming in the hallway made me flinch. As I slid into my chair in typing class, I read on the chalkboard that we were having a speed test. I turned on the electric typewriter in front of me and opened my typing manual to page thirty-seven, as instructed. With our papers rolled into the carriages, we were all poised with fingers on the home keys, waiting for the signal to begin. Mrs. Hall rang the bell at her desk, and the "clickety clack" commenced. "Ding" went the carriage returns of the students around me. "Ding, ding!" "Clickety clack"—the keys struck the letters onto the page. I glanced at the paper in my typewriter and saw a mistake. Several mistakes. I was hitting an *r* when I thought I was hitting a *t*. "Clickety clack!" "Ding!" I leaned my elbows on the desk and held my forehead with both hands. I stared at the page. Time was going by. I couldn't catch up now. I would fail. Tears began to sting behind my eyes.

I felt Mrs. Hall's gentle hand on my shoulder.

"My teeth hurt," I quavered, not looking up. "I got my braces tightened yesterday." That was the excuse I gave her. And it was partly true.

But there were other things I wanted to cry about. The boy I liked had been walking hand-in-hand down the hallway with another girl. Sasha, my locker partner, had greeted me that morning with a sneer at the blouse I was wearing. "Unbutton that top button," she had scoffed. "You'll never catch a boy like that."

"Don't worry about this," Mrs. Hall reassured me. "I won't count this test in your grade." She looked at me kindly. "I'll write you a pass. Why don't you go to the nurse's office and get some Tylenol?"

I was so grateful. I packed up my things and stepped out into the empty hallway. Leaning my back against the brick wall, I let the tears flow.

The orthodontist had convinced my mother that I needed jaw surgery. I had a pronounced underbite, and in order for my teeth to meet properly I would need to have my lower jaw pushed back. More graphically, they would go in through the inside of my mouth, remove a small piece of bone from each side of my lower jaw, push it back together, and wire my mouth shut for six weeks so that the bones would heal.

Following months of appointments with an oral surgeon, orthodontist, and various other people poking around inside my mouth, I was scheduled for surgery after school got out in May.

I awoke in a hospital room with my mother at my side. She was holding my hand. My head was wrapped tightly in white bandages to keep the swelling down, and I couldn't open my mouth. My mother offered me a sip of water, through a straw that had to be wedged between my swollen cheek and my back teeth. But the general anesthetic had made me sick to my stomach, and the water soon came back up. My mother held a plastic bowl for me while I leaned over it, letting the vomit drain out between my teeth. I leaned back against the pillows and went to sleep.

I dreamed of nurses wrapping my head in white bandages. Around and around my head the strips of cloth went. Around my jaw, around my face, like a mummy. I began struggling against them, tearing at the bandages, trying to push the nurses away, but they kept on wrapping around and around . . .

I awoke with a start. My mother was by my side, soothing me. "It's okay." She stroked my arms softly. "It's all right. You were just dreaming." I opened my eyes fully and took in the beautiful face of my mother. She had been crying.

There was a lovely basketful of daisies and chrysanthemums on the bedside table. "They were sent by Grandmother Butler," she told me. "And Grandma and Papa are flying in tomorrow."

I slept quite a bit over the next couple of days, before the nurses peeled off most of the bandages and sent me home, where I set up residence on the couch in front of the TV. Grandma sat in the chair nearby, crocheting, while Papa worked on a jigsaw puzzle at the kitchen table, whistling. My mother was busy in the kitchen preparing a roast beef dinner, with potatoes and carrots and peas. A jar of home-canned sweet pickles and fresh biscuits finished off the display of food on the dining room table as the family gathered around.

"You don't have to join us," my mother whispered to me as I took my seat. But I wanted to be with everyone. My dad said the prayer, and then the bowls of delightful smells began to be passed around. I handed the steaming potatoes from Serena to Grandma. Then the mouth-watering gravy. I soon realized that this was going to be dreadful, just sitting there watching everyone else eat. "You don't have to stay," my mother reiterated.

I went back to the couch. She brought me some warm beef broth in a mug, with a straw.

Over the next six weeks my mother became an expert at making smoothies and milkshakes. I actually gained weight. She bought protein powder to mix into my daily chocolate shakes. She pureed my favorite soups for me. And when I had a craving for a hamburger she put a beef patty in the blender with beef broth and a little ketchup and mustard. That was the best burger I ever drank through a straw.

CHAPTER 14

DEXTERITY

Twist ties. Bread clips. Little packages of ketchup at a fast food restaurant. Little bags of peanuts or pretzels on an airplane. Packets of sugar at the coffee shop. Peel-open small containers of cream. Or butter. Or jelly.

Buttons. Snaps. Small buckles on shoes. Stud earrings. Clasps of necklaces and bracelets. Zippers with tiny pull-tabs. Bobby pins. Regular-sized fingernail clippers.

Thumb tacks. Paper clips. The tear-off plastic strip on an ink cartridge.

These are all things that are challenging for me. Some I can no longer manage at all, and I have to ask for help. Some I have learned to deal with.

I keep several clothespins handy in my kitchen to replace the twist ties on bread or crackers or bags of frozen vegetables. Zip-lock bags are becoming increasingly more difficult, so I have started buying only the kind with a sliding lock. These are not available in the sandwich bag size (at least I haven't found them in the store) . . . so, oh well. We're going to save that handful of goldfish crackers in a quart-sized bag. I keep a small pair of scissors in my purse to use at restaurants to open small packages like ketchup or sugar. And I have been known to stab the peel-off lid of the tiny tub of cream with my fork, strategically holding it over my cup of coffee and praying that it doesn't spray out onto my blouse.

I usually wear shirts that I can pull over my head. Even button-up shirts go through my laundry with their buttons already fastened, leaving just enough room for me to push my head through the collar opening. Forget snaps. I'm not wearing anything that requires snaps. Also, forget shoes with buckles. I'm strictly a tie-on or slip-on shoe person now.

Zippers are another story. If the pull-tab is just too small for my half-numb fingers to grasp, I will grab a pencil and jab the point of it into the square hole in the pull-tab. Voila. A few times I have panicked in a public restroom, trying to zip up my jeans, and have had to scramble for a pencil in the bottom of my purse.

Large toenail clippers are the only way to go for me. Yep, I trim my fingernails with them. Tweezers are a little tricky. I pluck my eyebrows holding the tweezers back in the palm of my hand, squeezing them with my middle and ring fingers. It looks funny to watch me, but it works—and, believe me, I am picky about my eyebrows.

I shop for mascara based on the shape of the tube. It's got to be something other than a smooth cylinder—something with edges I can grip to open it and then hold firmly while painting my lashes.

As for jewelry, fish-hook type earrings are the only ones I'll wear. And I'll have to admit I am somewhat of an earring hog. You might find more than twenty pair strewn about my dresser. I also love necklaces. A few years ago I discovered magnetic clasps for the ones that are too short to pull over my head. Once my husband attaches the magnets to the existing clasp I can do it myself and am free to choose from the array of chains that hang from my bedroom mirror.

Thumbtacks, however, are impossible. Ditto for pushpins. If I need to pin up a poster on the church bulletin board, get me a stapler. And I buy only the large kind of paper clips, which I keep in a little square, magnetic holder on my piano. My students all know this quite well, as we clip the pages of their books to mark our place and hold the pages back while playing. I also clip their practice sheet to the front of their lesson book each week so that it doesn't become strategically "lost."

Occasionally I run into some new challenge that I no longer have the dexterity or the feeling in my fingertips to handle—a new conundrum for me to figure out. This month it is cough drops.

I have caught a little cold. There hasn't been much to the sniffles, but the irritated throat and post-nasal drip have lasted for weeks. I keep myself awake coughing at night until I give in and take some medicine. And during the day, whenever I open my mouth to speak, I can't complete a full sentence without breaking into a coughing fit. The only relief I have found (besides not talking) is cough drops. If I keep one in my mouth through an entire piano lesson, I can avoid coughing along to the rhythm of the music. But unwrapping those little buggers is a challenge. The paper is twisted around them, with not much to hold onto.

I *can* do it. It just takes me a while. So I unwrap a whole handful of them before my students arrive and cue them up at the piano. They are lined up next to the metronome, sitting on top of their wrappers, waiting for me to grab them as needed.

I also did this at the piano at church last Sunday. Before the service started I lined up a row of cough drops just above the keys, where I could easily pop them into my mouth during the worship songs. My sweet friend Tia, who sings on the worship team, saw me struggling to unwrap them in the moments before we were about to start. She held out her hand, offering to help. But I had almost completed the task, and I was being stubborn.

"No thanks," I smiled at her. "I am determined to do it myself."

CHAPTER 15

JILL

After picking me up, the junior high bus would labor up the hill to the newest part of the housing development, where the early morning buzz of hammering and sawing told of the various homes being built. It was up this road and around a freshly paved cul-de-sac that the bus stopped one morning for someone new. A girl who looked a lot like me climbed onto the bus and sat down in the empty seat in front of me. I don't remember whether I spoke to her that first day, but soon we got to know each other quite well. Jill was a year younger than me. Her family had moved to Seattle from Japan, where her dad had been stationed in the Navy. And when they also started coming to our church, I knew God had sent me a friend. Jill and I became inseparable. We looked so much alike with our long brown hair and bangs that people often got us mixed up. On the way to school each morning, as soon as she sat down next to me on the bus, I would ask her if my mascara was clumped. Together we considered whether our blush might be a little too pink or if our jeans were in style.

Our time together on the bus was never enough. After school we would talk on the phone until our parents insisted we had better things to do. But I could stretch that curly phone cord all the way across the kitchen into our carpeted dining room, where I would lie on my back, spiraling the cord around my fingers, and talk to her about school, about boys, and about God.

We discovered one day that if we lay on our backs with our feet sticking up in the air, we could not stop laughing. This became our regular game on the phone, to raise our feet together and see who could go the longest before bursting out in giggles. But we also had serious talks about our faith.

When a summer discipleship class was offered at our church, we both signed up. This involved memorizing Scripture passages, along with some serious Bible study with questions to answer each week on assigned passages. Jill and I quizzed each other in the backseat of her mom's car on the way to the class.

In the summer we had countless sleepovers, talking long into the night. We helped each other with chores our mothers gave us, like scrubbing a bathroom together. Jill insisted that we use an old toothbrush to clean around the faucet. Together we watered her dad's vegetable garden, and with a silly grin she spoke softly to the plants as she sprinkled them with water: "I am the rain."

Our parents also became great friends, and it wasn't unusual to find our two families together for backyard campfires and holiday dinners.

That winter our youth group had a weekend retreat at a chalet on Mt. Baker. Jill and I shared bunk beds in a dormitory-style room with other girls from our church. We had morning devotions around a beautiful fireplace where our youth pastor led us in worship songs. There was a game room with ping-pong and air hockey tables and an intimidating, long and steep sledding hill just a few steps outside the back door. The first evening we were there the whole group went outside under the stars. People were taking turns going down the hill on sleds and inner tubes. Jill and I found a big inner tube and jumped on together. Bundled up and laughing, we linked our elbows back-to-back and started down the slope. But not far from the top we hit a bump and overturned, and I was thrown forward. I took the entire hard-packed, icy hill face first, scraping my chin the whole way down. The braces on my teeth cut into my bottom lip, and when we finally stopped at the bottom of the hill I managed to press my snowy mitten to my chin. It was bloody.

Jill helped me back inside and helped me get cleaned up. But as much as it hurt, my main concern for the rest of the weekend was how hideous my face looked.

Jill stayed inside with me the next afternoon, while most of the other kids went skiing or sledding. We decided to play ping-pong, and in her usual comical way she invented all kinds of silly strategies: holding the paddles upside down, twirling around between shots, shouting Spanish numbers as we volleyed back and forth. At one point we were laughing so hard that when I hit the ball it bounced right into Jill's open mouth! That did it. We were rolling on the floor, hardly able to breathe from hysteria. From then on we were known fondly in the youth group as "Ping" and "Pong," and for a long time afterward we would sign cards or notes to each other with, "Don't eat any ping-pong balls!"

As I started high school, my lessons with Mrs. Downhour came to a bittersweet end when she gave birth to twins. My mom and I went to see her in the hospital and admire the two tiny babies. My normally sophisticated teacher was wrapped in a hospital gown, with her beautiful dark hair pressed against a pillow. But she smiled and sat up to greet us when we quietly walked in. I shyly offered her a gift bag that contained two toy humpty-dumpties, which my mother had sewn together and stuffed herself. As we chatted by her bedside she suggested that we look for a teacher who could challenge me to go farther in my piano studies. And then she mentioned that, really, I was advanced enough to take on students of my own.

The following Sunday after church, my mom asked our minister of music if he would consider teaching me. He was, after all, the prominent pianist at our church. But he admitted that having a piano student would be new for him. He did agree to meet with me one day after school that week.

At our first lesson together, sitting at the grand piano in his house, he opened the hymnal to "Fairest Lord Jesus" and set it in front of me. "Okay, tell me what key this is in."

I had no idea. "It . . . has three flats."

"Yes—what key is that?"

"I . . . don't know."

"Okay, it's *E flat*. Now, what chords do you see?"

I was totally baffled.

So, patiently, he showed me the difference between major and minor chords and how they were built of thirds. We played through the first few chords, and he had me flip the notes around until I could tell him the root, and whether the chord was major or minor. His assignment that week was to take that hymnal home and write the name of each chord for that song above the staff. There was a chord for each syllable of the verse. We did the first few together, penciling them in above the first phrase. I was excited to do this, finding it fascinating.

He began teaching me about common chords to look for, depending on the key. I learned seventh chords, suspended chords, and relative minors. He showed me that I didn't have to play the notes as written but could rearrange them under my hands to play the chord "flipped over" or with arpeggios instead of all together. This opened a whole new world for me.

My mother spread the word among the ladies in our neighborhood that I was looking for piano students, and before long eight-year-old Bryce and then seven-year-old Julie signed up. In a phone conversation, Mrs. Downhour referred me to a curriculum that printed a teacher's guide, and I was glad to make use of its suggestions for introducing note values and reading treble and bass clefs. I bought a big poster board at the drugstore, along with a package of sticky gold stars. Sitting in the middle of our kitchen floor with a yardstick and a permanent marker, I drew a chart with enough space for ten names (even though I had only two students). I drew in squares in which I could reward them with a gold star for each week of good practice.

So, as a fifteen-year-old, for five dollars a lesson, I sat at the piano with Bryce, and then with Julie, after school once a week and began learning how to teach piano. Jill also asked me to give her piano lessons, and we did sit at the piano together a few times, but our sessions inevitably ended with a round of giggles.

CHAPTER 16

LIGIA

I pull into her driveway, wondering whether she will be outside in her garden. She isn't expecting me. I've come on a whim.

Lois is babysitting all day today, and Lisa is cleaning my house, so I've decided to get out of the way and go get coffee at the little cafe on Main Street. At the first stop sign it occurs to me that this would be more fun if a friend were to come with me, so I flick on my blinker and head around the block to her house.

There she is, lying in a hammock on her screened in front porch, reading a book. Gladiolas and coneflowers are blooming around the porch. Two wooden chickens, painted with bright polka dots, stand guard next to a rosebush and the wide green blades of irises.

I roll down my window as she looks up from her book. "Want to go get coffee with me?"

"Sure!" She rolls out of the hammock and slides her feet into flip-flops before skipping down her front steps. The screen door thwacks behind her.

She is Ligia. The only Ligia I have ever known. In many ways.

The name is pronounced LEE-hee-a, and she often chuckles at people when they try to say it for the first time. When you hear her say it, the *g* is actually more like clearing your throat. I try to use my best Spanish pronunciation, but I have no doubt that, to her, it is not quite right.

I first met her when my husband accepted an engineering position here in Vermont twenty-three years ago. The first time we visited the Panton Church, she and her husband, Peter, were seated in the pew directly in front of us. Her thick, dark hair was shoulder-length then, a beautiful, semisweet chocolate mass of curls that I longed to touch. When it was time to shake hands with the people around us, she and Peter turned around, and it was clear that she was very pregnant. I was holding one-year-old John at my side, and Peter held the hand of their two-year-old daughter, Maria. I knew instantly that we would be friends.

Ligia, born and raised in Honduras, speaks both Spanish and English. She met Vermont-native Peter when he took a teaching job right after college in San Pedro Sula. He returned to Vermont two years later with this princess on his arm. She had agreed to date him in Honduras on one condition: that he go to church with her. Missionaries had shared the gospel with her as a teenager, and her faith in Jesus was unwavering. Soon Peter became a believer as well, and the two of them began their marriage committed to Christ and to each other.

She is one of the happiest people I have ever met. Even when she is grumpy, she laughs at herself for being such a grouch. I remember a day when our kids were young and she was getting something out of her trunk for me. We were standing in her driveway, and just as she opened the trunk there was a gust of wind. She had been stashing plastic grocery bags in there, and the wind took them. They flew in all directions. She ran, laughing and chasing plastic bags through the yard and snatching them out of the air.

Years ago, when our children were all still at home, there was a severe snowstorm that virtually shut down the town. Even our Sunday morning church service was canceled. That morning my husband suggested that we call Peter and Ligia and see whether they would like to walk over to our house for our own private church service. They did. I threw together something in the Crock-Pot and watched out the window for them. Soon we saw their family trudging through the snow, bundled up like Pa Ingalls, up to their thighs in white powder, laughing. After peeling off their layers of hats, scarves, mittens, coats, and snow pants, we gathered our two families in the living room and belted out favorite hymns as I played them on the piano. Peter and my husband took turns reading passages from the Bible. My kids still talk about the time we "did church" in the snowstorm.

Ligia and I have an unspoken appointment every Monday night in the summer, at the concert in the park. Here, in our quintessential New England town square, the city band plays in a typical gazebo, while people relax in their lawn chairs and kids run circles around the great marble war memorial. Our spot is under the oak tree on the north side of the park. My husband sets up our lawn chairs, and soon Ligia will appear with a blanket to throw on the ground, having biked up or walked up from her house. Occasionally Peter comes too, if he isn't teaching a summer class. She'll bring a deck of cards or a knitting project.

Last Monday she reached into her bag and pulled out something she had sewn at her machine that day. It was an ingenious bookmark/pen holder made from elastic and scrap fabric. The elastic band can go around the book, and it includes two perfect pockets for a pen or pencil to slide into. I admired it, and she said, "It's yours!" with a flip of her hand and a huge smile. I have it around my Bible now, holding my favorite pencil, ready for taking notes on the next chapter of Matthew.

Ligia is serious about knowing her Bible. At the weekly Bible study that meets in my living room, she will be scribbling thoughts in a little notebook, her reading glasses perched on the end of her nose. But more than that, she is earnest about following Jesus. When faced with temptation, either of us will contact the other with a simple request: "Pray for me." Once or twice she has very gently but sternly corrected me when she saw me heading down a path toward sin. "Susana," she says with love beaming from her deep brown eyes, "You know the right thing to do."

But today we are not being serious. We are just sipping coffee together at a table on the sidewalk, wondering out loud what our grownup babies are doing today, pondering the beauty of the begonias in the planter next to us, and laughing at our "old lady" ailments.

She offers me her elbow as we rise to head back to my car. "Do you need an arm?"

But today, with my cane, I am feeling pretty steady. "No, I think I'm good."

We stop to look in the window of the antique store and admire an old ladder-back chair that has been re-caned, using colorful old belts. "That is so cute!"

"You could do that," I whisper to her.

"What I need is another project," she giggles.

Friend. Amiga. Sister. Ligia.

CHAPTER 17

STEPHEN

On Easter Sunday Stephen brought me an egg. He placed it in my hand as I came into the Sunday school classroom where we taught the junior high class together. It was incredibly light and felt fragile in my palm. He had blown it himself and hand-painted it with acrylics in shades of bright blue, with puffy white clouds and a rainbow. And circling around and around it he had written one of his favorite Bible verses, Acts 1:11: *"Men of Galilee, why do you stand looking into the sky? This Jesus, who has been taken up from you into heaven, will come in just the same way as you have watched Him go into heaven"* (NASB).

I brought it home and set it carefully on the shelf in my room, next to my bed, poised on a little white plastic ring my mother found for me in her sewing drawer.

We were at a roller skating party with the youth group that spring when Jill told me that her family was moving to Oregon. Sitting together on a bench to lace up our skates, I could barely hear her over the pounding beat of the disco music. "We're moving."

"What?"

"My dad's job."

We stood and clumsily skated across the carpeted floor to the edge of the rink. Clutching the railing, I cautiously stepped down onto the polished floor to join the parade of skaters circling the arena. A disco ball hung from the center of the ceiling, and the lights danced across Jill's face. We locked elbows and did our best to appear graceful. My gold velour V-neck sweater felt sticky against my skin as I tried to let go of Jill and skate without her. She skated on ahead to join a group of girls. I hugged the carpeted wall to keep my balance.

Stephen skated up to me, his unbuttoned flannel shirt fluttering behind him, showing off his *ichthus* T-shirt. He had to shout over the music: "Hey, Xanadu!" He offered me an elbow, and I gladly accepted, as we finished one loop of the rink. We stepped up onto the carpeted floor, where the skating was easier with the traction of the carpet.

"Want to get a Coke?" he shouted.

I landed at a table near the concession booth while he went up to order two Cokes for us. My heart was pounding. I don't think it was the skating, or even sitting with Stephen. It was pure dread. Jill was moving away.

Echoing in my mind was the prayer I had recently prayed at our church revival. Hadn't I knelt in the aisle and surrendered every part of my life to God? And now he was taking Jill away.

As soon as school ended that May, Jill's family packed up to move. On a sunny Saturday morning their station wagon pulled into our gravel driveway, on their way out of our subdivision. In tears, we stood for a long time and hugged, not wanting to let go. Our mothers hugged each other as well, while our fathers shook hands and hashed out the best route to Corvallis, Oregon.

Then Jill got into the back seat and closed the door, waving to me as they pulled out of our driveway and down the road.

It wasn't long afterward that I found out my own family would be pulling out of the state of Washington. And saying goodbye to Stephen would be just as difficult. My parents and I would be moving to Missouri in August. I had one last summer in Seattle, and I spent most of it with Stephen.

One afternoon found us over at his house, where he wanted to show me the irises he had planted near the front door. They were blooming a brilliant purple, with fuzzy yellow beards. He told me he had planted the bulbs in the fall and watched for them to grow this spring. I was amazed. His mother was outside, hanging some lace to dry on a clothesline she had strung between two trees. We wandered over to her, and she showed me the doilies she had crocheted herself. They were so delicate. She had washed and starched them, she explained, and wanted them to dry in the sun.

As we all came inside, she offered Stephen and me some lemonade, and we went into his room to visit his birds. He had two tiny finches in an elegant bamboo birdcage that hung in the corner of his room. They flitted around as we came in, and Stephen greeted them in falsetto: "Hello, Mr. and Mrs. Finch." They knew his voice and chattered away as we talked in his room. He showed me a pastel painting he was working on, one of his sky-scapes with wispy cirrus clouds against a vibrant blue. "It makes me think of Jesus coming back in the clouds," he explained softly. "Someday he's going to BURST through the sky!" His eyes sparkled as he suddenly got loud, teasing me.

On a Saturday afternoon in June, Stephen came over to my house as usual to prepare our notes for our Sunday school class. We were sitting on the living room floor in our typical fashion, with Bibles and papers spread out. I got up to get us some chips from the kitchen pantry. But as I stood, I paused for a moment to take a mental picture. He was reading and deep in thought. I stared, engraving the image in my mind. I wanted to remember this moment forever. I wanted to remember the lines of his hair, the curve of his nose, and the darker skin tone around his eyelids. I thought, *Even if I don't have a photograph, I want to remember this. I want to remember him forever.*

That evening, as we said goodbye in the front hallway, Stephen leaned against the door. "Sue, we have to talk."

I brushed my hair behind my ear. "Talk about what?"

"About us . . . You and me."

I took a deep breath and put my hands in my pockets. "Okay."

"I . . . I don't want to start something now, right before you move away. I mean, we're best friends. And I know it could be something more, but . . . well, you're leaving, and I just graduated, and I'm starting college classes in the fall, and you're . . . you're moving to Missouri, where you're going to turn into one of those sweet Southern belles."

I stared at the doorknob where his hand rested. "Okay."

"Okay?"

"Yeah."

He reached out to hug me, as he always did, and I rested my cheek against his soft flannel shirt. "Okay."

In July our youth pastor, Rick, asked Stephen and me to come with him to kids' camp for a week. Not as counselors, but as co-directors. Stephen would speak at the chapel services each morning, sharing the parables of Jesus, and I would lead the singing. We slept in cabins with the kids and the counselors and ate all our meals together at picnic-style tables in the mess hall, chatting and laughing with our little congregation. Honestly, I spent the week trying not to fall in love with Stephen as I listened to him tell Bible stories to the kids. We met with Rick every afternoon. He coached Stephen on his storytelling skills and gave me pointers for introducing hand motions and keeping the kids engaged. I believe I must have glowed, standing in the front of that rustic chapel teaching the kids our theme song for the week. I sang out a line, and they echoed back:

> *King Jesus is all*
> *My all in all*
> *I know He'll answer*
> *Me when I call*
> *He's walkin' by my side*
> *And I'm satisfied*
> *'Cause He's all*
> *My all in all.*

After camp we had only a few days left before my parents and I would fly to Springfield, Missouri. I stayed up late one of those nights, curled up in my dad's easy chair after everyone else had gone to bed. The reading lamp next to me was the only light in the silent, shadowy main floor of our home. My Bible lay closed in my lap—the Bible I had toted back and forth to youth group and Sunday school so often. The binding was falling apart, and the corners of the cover were ragged. There were highlighted passages and verses underlined in red pen, but I was at a loss.

"Lord," I prayed, "*I don't know how to do this. How can I say goodbye? How can I leave this place? You are asking so much of me. I don't think I can do this.*" I opened my Bible randomly, and the pages fell open to Philippians 4. I looked down and read the words of verse 13: "*I can do all things through Him who strengthens me*" (NASB).

The next day a huge moving van pulled into our driveway, and strange men were in our house, wrapping all our dishes and knickknacks in white paper and stuffing them into boxes. Even in my bedroom a man wearing a blue uniform was putting all my books and stuffed animals into a box marked "Girl's Room #2."

Serena was busy in her own room, packing her boxes and sorting through what she would take to college and what she would send to Missouri with us. She packed our car with her clothes and bedding and took a load of her things over to her best friend Cathy's house. Cathy had also just graduated with Stephen and Serena and would be her roommate in the dorm at Western Washington University. Since her bed was already loaded onto the moving van, Serena was to spend the next few nights at Cathy's before they would venture off to college the following week.

One of the families in the neighborhood offered to let us sleep at their house on that last night, when all our earthly possessions, except for a few suitcases packed with clothes, were on board that enormous van in our driveway.

That final evening Stephen and some of my other friends said they wanted to take me out for pizza. Stephen picked me up, squeezing his tan Ford Pinto into our driveway next to the moving van. As I opened the passenger door to get in, I noticed a long cardboard tube lying in the backseat, something like an empty roll of wrapping paper. Stephen reached back and picked it up, then handed it to me. "This is for you."

I pulled a large, rolled paper out of the tube and carefully uncurled it. It was the pastel painting I had seen in his room that day, now finished with a skyline of ancient Jerusalem at the bottom of a wide, hopeful sky with feathery, light clouds.

This was his heart.

"Oh, Stephen, it's beautiful." I leaned across the gearshift to hug him.

"I think it will survive in your suitcase if you keep it rolled up in the cardboard."

"Yes, I'm sure it will be fine. It's amazing."

After our pizza with friends, Stephen drove me back to my house. We were both quiet. My heart was in my throat, knowing that this was it. When we pulled into the driveway the van was gone, and the house was completely dark. "My parents must already be at the neighbors.'"

"Want to go sit on the steps?" Neither of us was ready to say goodbye. The front steps seemed cold and dark. We wandered around to the backyard, where the log benches my dad had built sat deserted around our campfire pit. We sat staring at the heap of cold ashes, not saying anything. The moonlight shining through the pine branches cast a shadow across Stephen's face. More than anything else, I wanted him to kiss me. He picked up a long stick and stirred the ashes. Why didn't he kiss me? The minutes clicked by, and we just sat there.

I looked down at my feet. "I guess we should go. My parents will be wondering where I am."

We stood to walk back to his car, and I boldly reached for his hand. It was an awkward grip, but I wasn't going to let go. I held on, and he seemed to be holding on too, until we reached the car and he let go to open the door for me. I looked up at his face, but he made no move toward me. I got in, and he went around to the driver's side. Then we backed out of my lonely driveway in silence and down the street to the neighbors' house.

"I'll see you tomorrow at the airport," he finally said.

"You're coming to the airport?"

"Yeah, I'll come and see you off."

That night, trying to fall asleep in my neighbors' guest bedroom, I imagined the scene. We would be ready to board the plane, and just as we would start to walk away Stephen would grab me and kiss me. But it didn't happen that way.

Serena went with us to the airport the next morning, with Shag in the backseat, not knowing what was happening. I stroked the black fur on the top of his head as he laid his chin in my lap.

As we walked through the big glass doors we were surprised by a whole group of friends with Stephen, all greeting us with cheers and hugs. They waited as we went to check our bags. My mother had to convince Shag to get into a big dog crate and then fed him a sedative for the long ride he would endure in the cargo belly of the plane. We watched as the dog crate, with Shag's fluffy tail sticking out the back, traveled along the conveyor belt with our suitcases, on its way out to the plane.

Serena, Stephen, and our friends walked with us to the gate and hugged us all good-bye. My mother held Serena for an extra minute before we turned to go. And as I started walking down the jet bridge with my mom and dad, I looked back to catch one final glimpse of Stephen, wearing his T-shirt and jeans, waving.

CHAPTER 18

RUNAWAY BREAKFAST

My phone dings as I am putting a container of leftover green beans in the fridge after supper. My husband is loading the dishwasher for me, as he always does, and my usual job is to "store the lefties." I glance at my phone on the kitchen counter.

It's my friend, Annette. "Want to do breakfast with me tomorrow?"

"Sure!" I type back.

"I'll pick you up at eight."

"Should I dress up?" We have sometimes gone out for a fancy breakfast at a local B&B where her daughter works.

"No. We're running away."

Hmm. I wonder what she has up her sleeve. Annette and I have had a few adventures together. Our friendship started that fateful day when my husband and I walked into the Panton Church. She wasn't sitting near me like Ligia, but after the service she made a beeline over to me. "You must be new here. Can you come to my house for lunch one day this week?" I was a young wife and mother who didn't know a soul yet in this small town. Two days later I found myself at her kitchen table eating delicious homemade pizza surrounded by her three little children and my toddler, John. The face of her youngest, covered in tomato sauce, matched the orange jack-o-lantern bib he was wearing that day.

She knocks on my door a few minutes after eight.

"Come on in!" I holler from the kitchen, where I am sorting through a stack of junk mail on the table.

She opens the door and steps into my front hall. "Good morning! You ready?" She pushes her sunglasses up and over her thick brown hair, like a headband, revealing her steel-blue eyes.

I walk over to hug her. "Yeah—where're we going?"

"Do you have some good walking shoes on?" She looks down at my feet and smiles at my sneakers. "I thought we would go up a mountain."

Now, Annette has climbed all of the mountains in Vermont. In fact, she has hiked the Long Trail from the Massachusetts border, following the ridge of the Green Mountains, all the way to the Canadian border. She has spent many a night under the stars in a sleeping bag that she carried on her shoulders above a backpack. Mountains are home to her.

There are several smaller mountains within a half-hour's drive from my house, each somewhere between nine and twelve hundred feet in elevation. And I am proud to say that I did hike up one of those trails years ago, with my hubby and the then two-year old John. I couldn't do it today. But there is one mountain, about twenty minutes north, that has a paved road to the top— Mt. Philo. What a perfect name. It means "loving friend."

"Should I bring anything?" I ask Annette.

"Nope, I've got everything in the car."

"I'll go through the garage and meet you out in the driveway," I say, as I open the door from my kitchen to the garage and press the button of the garage door opener. I need to go out this way so I can use the ramp instead of our front steps. Annette heads back out the front door, and I hear her pulling it closed. Now she comes to the open garage door to wait for me.

"Hold on. Let me grab the remote from the car so I can get back in." I open the car door and reach up to the visor where the remote is clipped. I slide it off and put it in my pocket. "Did you get up early this morning?" I ask my friend.

"Oh, you know me. I'm up with the sun!" she chuckles.

I grab my garden walking stick from the corner of the garage, near the open door, and walk out into the sunshine. As I open the passenger door of her car, I spy a picnic basket on the backseat, covered in a blue checked cloth. "You've been busy this morning!"

I set my body down into the front seat, and she smiles as she turns the key in the ignition. "Sometimes you just have to run away with a friend," she announces.

The morning is warm and clear. The blue sky and billowy white clouds promise that it will be a beautiful summer day. We chat effortlessly as we drive up Route 7, then turn onto the side road that takes us over to the foot of the mountain. Annette slows to a stop at the little booth just inside the park gate, and a ranger steps out. "Good morning, ladies!"

"Good morning!" we answer in unison.

Annette hands him her park pass, and he takes a hole puncher from his pocket. "Should be a lovely day up there.

Stay to the right on your way up." He hands the punch card back to Annette.

We begin our ascent through maple trees and pines. Wild grapevines have entwined themselves around saplings near the road, and the raspberry canes lean against the milkweed, with rosy blooms attracting little bees. The road gets steeper as we come to a fork, with a sign pointing us to the right, and we follow, turning sharply around a huge boulder. Then, up and around—I think we are circling the mountain. To my right, as it slopes off, the woods are carpeted with a layer of graying leaves, and old logs are strewn about. The Queen Anne's lace has found a few open spots to bloom, especially near the road.

At the top the pavement opens up to a small parking lot, and Annette pulls into a spot close to the wide trail that leads to the pavilion and the open viewing area. We both step out of the car, and I reach back in for my walking stick. The trees are blocking the view from here, but I know we are about to see something spectacular just up the trail.

"Let's see . . . How should we do this?" she ponders out loud as she pulls the picnic basket out of the back. "Will you need an arm?"

"I'm not quite sure." I wish I could help her carry something. "Why don't I try it, and if I need you, I'll grab you."

"Okay." She hooks the handle of the basket over her elbow. Which side do you need me to be on?"

"Um, my left, I guess." But as we begin walking up the path, it seems fairly flat and even, so I think I'll be all right with just my stick.

About halfway to the pavilion is a little trail sloping down to the left, where a picnic table is poised perfectly on a bit of level ground and the trees open up for a view of the valley below.

"Can you make it down there?" Annette asks me.

"Um . . . I could try." I take a few steps, but there are some tree roots that are definitely going to be a problem for me at this angle. I reach out to steady myself on the trunk of a small maple.

"Here. Wait right there, and I'll come back for you." Annette walks easily to the picnic table and sets down her basket. "Wait till you see the view from there," she exclaims as she comes back up.

I take her elbow and we start down, pausing twice as I step over roots. The trail isn't really wide enough for two people, so at one point we have to turn sideways and sashay between two big rocks. She walks me right over to the picnic table, and I sit down on the bench.

Finally I look up, and the scene takes my breath away. Lush green fields spread out below. Darker green cushiony treetops outline farms and estates. Tiny white roofs of houses reflect the sun here and there, with thin, silvery roads leading between them. Beyond that Lake Champlain is a cerulean blue, with jade-colored peninsulas defying the water, stretching out and forming little round bays where the white specks of boats can be detected if you squint. And, standing broad and regal above the waters, four or five distinct layers of the Adirondacks are brushed in varying hues of indigo, cobalt, and sapphire.

I cannot sit here at the table. I've got to get closer. I lower myself down onto the ground and do a little crab walk over to the edge. "Annette, let's have our breakfast over here," I nearly whisper as my view becomes more panoramic.

She brings the basket and sits down at my side on the rock ledge. I could almost dangle my feet over, but I shrink back and sit as close as my nerves will let me. She folds back the cloth from her basket and pulls out a little metal pot, a can of sterno, a box of matches, and a bottle of water. "I thought I would make us some tea," she announces, as though this were an everyday occurrence. She has also brought two china tea cups with saucers, wrapped in cloth napkins, as well as two spoons and two china bowls. There is a plastic container of fruit salad, and from a smaller basket, wrapped in a tea towel, emerges the best surprise of all: four of her scrumptious blueberry muffins, each adorned with a little paper fairy on a toothpick.

"I can't believe you did all of this." I beam at my precious friend.

"Oh, Suzanne, I needed it as much as anybody."

We sip our tea and savor the fruit and muffins while commenting on the majesty of our Creator. And then Annette reaches into the basket once again and pulls out a book. "I wanted to read a chapter of this out loud while we are here," she says. I recognize the cover at once. It is Hannah Hurnard's classic novel *Hind's Feet on High Places.* "Have you read it?" she asks.

"A long time ago." My mind travels back to Stephen storing the book in our school locker and encouraging me to read it.

She opens the book and begins to read about little Much Afraid walking up the mountain with her companions, Sorrow and Suffering. I gaze out at the mountains across the lake as she reads, aware of my own companions and the significance of this allegory. Her voice is clear in the quiet of this morning, competing only with the gentle calls of finches and the breeze rustling the pine boughs. I know that she, like me, is Much Afraid at times, calling out to the Good Shepherd in desperation.

Years ago I sat at Annette's dining room table after church one Sunday afternoon when she and her husband, Eric, had invited my little family over for lunch. I was pregnant with Lois at the time, and I had just received the news that my three-year-old, John, had inherited my tainted gene for CMT. My darling little blonde boy had sat so still, holding my hand while they drew his blood. "Look at me, John," I remember saying. "It won't take long." Indeed, that part went quickly, but getting the results took longer than this praying, impatient mother thought she could bear. It was weeks before the pediatric neurologist called with the dreaded news that yes, John had CMT. I had sat with Annette in tears at her table. "How can I trust God?" I had asked, rubbing my belly, "when I pray that *this* child will not have it?"

As Annette finishes reading the chapter, it seems only natural for us to pray together. We praise God for showing us His astounding beauty. We thank Him for His goodness, His faithfulness, and His mercy. We pray for our little church, and for individual lives within it that need His tender care. We pray for our husbands, working in the same engineering company and also serving together as a lay pastor and elder within our humble congregation. We pray for our children, one by one, her four and my two, that each would be following after the heart of God. And then she prays for me, and I for her, that we would each continue in our walk with Christ, in our climb up the mountain, held by the hand of our dear Savior.

CHAPTER 19

SPRINGFIELD

My first day of eleventh grade at Glendale High School in Springfield, Missouri, was hot and sticky. There was no air-conditioning in the three-story building, and when I leaned back against the wooden chair in my history class my pink cotton blouse stuck to the varnish.

I had awakened that morning in the hotel room where I was staying with my parents while we waited for our moving van to arrive with our beds and the rest of our furniture. My dad had taken me to breakfast at McDonald's and then driven me to the daunting front entrance of the school in his new company car. As I walked in, other students were greeting each other, boys slapping each other on their backs and girls squealing as they hugged. I had been to the school the day before, to get my schedule and a map of the building, and it hadn't seemed so scary then. But now the hallways were filled with teens who obviously knew each other better than they would ever know me.

The girl sitting next to me in my English class seemed equally nervous, so I introduced myself. Her name was Lori, and she had just moved from Oklahoma. I told her I had just moved from Seattle, and the smile we exchanged as our teacher started class confirmed that we were instant friends. We agreed to find each other at lunch.

My next class was chorus, and I was excited to have an hour of singing in my schedule every day. I walked into the large room where choir risers were pushed against a wall and forty or fifty high schoolers were gabbing and laughing. The chairs were arranged in sections, four rows each for sopranos, altos, tenors, and basses. I sat down in the front row of the alto section, hugging my schoolbooks to my chest. The other girls were chattering with each other until the director, Mrs. Kugler, called us to order. We sang scales first, and she introduced hand motions for the different notes. She handed out some sheet music, and as we passed it down the row I noticed the gold pin on the collar of the girl sitting next to me. It said "Jesus First."

I couldn't wait until after class to ask her about it. But what should I say? She had beautiful, long, wavy blonde hair and the face of a model. As she wrote her name at the top of her sheet music, I saw in lovely script, "Tuesday."

Finally, when Mrs. Kugler dismissed us, and we were gathering our books to leave, I turned to her bravely. "Is your name Tuesday?"

"Yes!" She seemed so self-confident. "What's yours?"

"Sue." I mustered my courage. "I noticed your pin. I . . . I think it's important to put Jesus first." *That sounded totally stupid.*

"I agree!" She looked down at the pin. "I got this at a conference at my church." Some other girls were waiting for her over by the classroom door. "I'll see you tomorrow!"

When school ended that day, my mom was waiting for me in the car outside the front door of the school. She drove me to our new house, where the same huge moving van was now parked and furniture was being unloaded. Shag greeted me, his tail wagging vigorously, and I took a few moments to scratch his ears and stroke the fur under his chin.

Our new home was a picture of the American Dream. A circle driveway brought you to the brick steps at our front door. The front hall featured a tiled floor and an elegant staircase. To the left was a formal living room, where the piano now sat waiting for me. Straight ahead was the kitchen, where I dropped my books on the table. Looking past the refrigerator and stove, I could see our dining room furniture being arranged by the movers in a carpeted room with a bay window. And back to my right, two steps down from the kitchen, was a large family room with French doors that led out onto a patio.

Upstairs, I had chosen the bedroom at the front of the house that had a little nook where a padded window seat was tucked into a dormer window. I could sit there and gaze out at the quintessential pasture across the street from our home, where old oak trees graced the edge of a pond and two chestnut horses had their noses in the grass. A barbed-wire fence provided the perfect border between the old road in front of our house and the horses' domain.

When my bed was set up and my dresser had been placed against one wall, I decided to get to work unpacking the boxes that the movers had stacked in my room, "Girl's Room #2." Here were my winter sweaters that were to go into my bottom drawer, and the lamp I set up on the table beside my bed. Here was my yearbook, and my clock radio, and a framed picture of Jill and me standing arm-in-arm in front of my house in Seattle.

Then I reached into the box and pulled out a wad of paper. What was in here? I unwrapped it cautiously, slowly revealing Stephen's precious egg—smashed into little pieces.

My back teeth clenched tightly together, and I could feel the sting behind my eyes. I carried the wrinkled paper, cradling my shattered treasure, down the stairs and found my mother in the kitchen unwrapping glasses and setting them in the cabinet. I couldn't say anything. I just held it out to show her. She looked down at the carnage in my hands and sighed deeply. Pulling me close, she wrapped her arms around me and let me cry.

Over the next few days at school, I made sure to sit in the same choir seat next to Tuesday, who always greeted me with a warm smile. And then Lori and I would eat lunch together, exchanging woes over leaving behind old friends and getting used to the way things were done at our new school. Lori had a boyfriend back in Oklahoma who often wrote to her. She wore his high school ring on a chain around her neck. I told her all about Stephen, and that I wondered how, or whether, I would ever see him again. We compared notes from our English class and decided that this teacher required way too much homework in comparison to our previous schools. And together we noticed that the fashions here were different. Girls dressed up for school in skirts and blouses. If they did wear jeans, they were tapered at the ankles, not bell-bottom like all of mine were. Lori and I quickly realized we were both out of style. So as soon as my mother's sewing machine was unpacked I turned all my jeans inside-out and sewed down the outside seams, tapering the legs until they looked like what the other girls were wearing.

After school the bus would let me off right in front of our house, and Shag would be waiting for me, his tail going wild. After a ruffle of his mane, I would go straight to the mailbox to see whether there was a letter for me in Stephen's handwriting. To my delight, about every third day I would find one; I would tear into it before I got inside the front door. And of course, I wrote back, telling him all about school and our new home.

Mom and Dad and I visited several Baptist churches in Springfield. There were so many to choose from. We finally settled on one that had a couples' Sunday school class for my parents, good preaching, a full choir in the loft behind the pulpit, and a youth group of fifty or more teens. Some of these teens I had seen at the high school, even though none of them had ever spoken to me.

My Sunday school class would start each session as a large group in the youth room, where we sat in metal folding chairs and ate donuts before breaking into smaller groups. The eleventh-grade girls' group filed into a side room and sat in a circle of seven or eight chairs with our teacher, who was the mother of one of the boys in the other room. We cracked open our Bibles, and someone would read a passage out loud. I expected a discussion to follow that would apply the Scripture to our lives. Instead, the girls began talking about which boys were cute and how stylish their new clothes were. One stood up to model her new plaid wool skirt, pleated at the waist. She sat down and smoothed it over her lap.

One girl asked our teacher, "Do you think it's a sin if you're at a party and you just hold the cup of beer in your hand but don't actually drink it?"

Another girl chimed in, "Oh, I just go in the bathroom and pour a little down the sink, so it looks like I've been drinking it."

I sat in stunned silence.

My mother asked around for a piano teacher, and she got the name of a retired music professor from the State University. She picked me up after school one day and drove me to his house in an older part of Springfield. He welcomed us into his small home, where a huge grand piano encompassed most of the front room. A dusty old couch was pushed against the front window, and my mom took a seat there while I sat down at the piano bench.

He dropped to the carpet next to me and sat cross-legged on the floor. "Do you have something prepared that you could play for me?" Nervously, I began playing through Michel Legrand's "Brian's Song." I had worked on it with my music minister/teacher in Seattle before we moved, perfecting all of the dynamics and tempo changes. He closed his eyes and sat still, listening as I got to the majestic second chorus, with loud, powerful, eighth-note chords. "Yes, yes, yes." He hugged his knees.

As I finished the piece with simple, quiet, rolled chords, he began shuffling through a stack of music on the floor under the piano. "Here, try this." It was a complicated piece by a name I didn't recognize. He stuck it on the rack in front of me, and I fumbled through the first few lines. "Yes, take that home and see what you can do with it."

I left feeling aimless and missing my former teacher. I muddled through a few more sessions with this eccentric old man before my mother, driving me home from a lesson and sensing that I was unhappy, relieved me. "You don't have to continue if you don't want to."

I sighed. "Maybe I could see about getting some students, though?"

She helped me call the newspaper to put an advertisement in the classified section: "Beginner Piano Lessons, $5 per half-hour session" with our phone number. I got one call from a woman who had a daughter who was interested. But when she asked me about details and found out that I was a high school student, she changed her tone. "I hope this doesn't sound unkind, but aren't you a little young to be doing this?"

"Well, I've had two other students, when we were living in Seattle last year."

But I never heard from her again.

CHAPTER 20

DUCT TAPE

Our car is packed to the gills. That's what my husband says. It's all of my daughter's stuff, plus one suitcase that my husband and I are sharing. We are taking Lois back to college. I hate goodbyes, and this is going to be a long one.

It's nine hundred miles from our home in Vermont to Wheaton, Illinois. We left yesterday morning, starting out by crossing the Lake Champlain Bridge, and then drove all the way across New York, the corner of Pennsylvania, and all of Ohio. Once inside Indiana, our three tired bodies were more than happy to stretch out on the beds in a hotel room and watch the tail end of an old movie.

This morning Lois has gone down to the lobby to see if they have any decent coffee while her father takes a shower and I get dressed. I am sitting in the desk chair putting on my leg braces when I notice that my nylon is caught on something. I look down carefully. There is a crack in the white plastic brace, right at the curve from my foot to my ankle.

"Oh no!" I know from experience that this is not good. I take my foot out of it and bring the brace into my lap to get a better look. I gently press against the foot section to see how bad the crack is. As I put pressure on it, the crack opens up, about halfway across the back of the ankle. "Oh no!"

"What's wrong?" My husband calls from the bathroom, where he is brushing his teeth.

"There's a crack in my leg brace."

"What?" he asks, walking over to me, toothbrush still in hand.

"Look at this." I push on the foot part again, showing him the crack as it opens up. I might be wrong, but it seems as though it goes further this time across the ankle. It won't be long before the whole thing goes.

"Oh. . . . That seems bad."

"I know! What am I going to do?" I hand the brace to him, and he turns it over, inspecting it.

"Hmmm. We could duct tape it."

"Are you serious?"

"Well . . . is there someone you could call?"

We look at each other. This might change all our plans. After dropping off Lois in Wheaton, we were going to spend a few days with his parents in Detroit and then take our time driving back to Vermont, perhaps spending a night in Stratford, Ontario, and taking in a Shakespeare play.

I open the desk drawer and pull out the phone book. "I don't even know what to look for. 'Technician,' I guess. 'Orthotics.'" I thumb through the yellow pages. "Ugh." I should just look it up on my phone. "Should I look for someone in Chicago?"

"I guess . . . ," he sighs.

I type "Orthotics technician Chicago" in the search bar, and a whole list of businesses pop up. "Prosthetics and Orthotic

Technicians." I call the first one. No answer. I guess they are not open yet.

"You know, it's an hour earlier in Illinois," my husband reminds me. I look at my watch. It's almost nine, which means it's almost eight in Chicago. I try calling the second one.

A very kind woman answers.

"Oh! Good morning," I try to sound calm as I explain my situation.

"Did you have the braces made here at our office?"

"No, I had them made in Vermont, where I live."

"I'm sorry, but we only repair pieces we've made ourselves. You'll have to contact the technician who made them."

"But I am here. I'll be in Chicago today. I just need someone to fix them . . . to hold them together until I get home."

"I'm sorry. It's a liability issue."

Sigh. "Okay."

I guess I had better call the guy in Vermont and see whether he knows anyone in Chicago. Maybe he has some colleague who would help me out. I'm trying to think of his name. Or at least the name of his business. *Think. Think.* I should just search it on my phone. "Orthotic technician Vermont." Bingo.

His receptionist answers.

"Hi. This is Suzanne Rood calling."

"Hi, Suzanne, how are you?"

"Well, I'm outside of Chicago, bringing my daughter to college . . ."

"How can she be that old already? I remember that sweet little girl."

"I know—the years fly by. Um, I just noticed there's a crack in one of my braces, at the ankle, about halfway across the back."

"Oh, dear. Let me go get Dave."

The phone goes silent. I picture her getting up from her office chair and going down the hall to find Dave in some back room where he is sanding down someone's prosthetic.

When he picks up the phone, I explain my situation once again.

He pauses. "Uh . . ." I can almost hear the gears turning in his head. "Do you have any duct tape?"

"Ha, ha."

"No, I'm serious. No one in Chicago is going to touch them if they didn't make them. Wrap some duct tape around them until you get home. That should keep the crack from getting any bigger, anyway. Can you come in next week?"

"Um, yes. We should be home by next Wednesday, I think." I look up at my husband as he nods.

"Okay. Why don't you come in on Friday, and we'll make you some new ones. In the meantime, wrap the tape around them three or four times. Do you have an old pair?"

"Well, not with me. But yes, at home I do."

"Good. So you can hopefully wear those while you're waiting for your new ones to be ready."

Ugh. I know this process could take weeks. First, he will wrap my foot and lower leg with strips of gauze dipped in plaster of Paris, like the doctor setting my broken arm so many years earlier. He will hold my foot in position while it hardens and then cut off the cast with an electric rotary saw, with one straight cut down the front. He will remove the cast gently, because after my appointment he will use it to make a white plaster statue of my leg. Then he can wrap a sheet of heated plastic around it, cutting it, sanding it, and molding it to the exact shape and size of my leg.

"I'll let you set up an appointment time with Cara."

He hands the phone back to her, and she asks if I can come in at 1:00 next Friday.

"Sure. See you then."

As I hang up the phone I am thinking about that old pair of leg braces that are hidden underneath the ruffle of the blue chair upstairs in my bedroom back home. I think there might actually be two old pair under there. An idea hits me. I open a new text message on my phone to Ligia.

"Hey, are you home? Can I ask a big favor?"

"Yes," she types. "What do you need?"

"We're on our way to Chicago and one of my leg braces is breaking."

"Ay! Caramba!" she types.

I explain to her where to find the spare key to our house, where to find my old braces, and ask whether she can mail them overnight to my in-laws' house. "We're headed there tomorrow after we leave Chicago. I'll pay you back for the postage."

"Not a problem. What's the address?"

I look up at my husband, who is putting on his shoes to go buy some duct tape. "Honey, what's your parents' address? Ligia's gonna overnight my old braces to me."

I type in the address as he dictates it and then add, "I don't know how many are actually under that blue chair, or what condition they are in, or if they are right foot or left. Just send them all."

I hang out in the desk chair, shoeless, waiting for my husband to return from the store. Lois comes back to the room and suggests that we go through the Starbucks drive-through on our way out of town. From my confined place in the desk chair, I show her my situation. When she sees the crack she wraps her arms around my shoulders, leaning her head against mine. "Oh, Mama."

With my brace now wrapped in duct tape, I have made it to the car. I am cautiously grasping my husband's elbow with my free hand, and probably leaning on the cane more than usual. With every step I hear a click as the raw edges of the crack scrape against each other, like someone flicking their fingernails. I wonder if at some point it will snap mid-stride. But for now I am just riding in the car, and the Starbucks drive-through is a welcome distraction.

Once inside Illinois we catch a glimpse of the Chicago skyline, and I wave in that direction, "Hi John-John!" knowing that he is probably sitting at his computer in one of those high-rise buildings, just a block away from the Willis tower, writing some kind of software code that I will never wrap my brain around.

Lois has been texting madly with her boyfriend, Mike, for about the last hour. And finally, as we pull into the parking lot of an apartment building near the train tracks in Wheaton, Mike simultaneously pedals his bike down the side street to meet us. Lois is out of the car just as soon as we stop, and Mike's bicycle is lying in the grass as he wraps her in a bear hug.

My husband steps out of the driver's seat, and Mike reaches out to shake his hand. "Can I help you carry stuff in?"

"Um, I don't have a key to get in the front door yet." Lois looks around. "And I don't know if any of my roommates are here." At that moment someone walks out of the apartment building, and like a bolt of lightning Mike runs to catch the door before it completely closes.

I step out of the car as my husband opens the trunk. "If you can hold the door, Suzie, we can bring stuff in."

That's a good job for me. Except that there are three cement steps up to the door. My husband has to walk me—more like *pull* me up the steps—while Mike stands holding the door. But once we are up, I trade places with Mike and he skips down the steps to go grab an armload of stuff.

"Has anyone texted Aunt Serena?" I yell toward Lois.

"Yeah, she's on her way!" she yells back.

Serena now works as a regional manager for Operation Christmas Child and conveniently has an office here in Wheaton. Her apartment is only about fifteen minutes away, and Lois has taken advantage of the situation by storing a laundry basket full of linens and a box of winter clothes there over the summer.

Mike hops up the steps carrying a large tote filled with clothes, and I open the door wide. Inside the hallway he bounds up the staircase to the second floor, where Lois will be sharing an apartment this year with three other girls.

Lois carries a suitcase through the door and up the stairs, and my husband follows with a box full of books. After a couple more trips the parade of stuff is concluded, and my husband comes back down the stairs to me. "Do you want to go up?"

I eye the staircase. It's pretty steep. There is a railing on only one side. "Yeah," I answer hesitantly. He offers me an elbow, and we start upward. Left foot up, pull on the railing, right foot up. Click. A student starts coming down the stairs above us. My husband retreats down a step, and I hug the railing so she can get by. Then he is back at my side, and we continue our climb.

"Do you feel like it's holding?" he asks.

"I think so."

Left foot up, pull on the railing, right foot up. Click. We keep going.

It is an adorable apartment. Small, but clean. There is a living room area, where one of the girls has thrown a quilt over the back of a couch. A small kitchen table fills one corner of the kitchen. I go right to work unpacking Lois's mugs and dishes from a box on the counter, stacking them in a cabinet. I can hear her talking to her dad and Mike in her bedroom. "Can we put the desk over here?"

In the bottom of the box there is a little pad of cute floral paper with a magnet to hang on the fridge. I fish a pen out of my purse, write my daughter a love note, and hang it up.

She walks in from the bedroom, looking at her phone. "John says his train gets into the Wheaton station at 5:27."

"Okay. Did you tell him Dad will pick him up?"

"Yeah . . ." She is texting. "Oh! Aunt Serena is here. I'll go meet her."

I hobble toward the bedroom to see what the guys are doing. Mike is lifting up one end of the bed while my husband is maneuvering a bookshelf to go under it. I imagine my girl climbing up into that bed every night to snuggle under the covers. A train whistle blows, and the clickety-clack gets surprisingly loud as it passes by. I wonder how she will ever sleep through that.

"Hello!" I hear Serena's familiar voice as she comes into the apartment with Lois, and I do my best to hurry to greet her. She sets down her load on the floor, then reaches out to hug me. We are the same height, and our chins fit perfectly over each other's shoulders as we embrace each other tightly. I steady myself with my cane as we let go. I look into her familiar eyes. The older we get the more alike we look. Except that she has our mother's hazel eyes, and I have our dad's dark brown.

"How was your trip?" she asks.

"Oh, fine." I don't really want to tell her about my broken brace right now. "I think John is on his way out here as soon as he gets off work, and we can all go to dinner together."

"Do you want any help unpacking?" she offers.

"Nah," Lois replies, "It's going to take me awhile to figure out where I want everything."

Serena looks at her watch. "Well, maybe I'll go back to the office for a while. I'm supposed to have a video meeting with someone. Where do you want to meet for dinner?"

"There's that Mexican place we went to before. Do you like that?"

"Sure."

"Okay. We're meeting John at the train at 5:30. How 'bout we meet you there right after that?"

"Yep. Okay," she nods. "Hey, Lois, I washed the sheets that were in here. So you can just put them right on your bed." She turns to head back down the stairs.

"Aw, you're the best!" Lois reaches down to grab the laundry basket and take it to her room.

I limp out into the hallway to see Serena off. "Thank you so much, Serena."

"Sure thing." I watch as she grabs the railing to steady herself on the stairs. Despite her having inherited the same condition, she handles them a lot more gracefully than I do, without a cane and without anyone's arm to cling to.

"See you soon!" She waves back at me as she heads outside.

I can't get out of the car fast enough when I see John jogging toward our car from the train. He is tall and thin, just like his father was as that age, with the exact same dark hair. He has grown a full beard but keeps it trimmed short, and as he bends down to hug me I kiss his whiskery face.

"Heeeeeeyyyyy!" he flashes his sweet smile and throws a wave toward his dad in the front seat before climbing into the backseat with Lois and Mike. Lois, seated in the middle, throws her arms around her brother before he buckles up.

My mind travels back in time to when they were young, giggling in the backseat together over some silly lyrics to a song they had made up. I think it was something about brushing teeth and involved John beat-boxing while Lois rapped. For a moment they revert in my mind to the ages of eight and twelve. Then I blink and look back at them, and they are once again twenty and twenty-four.

"We thought we would go to that Mexican restaurant again," my husband tells John.

"Oh yeah, that sounds great!" he answers.

The hostess seats the five of us at a table for six, next to a window. I take a chair near the wall and lean my cane against a window frame. My husband looks out into the parking lot to see if he spies Serena's car.

"I'll go watch for her," Mike offers politely as the rest of us settle in.

My husband sits down next to me and whispers, "How's it holding up?"

To be honest, the clicking has gotten louder throughout the day. "So far, so good," I whisper back. I'd rather not make it a topic for our dinner conversation.

I open the menu and start reading, but soon set it down as I look across the table. Here we are. Just the four of us, as it used to be for so many years. My daughter looks radiant. Her dark brown hair is pulled back in a cute ponytail, with stylish bangs just above her bright blue eyes. My son's similar eyes are framed in dark-rimmed glasses. And as he glances through the menu I can't help but think once again that he looks exactly like my husband did when I married him.

He looks up. "Can we get the tableside guacamole?"

Lois answers quickly. "Yeah—duh!"

"Oh, here's Aunt Serena!" John exclaims, as he sets down his menu and stands up to hug her.

Mike rejoins us as well, taking the seat next to Lois.

"How was your video meeting?" I ask.

"Oh, fine. I have to go to Minneapolis later this week." She picks up a menu as the waitress comes over to fill our water glasses.

"When do you go to the Philippines?" I honestly can't keep track of all her travels.

"In a couple weeks."

She amazes me. Single, traveling the world on mission trips, learning foreign languages, organizing volunteers, and speaking at churches.

"You know you are welcome to stay with me." She politely double-checks with me.

"Thanks. I know. We'll take John home downtown tonight and then start back toward Michigan. We'll probably stay somewhere in Indiana."

"Okay. But you guys should all come over after this."

Our waitress has returned now with chips and salsa and asks whether we are ready to order.

After stuffing ourselves on enchiladas and guacamole and quesadillas, we all head over to Serena's place and crash in her living room. I am thankful that she lives on the first floor and that there is just one little cement step up to her front door. John sits down on one corner of the couch, extending his long legs straight out into the room and crossing his ankles. Mike and Lois sit together at the other end, and he throws an arm up comfortably behind her. I plop down on my sister's red checked loveseat, across the room from her bookshelf, where photos of our parents and grandparents are displayed in a variety of frames. And she leans back in a comfy chair over by the fireplace, where souvenirs from different countries she has visited are displayed on the mantle. Her coffee table holds a teapot and cups she brought back from Bulgaria, and sitting under the lamp next to me is a doll dressed in traditional kente cloth from Ghana.

"Want to play twenty-million questions?" my husband asks as he stretches out on the carpet.

This is a game he started playing with our kids when they were barely old enough to understand it. A variation on Twenty Questions, someone chooses a person, place, or thing and the others take turns asking yes or no questions until someone guesses the answer. But over the years the "things" have gotten more and more obscure and hilarious. Frankenstein's left big toenail. The buffalo that was walking down the middle of the road at Yellowstone Park during our vacation there one summer. The strawberry that fell off a table once at a farmer's market—we had all watched as it rolled under the wheel of a passing stroller and got squished.

"Pick something we will all know," I suggest to my lounging husband, knowing that this game will be new to both Mike and Serena.

"Okay, I've got something," he answers, folding his hands behind his head.

Lois asks first. "Is it edible?"

"No," he chuckles.

Now it's Mike's turn. "Is it bigger than a bread box?"

"How big is a bread box?"

"You know, about this big." Mike holds his hands up, about two feet apart.

"Hmmm. I would say . . . no."

My turn. "Is it something we saw tonight?"

"I don't think so."

Now Serena: "Is it man-made?"

"Yes."

Then John. "Do you need a license for it?"

"Ha! No."

It takes us a while before we finally narrow it down to the sticky paper that is wrapped around a pair of socks when you buy them.

We all hug Serena goodbye before the five of us pile back into our car to drive Lois and Mike back to her apartment near campus.

"Do you want us to take you back to your place? Oh, I guess your bike is still at Lois's apartment." My husband is addressing Mike.

"No, that's fine. I'll bike back."

In the parking lot we all get out of the car for another round of hugs.

Mike shakes my husband's hand as I wrap my arms around my girl.

"I guess I'll see you at Thanksgiving." I am starting to get choked up.

"I love you, Mama." We hold each other for an extra moment, but not long enough. "Okay, rip the Band-Aid off," she says, which is her analogy for "Let's get this over with," and she lets go. I climb back into the car, and we pull out of the dusky parking lot, waving at the young sweethearts standing there hand-in-hand.

Now we have nearly an hour's drive to get downtown to John's apartment. This gives me a chance to ask him all about work, and what kind of software he has been writing (not that I would understand any of that). I twist my body around from the front seat so I can see his handsome face as fully as possible. We talk about the worship team at his church. He usually plays drums or runs sound for them. I ask about what new songs they have been doing lately. Then he shows us a recording of a song on his phone that he has been composing, using a modular synthesizer and some other electronic equipment that he tries to explain to me. It has a very cool drum pattern, and a unique chord structure that modulates between keys. I'm extremely impressed.

My husband pulls up slowly to the sidewalk near the gate at John's apartment building. I don't like this moment. We step out of the car under the light of a street lamp. There are city sounds of traffic and people laughing in the distance. My husband and I take turns hugging our boy, as our shadows on the pavement embrace each other, too. I kiss John's bearded cheek once again before letting go. "I love you, Johnny Cakes."

"Love you, too!" He says matter-of-factly as he hops up onto the curb. "I'll call you next weekend, like always." He unlocks the gate and waves to us as we pull away.

I watch until he disappears inside, gratefully praising God that John's CMT symptoms are so minimal. I turn in my seat to face forward now, and my husband reaches over to grab my hand. We drive on in the dark, through the city toward Indiana. And tomorrow we will get to Detroit, where my old leg braces will be waiting for me in a box at my in-laws' house.

CHAPTER 21

GRIEF

Serena flew home from college for Thanksgiving. Well, it wasn't exactly "home" to her, since she had never been to Springfield before. But we were there. My mom and I made a huge paper banner that announced, "Welcome Home, Serena!" and hung it across the wide kitchen doorway so that when we walked in from the garage after picking her up at the airport it would be there to greet her. The four of us sat at the kitchen table for a late-night piece of pecan pie as she told us all about life in the dorm.

I was excited to show her to her bedroom upstairs. My mom had bought a new comforter for her bed that complimented the floral wallpaper. There were moving boxes stacked against one wall waiting for her to unpack, because we thought she would like to arrange her things on the walls and on her dresser the way she wanted them. I sat on her bed while she told me stories about her roommate and suitemates late into the night, long after Mom and Dad had gone to bed.

The weekend went by too quickly, but we knew she would be back in a few weeks for her Christmas break, and Mom and Dad were talking about the four of us driving down to Florida to visit all the grandparents and cousins for the holidays.

One December morning there was a dusting of white powder lining every branch of the locust trees around our house. From my bedroom window I could see the horses across the street putting their noses down into the snow to nibble on the grass underneath.

When I got off the bus in the afternoon I was surprised to find Shag, not running to greet me, but lying on his side in the snow near our front steps. I stooped down to stroke his forehead and scratch behind his ear, but he didn't even raise his head for me.

"Mom," I cried as I burst through the door, "there's something wrong with Shag."

"I know," she sighed from the kitchen sink. "He's been like that all day. I think he's running a fever. I've got an appointment tomorrow with the vet."

While I was at school the next day she coaxed him into the car and drove him across town. The vet decided to keep him overnight. In fact, Shag continued to stay with the vet while the four of us drove down to Florida for Christmas.

My dad was especially eager to see his mother because she had recently gone into the hospital to have a tumor removed from her throat. We stayed at my Uncle Wayne (my dad's youngest brother) and Aunt Linda's house, and all the girl cousins slept on the living room floor in sleeping bags, chatting long into the night with the lights from the Christmas tree casting a multi-colored glow onto the ceiling.

The next morning we filed quietly into my grandmother's hospital room. My mother was carrying a bright red poinsettia with a crinkly gold bow. Grandmother was sitting up, her little frame covered in a light pink hospital gown. She could barely speak, but she was moved to tears to see her beloved son and hugged us all, one by one. A box of tissues was in her lap, and now and then she had to spit into a tissue and gently wipe her mouth. "I'm so sorry you have to see me like this," she whispered. "I can't swallow."

My grandmother was a woman of quiet dignity. She had survived the Great Depression as a teenager in rural Georgia. She had raised five children and struggled through a failing marriage with an alcoholic husband. She had kept her head above water after her divorce by working as a cashier and renting out a bedroom in her little house. But every Sunday you would find her in the same pew at the Baptist church in Fort Lauderdale, singing hymns to her Savior.

My dad sat on the edge of her bed and held her hand. We didn't stay long. I could tell it was difficult for her to allow us to see her suffering like that. Even as she wiped her mouth with a tissue, she did so with a grace that denied the pitiful condition to which she had become victim.

It was raining hard as we began the long, two-day drive back to Missouri. Serena and I were quiet in the back seat. The rain beat against the roof of the car, and the scene out my window was smeary. I was supposed to be reading Ernest Hemingway for my English class, but I was procrastinating. The book was lying on the seat beside me.

My dad cleared his throat. "I need to tell you girls something. We got a phone call from the vet while we were staying at Uncle Wayne's house."

Then I remembered the phone ringing early that morning while I was still dreaming, wrapped in my sleeping bag on the floor.

"Shag died."

He let that sink in. I focused on the windshield wipers sloshing back and forth.

"He thinks he must have had some kind of infection."

The raindrops raced sideways along my window. I could remember being in the backseat of the car with Serena when we were little during a rainstorm, watching the raindrops scurry across the glass. "Crazy cars," we called them. She would point to one, and I would choose another, and we would watch them race in a jagged pathway to the back edge of the window. Sometimes they would run into another drop of water and become a bigger, slower vehicle, driven by the wind until it reached the finish line at the chrome frame of the car door.

I watched the crazy cars for a long time, not wanting to believe that I would never again hear the jingle of tags around Shag's thick mane as he ran to greet me after school.

Serena flew back to college, and a new semester began for me at Glendale High School.

My grandmother died in March. I was in the middle of typing a term paper upstairs in my room when Uncle Wayne called. It took me a few minutes to realize that I didn't need to finish typing my paper. I had to pack a suitcase.

Mom and Dad and I drove down to Florida, spending a quick night at a cheap motel somewhere outside Atlanta. We got to Uncle Wayne's house with barely enough time to shower and dress for visiting hours. All of my dad's siblings were there, and most of my cousins. But I missed Serena.

The next day the chapel was packed with people who had loved my little grandmother. As we stood near the door to greet family and friends, the organist interrupted us quietly to ask my dad if she should keep playing. She had played through all of my grandmother's favorite hymns, but people were still coming in. "I'll just start at the beginning and play through them all again," she decided.

My grandmother was lying beautifully in her coffin, with her soft brown hair curled around her face and her cheeks brushed with pink powder, just as I remembered her. I stood looking at her delicate hands folded across her chest, half expecting them to move as she took a breath. Next to me my mom whispered with my dad's sisters about how lovely she looked and what a nice gown they had chosen for her.

The day after the service, before making the long trek back to Missouri, Mom and Dad and I stopped by her grave at the cemetery for one last goodbye. There was no one else around—just the three of us standing in the grass in front of the fresh mound of dirt. My dad reached over for my mother's hand and began to cry. Then he buried his face in her shoulder, and I stood silently while he took deep, staggered breaths between sobs. I had never seen him cry like that. Honestly, I couldn't remember if I had ever seen him cry at all. Maybe he had shed a tear during his father's funeral when I was five, but I had only a vague memory of that event.

Usually my dad had a twinkle in his eye that made me suspicious of some silly joke he was scheming. If he helped me set the table for dinner, he might load up my mother's plate with all the condiments: the salt and pepper shakers, the bottle of ketchup, and the sugar bowl. If he had to wake me up on a weekend morning, he would do it by grabbing my toes. Other people knew his silly character, too. When our next-door neighbors planted a small strawberry patch, he snuck over and staked up a sign that said, "Strawberries, U-Pick." And he could never keep a straight face. A low chuckle would start deep down in his chest and then burst out of his smile.

But now, as we stood in the bright morning Florida sun, I was watching him grieve. For me this was a glimpse into the heart of my daddy, who had loved his precious mother deeply. Perhaps I was not the only one who had found it hard to move around the country so far away from family and friends.

CHAPTER 22

COFFEE SHOP

It's a rainy September morning, and there's nothing on my calendar until my piano students after school. I roll out of bed, and a happy thought crosses my mind: I could take my laptop to the coffee shop on Main Street and work on my book. What a perfectly romantic idea. I dress in my most trendy clothes and put on my makeup. I decide I should eat breakfast at home first to save a little money, so I fry myself an egg, make cinnamon toast, and sit down to a leisurely breakfast, checking emails on my phone and sipping my tea. I feel absolutely chic.

I pull my Bible off the seat of the empty chair where I keep it in the corner of my kitchen, and it falls open to the chapter I've been working on, Matthew 5. I read the opening verses over and over, trying to memorize them: *"Blessed are the poor in spirit, for theirs is the kingdom of heaven. Blessed are those who mourn, for they will be comforted. Blessed are the meek, for they will inherit the earth."*

I rinse my dishes and stack them in the dishwasher before going to the front hall closet to get the little backpack I like to use for carrying my laptop. It is lightweight, with simple pull-cords that I can easily put my arms through, allowing me to

150

walk with free hands. Well, at least one free hand. My right hand will be holding my cane, of course.

But the closet door is stuck. I turn the knob and pull as hard as I can. It's really stuck. Must be all this humidity. Oh, the joys of living in an old house. I grasp the knob again and jiggle the door back and forth. It seems to be stuck at the top of the doorframe. I try to push down on the doorknob as I pull with all my might. Nothing.

I try to think of another bag somewhere else in the house I could use for my laptop. Most of my other tote bags are in this closet. There might be something upstairs in my daughter's closet, but it wouldn't be as good. The one trapped in this closet is such a perfect backpack. It is light enough that it doesn't throw me off balance. For a moment I try to imagine myself carrying a tote bag down the sidewalk in town, with my cane in one hand. Would the handle stay on my shoulder? Would it slip down to my elbow as I tried to open the door of the coffee shop and throw me over? Erggg! I really want that backpack. I am feverishly yanking on the doorknob now, but I can feel that my leg muscles are just not strong enough to support me much longer in this battle.

I go back to the kitchen table and sit with my chin in my hands. *"Really, God? All I wanted to do was go to the coffee shop and write."* I call my husband. Not that there is anything he can do about it from his desk at work, but if there is anyone I should be able to complain to about these stupid little inconveniences in life, it should be my husband. He doesn't answer. I write an email to him from my phone.

I suppose I could just sit here at my kitchen table and write on my laptop. Maybe God wants me to stay home today. I suppose I could set myself up in the dining room. It's not the same, but I guess it will be fine.

I think I'll try one more time. I have an idea. I walk back to the closet. Across the hall from it I sit down on the stairs. I lower myself down to the wood floor and scoot myself over to the closet door. On my knees, I grab the knob with both hands and pull, hanging all of my weight on the door. It cracks open! Success! I scoot back to the stairs, push myself back up to my feet, and snatch the backpack from the shelf.

Returning to the kitchen table, I notice a red bubble on my phone, indicating that my husband has emailed me back. "Do you want to pick me up, and then I'll get the bag and you can drop me back here on your way to town?" Sometimes he surprises me with sweetness.

I type back, "I finally got it! Thanks for being willing, though."

My phone dings again. "I'm madly in love with you."

Leaving my car in my own private parking space, as I like to call it (the handicap spot in front of the coffee shop), I don the backpack and walk with my cane up the ramp, steadying myself with my free hand by intermittently grabbing the metal railing. It is wet from the rain, so I wipe my hand on my jeans before triumphantly pushing open the door to this, my conquest, the kingdom of coffee and Wi-Fi.

As I enter the bustling milieu, I serendipitously spot my friend and associate pastor, Travis. With headphones on he is staring at his own laptop, his Bible open on the table next to him. I walk in front of his table and stare him down with a goofy grin. He looks up, and a great big smile spreads over his face.

"Suzanne! Hey, sit down! I'm working on my sermon for Sunday."

"The book of James?" I ask, knowing he has been preaching through it for the past couple of months.

"Yeah, the last few verses. Let me ask you about this."

I plop down in the seat across from him and lean my cane against the table.

"I'm working through those verses about calling the elders of the church to pray over a sick person. I'm thinking that maybe it has more to do with spiritual healing than physical healing. Like, I don't want to deny that God can certainly heal people today, because I know sometimes he does, but when you read the verses around it . . ." Travis slides his Bible closer to himself and runs his finger across the thin page to find the place where he had obviously just been reading. The scribbled notes that fill the margins of his Bible display his struggle with these verses. He reads out loud from James 5:15–16 in the English Standard Version: "'The prayer of faith will save the one who is sick, and the Lord will raise him up. And if he has committed sins, he will be forgiven. Therefore, confess your sins to one another and pray for one another, that you may be healed.' That certainly sounds more like a concern for spiritual healing more than physical healing."

"Well," I confess, "I once called the elders of our church to pray over me."

"Oh! Tell me!" His eyes light up as he leans back in his chair.

"It was years ago. Some of the same elders we have now at our church were elders then, including my husband. Jim was our pastor then. We had a meeting in the dining room at my house, and they doused me with olive oil and prayed over me. It was pretty humbling. I remember Jim saying that since I had asked him about it a week before we had the meeting, he had spent that week really soul searching and confessing any sin. And at the meeting he asked me if I had any sin to confess. Then they gathered around me and prayed. But, you know . . ." I hold out my cane. "Here I am."

Travis nods. "Wow. Yeah, and I think Scripture is pretty clear that we *are* going to suffer. I mean, the verses right before that start with, '*Is anyone among you suffering?*'"

"Right," I answer. "And I often think of Paul, who prayed three times for his thorn in the flesh to be removed, but God said no." We chime in together to finish the thought, *"My grace is sufficient for thee" (2 Corinthians 12:9 KJV).*

A waitress comes by and begins to clear the table next to us. I wonder how much she is overhearing.

Travis continues, "But then there are those verses at the end of this section about Elijah. He was a man just like us, but when he prayed for drought there was a drought, and when he prayed for rain it rained. And what about Jesus' promise that if we have the faith of a mustard seed we could move a mountain?"

I sigh and nod. "Yeah, and I've heard people say that if I wasn't healed it must be because I didn't have enough faith. Or perhaps whoever was praying for me didn't have enough faith."

We are interrupted as someone comes through the door of the coffee shop and recognizes Travis. "Hey, man!" They chat for a while, and I excuse myself to get my coffee. But the question lingers in my mind even as I set up my laptop in a corner of the room and hang my sweater over the back of my chair. This is by no means a new question for me. In fact, I probably ponder it on a daily basis. Why has God chosen to plague me with this disease? Does it somehow bring Him glory? Does it somehow point people to Jesus? Perhaps it just serves to improve my character and make me more like Christ. I am reminded of Romans 5:3–4: *"We also glory in our sufferings, because we know that suffering produces perseverance; perseverance, character; and character, hope."*

Glory in our sufferings? I am reminded once again of Jesus' words that I've been memorizing from the beginning of Matthew 5, *"Blessed are the poor in spirit, for theirs is the kingdom of heaven. Blessed are those who mourn, for they will be comforted."* It is a constant paradox that the Bible calls me to *aspire* to: I am supposed to rejoice while mourning.

It seems as though I am on a colossal roller coaster of feelings, ranging from self-pity to bravery and determination, with an occasional peak (believe it or not) of pride that God would count me worthy to suffer for His glory. And somehow, while riding this range of emotions, I must go on living out the life He has designed for me: teaching piano students, directing a choir, leading worship, cooking dinner, folding laundry, pulling weeds, even having coffee with a friend.

Lord, Your grace is indeed sufficient for me. May I never forget that. But may I never, because of this disease, stop living and doing and serving. I want to be able to come to the coffee shop. I want to have conversations like that with people. I want to be able to open closet doors. I wish I could climb mountains. I wish I could play the piano as well as I used to. I wish I could walk as well as I used to. But for some reason, although I have asked You to heal me time after time, You have allowed me only to continue riding this ride. So I guess I have no choice but to ride it.

CHAPTER 23

RESCUED BY MUSIC

I found Lori in the cafeteria in our usual spot and plopped down at the table across from her to unpack my brown paper bag lunch. My mom had packed a bagel, spread with cream cheese, a baggie of grapes, and a fun-size Snickers bar.

"Hey."

"How is your day?" she asked, before taking a sip from the straw in her milk carton.

"Oh, alright, I guess. I got an extension on my research paper—thank goodness."

"I'm so sorry about your grandmother."

"Thanks." I looked over at her as I took a bite of my bagel. I was sincerely thankful for her friendship.

"Did you hear from Stephen?"

I shook my head. It had been more than a month since I had gotten a letter from him.

"Are you gonna write to him again?"

"I've written twice," I sighed. "I think it's his turn."

She swallowed a bite of her sandwich. "Hey, why don't you come to church with me Sunday night? I think you would like it."

"Maybe."

"There are some cute boys there." She winked at me.

"Maybe."

She knew I was feeling disappointed and left out by the youth group at my church. "My mom could pick you up."

"Okay."

It was a small congregation, with a dozen or more teenagers who had a prayer and chat session with the youth pastor each week before the evening service. We sat in a circle on the carpeted floor of a Sunday school classroom. He asked the group for prayer requests, and kids really opened up about things they were going through: sick relatives, bad grades at school, friends who were hurting. The group was smaller than what I was used to, but these kids seemed to know each other well. After praying about those requests, the youth pastor handed out little strips of paper and asked us to write questions we would like to talk about. It could be anything, he said, and he would keep it anonymous. We could ask about doctrine, end times, sexual temptation, . . . or whatever we were wondering about. He would take the next few weeks of our time together to try to answer them from the Bible. I was so encouraged by this.

As the evening service started and we all found seats in the pews, I soon realized that this congregation also loved to sing. The pianist asked for requests from the hymnal, and someone eagerly called out a number. As soon as the introduction was played, people began belting out the song in four-part harmony. I tried my best to find the alto notes, while Lori sang out the soprano line next to me. It was great fun and went on for four or five songs.

This happened every week. Most weeks someone would shout out "Number 204! 'Wonderful Grace'!" and we would all turn to that page while the pianist began the introduction. This was a new song for me, but she knew it by heart—it was the most popular request. The verse was fun enough to sing, but then, when we got to the refrain, the men would reel off, "*Wonderful the matchless grace of Jesus . . .*" while the women echoed the phrase, "*the matchless grace of Jesus . . .*" The tenors had the fun line: "*higher than the mountain, sparkling like a fountain.*" And when we got to the last few measures, everyone sang their absolute loudest as the sopranos climbed to the high climactic notes: "*O magnify the precious name of Jesus, PRAISE HIS NAME!*"

One Sunday evening when the pianist had stayed home sick, the pastor asked at the opening of the service whether there was anyone present who could play. I shyly raised my hand and made my way to the piano bench. Someone called out a hymn number, and I flipped through the pages as they awaited my introduction. I muddled through the song, putting my sight-reading to the test. Halfway through the verse I realized I had forgotten to check the key signature and was missing all the *A* flats. The next song was better. One sharp. Key of *G*. I could hear my former piano teacher asking me, "What key are you in? What chords should you expect?" It was a crash course in church pianist-ism. I could have been embarrassed by all my mistakes, yet somehow I was energized by this crowd that sang loudly enough to cover over and forgive any wrong notes I was playing. From then on, about once a month I was called upon to play.

During our senior year Tuesday and I were glad to be singing together again in the choir and naturally sat next to each other in the alto section on the first day. But Mrs. Kugler, our director, decided to "re-blend" our voices, which meant rearranging our seat assignments. In groups of three, she had us sing a verse from a piece we were learning. The middle person of the trio got to choose which of the other two voices blended better with their own. That person would be assigned the spot beside them on the choir risers.

When it was Tuesday's turn to choose, Mrs. Kugler asked her to stand. Then she called on another alto to stand on one side of her. I held my breath.

"And . . . let's have . . . Sue." To my relief, she pointed at me.

I stood and sang through the verse with Tuesday and the other girl, realizing that, in fact, Tuesday could choose the other girl if she wanted.

We finished the verse, and Tuesday looked up. "Sue," she said confidently. It was true: our voices blended well together. But in my seventeen-year-old mind this was an unspoken confirmation of her friendship with me, and I was grateful.

When Christmastime rolled around we got a small group of our choir friends to go caroling in the subdivision where Tuesday lived. Meeting at her house just as the sun was setting, we were glad to find we had all four parts represented. We practiced a chorus in her driveway, leaning against our cars. It was a carol we had learned from Mrs. Kugler:

Wassail, wassail all over the town
Our cloak it is black and our ale it is brown
Our bowl it is made from the white maple tree
With our wassailing bowl, we'll drink to thee.

Looking the part, all bundled up with coats, hats, and scarves, we began strolling from house to house, ringing the doorbells and singing to anyone who answered. We came to a house where the driveway was full of cars. When the hostess came to the door and we began singing, she was absolutely thrilled to have our surprise addition to her Christmas party and invited us into the front hall, where candles glowed and people gathered with drinks in their hands. We squeezed in and began to sing again from the beginning. Tuesday and I were pressed against a hall table where candles were lit. We were into the second verse of our song when I looked down behind her, smelling something burning. It was a wavy lock of her long blond hair, which had swept across the open flame and was just starting to catch fire. Still singing, I reached over and pressed her hair against the back of her coat, smothering it under my mitten. She didn't even know what had happened until we walked back outside and I showed her the singed end of her hair and the black spot on my mitten.

CHAPTER 24

MEPHIBOSHETH

"Good morning, Aunt Suzanne!" I am greeted by my sweet niece, Lucy, as my husband helps me up the carpeted stairs from the basement. This beautiful home, owned by his brother, Joe, and his wife, Shannon, is on the outskirts of the D.C. suburbs, in a growing neighborhood of brand new houses. We have come to spend the weekend with their family, and so far it has been wonderfully memorable.

Yesterday our nephew, Jack, the oldest, allowed me to look over his shoulder while he practiced his violin, and then patiently taught me how to hold the bow and play "Hot Cross Buns." I will never be a virtuoso, but we had some good laughs. Our nieces, Lucy and Kate, showed us their gymnastics and dance routines in a cleared out space in the living room, and we all applauded proudly.

They took us to their favorite burger joint, and then on Saturday evening Shannon made everyone's favorite—chicken braid. The girls and I would like to say we helped, but in truth we were busy at the table with a project, weaving a keychain out of plastic laces. When we finished it they said I could keep it, so my hubby attached it to the key ring in my purse, where I plan to treasure it for a long time.

I should refer to him as "Uncle Smarty-Pants," since that is what his nieces started calling him last night when they found out he could solve the Rubik's cube. How many times did they jumble it and hand it back to him, giggling, "Okay, Uncle Smarty-Pants—how about now?"

Joe and Shannon have a lovely guest room in their basement with its own bath. When we first arrived, Shannon kindly suggested that if the stairs were too difficult they could set up a mattress on the main floor, in the room they use as an office. But with the solid railings and my husband's arm, I assured her I would be fine.

As we come up the stairs into the kitchen now, the aroma of bacon and coffee welcomes us. Jack is buttering some toast as Joe pours coffee and offers us some scrambled eggs. "Help yourself, guys. Just grab a plate. I'm gonna go check on Kate." He heads upstairs, leaving us with Jack and Lucy, who are already dressed for church, finishing their breakfast.

"Wow! This smells wonderful. Thank you!" I pick up a plate and spoon some eggs onto it with a slice of bacon, then set it back down on the counter, realizing that I can't carry it to the table without losing my balance. My husband picks it up for me without a word and sets it down at the table before going back to fix his own plate. I pour myself a cup of coffee. This I can carry by myself. I settle into a chair next to Lucy.

"Jack, do you go to a middle school class at your church?" I ask, before taking a sip of coffee.

"Yeah, we actually have our own service. It's in a building across the street."

"Oh, that's cool," Uncle Smarty-Pants sits down next to him. "You have your own youth building?"

Jack swallows a bite of toast. "Yeah, it's pretty nice."

Shannon hurries into the kitchen holding a hairbrush and a couple of hair elastics. "Good morning! How'd you sleep?"

"Great!" I try to sound cheery. "That's a great bed. And thank you so much for breakfast! The scrambled eggs are delicious."

"Oh good—I'm glad!" She stands behind Lucy and brushes her hair into a ponytail, then wraps the elastic around it in a flash. "Kate!" she hollers toward the staircase, "five minutes!"

After we finish eating my hubby carries our plates to the sink before running back down to our room in the basement to grab my purse for me. I rinse our dishes, and Jack and I stack them in the dishwasher.

Joe comes back into the kitchen with his car keys in hand. "Suzanne, I'll open the garage door so you guys can come out to the driveway that way. I assume we're all going in our van?"

"Thank you. Yes—can we all fit? I guess there are seven of us."

The steps out the front door of their home are lovely and wide, with shrubs and flowers, like the cover of a magazine, but there isn't a railing for me to hang on to.

The three steps down into the garage have a railing on one side that I think Joe constructed himself. It is solid, which is good, because I am about to pull on it with my entire weight. I hand my cane to my husband and grasp the railing in both hands, turning sideways to face it. He is standing two steps below me, ready to catch me as I lower one foot down, then the other. When I reach the garage floor I sigh audibly as he hands me my cane and offers me an elbow.

The rest of the family has already come outside through the front door and is climbing into the van. Kate greets us as we walk out into the morning sun. "Good morning!" She has a piece of toast wrapped in a napkin.

"Hi, Kate! You look nice."

My husband has to help me get one foot up into the van before I can grab the handle overhead and pull myself up, aiming for the seat with my rear end. If I can just get myself onto the corner of the seat, then I can scoot myself over to the right place.

When we pull into a space in the busy church parking lot, Jack bails out and waves as he walks off quickly to catch up with some other kids who are headed toward the youth building. "See ya, guys!"

"Meet us right here after church, at the van!" Joe hollers after him.

I take my hubby's arm as the rest of our group starts walking across the parking lot to the door of the church. There are scores of other people arriving, and we are all funneling through the glass doors. I tighten my grip on my husband's elbow as we enter the building, afraid that I might get accidently bumped and lose my balance. He feels the tension and slows his pace. The foyer is packed with people. We follow Joe's lead as he makes his way through the crowd to the open doors of the sanctuary. Some people notice that I am using a cane and step aside, giving me extra room. Some even grab the hand of their child and pull them away from me. "Watch out," I hear them whisper, as if I am some danger to be avoided.

As we reach the entrance to the sanctuary, there is an usher handing out bulletins. He smiles and offers one to my husband.

"Good morning." Then he offers one to me, but I don't have a free hand to take it.

"No, thank you." I force a smile.

The aisle slopes downward now, as Joe leads us to a row of seats. He motions for us to enter first, so he can sit next to his wife. The chairs are nicely cushioned, and as I lower myself into mine I wonder where to put my cane. I could rest it against the seat in front of me, but that would touch the person sitting there. My husband sees my predicament and suggests laying it at our feet. He sets it on the floor against the front legs of our chairs, and both of us put our feet over it.

A young man with a guitar comes onto the stage and walks over to a microphone. "Good morning! Let's all rise as we sing to the Lord." He begins strumming as other members of the worship team come onto the stage, and all the people seated around me stand up.

Joe and Shannon are standing now. My husband joins them. I lean forward in my chair and place both hands firmly on the front corners of the seat, trying to push myself up. There are no armrests, or I would have more leverage. My husband offers me his hand, but I seem to be stuck. Finally, he puts a forearm under my armpit and lifts. I stand, wobbly at first, and hang onto his elbow, wondering how many people behind us just watched that.

The music is full now, with piano and drums and bass joining in, and the words displayed on the screen are familiar. I start to sing along. I am doing fine until we get to the second song.

I hear the Savior say
Thy strength indeed is small
Child of weakness, watch and pray
Find in me thine all in all.

I cannot sing this without tears. I find that I have no voice at all. I am struck dumb, holding onto my husband's arm, eyes closed. My strength, indeed, is so very small this morning. Physically and emotionally, I am a child of weakness. I do my best to sing the rest of the lyrics, but I am only able to squeak out a word here and there. *"Jesus paid it all. All to him I owe."*

When we finally sit back down, I start looking for tissues in my purse. The pastor steps onto the stage and prays, while the worship team exits. I am not really listening. I am worried that my eye makeup is totally smeared.

He makes some cordial opening remarks, welcoming us, and then gives a brief introduction to his sermon. He has been preaching through the life of David, he says, and this morning we will be looking at a passage about David keeping a promise.

He starts by reminding us of a vow David had made to Jonathan when the two friends had parted ways in 1 Samuel 20. David promised that he would never cut off kindness to Jonathan's descendants. And now, in 2 Samuel 9, we see David remembering that oath.

The pastor begins to read the chapter aloud, and as he reads my heart begins to flutter. It's the story of Mephibosheth.

David asked, "Is there anyone still left of the house of
Saul to whom I can show kindness for Jonathan's sake?"

Now there was a servant of Saul's household named Ziba. They summoned him to appear before David, and the king said to him, "Are you Ziba?"

"At your service," he replied.

The king asked, "Is there no one still alive from the house of Saul to whom I can show God's kindness?"

Ziba answered the king, "There is still a son of Jonathan; he is lame in both feet."

"Where is he?" the king asked.

Ziba answered, "He is at the house of Makir son of Ammiel in Lo Debar."

So King David had him brought from Lo Debar, from the house of Makir son of Ammiel.

When Mephibosheth son of Jonathan, the son of Saul, came to David, he bowed down to pay him honor.

David said, "Mephibosheth!"

"At your service," he replied.

"Don't be afraid," David said to him, "for I will surely show you kindness for the sake of your father Jonathan. I will restore to you all the land that belonged to your grandfather Saul, and you will always eat at my table."

Mephibosheth bowed down and said, "What is your servant, that you should notice a dead dog like me?"

Then the king summoned Ziba, Saul's steward, and said to him, "I have given your master's grandson everything that belonged to Saul and his family. You and your sons and your servants are to farm the land

for him and bring in the crops, so that your master's grandson may be provided for. And Mephibosheth, grandson of your master, will always eat at my table."
(Now Ziba had fifteen sons and twenty servants.)

Then Ziba said to the king, "Your servant will do whatever my lord the king commands his servant to do." So Mephibosheth ate at David's table like one of the king's sons.

Mephibosheth had a young son named Mika, and all the members of Ziba's household were servants of Mephibosheth. And Mephibosheth lived in Jerusalem, because he always ate at the king's table; he was lame in both feet.

As the pastor reads, I know that this is exactly what I need to hear this morning. Even before he makes the first comment, I hear God whisper to my heart, "This is you."

Lame in both feet. Yes, that's me.

We find the explanation for Mephibosheth's disability earlier in the book of 2 Samuel, in chapter 4. When Mephibosheth is only five years old, his father, Jonathan, is killed in battle, along with his grandfather, King Saul. Fearing that Mephibosheth will also be killed, a nurse picks him up and flees. But in her haste she drops him. Both of his feet are injured, and Mephibosheth is crippled for life.

When we find him now, later in life, he is living at the house of a friend. Perhaps because he is not able to take care of himself. Perhaps he is financially destitute. Most likely both are true. His self-esteem is so low he thinks of himself as a "dead dog."

But God does not leave him there. From now on he will eat at the king's table. Now he owns land. Servants will look after his farm and bring in his crops for him. And he will always eat dinner with the king, as though he is one of the king's sons.

"This is you," God whispers to me. "You eat at my table."

> *Oh heavenly Father, this is so true. You have not forgotten me. 'What is Your servant, that You should notice a dead dog like me?' Look how You have provided for me. My husband, my children, my home, my friends, . . . even Lisa, who cleans house for me. Yes, heavenly Father, I dine at Your table every day. And You, my Savior, You sit with me at every meal, and Your constant presence is what I take for granted.*
>
> *Yes, Lord. I am Mephibosheth. Lame in both feet. But I am eating at Your table.*

CHAPTER 25

KEVIN

I f it weren't for my physical education class, I would have gotten straight *As* during my senior year of high school. But part of our grade included skill, and I just couldn't run around the track as fast as everyone else, no matter how hard I tried. Regardless, I was in the top ten percent of my class, and that gave me a small scholarship to Southwest Missouri State University.

I would have gone there anyway. It was in Springfield, so I could live at home. Plus, Serena had decided to move back in with us and attend there as well. Most mornings we rode together in her bright blue Volkswagen Dasher across town to the campus.

"Hurry up! You're going to make me late for class!" Serena would call to me as I was taking the hot rollers out of my hair. I would slip on my little white flats and grab my backpack of books before scurrying down the stairs to join her outside in the driveway. She would be hanging her McDonald's uniform in the backseat so she could go right to work after classes. I would hop into the passenger seat, and as soon as she turned the keys to the ignition the cassette tape of Sandi Patti would pick up right where it had left off the day before. We knew every lyric by heart and sang them through the streets of Springfield.

We parked in the lot behind the Baptist Student Union, a brick building that may have once been a church, across the street from campus. Between classes you could find either one of us there in the lounge. I should have been studying there, at the round tables with orange plastic chairs. But most of the time there was a card game of Spades going on, or fellow students napping on the old couches. It was a great place to be.

On Thursday nights we had a gathering there. "TNT" stood for "Thursday Night Thing." We would push the tables aside and rearrange the couches and chairs in rows in the lounge. People also sat on the carpeted floor. One of the students strummed a guitar as we sang together, and then someone would share a testimony, or the BSU minister would teach about a Bible passage. For me, it was like being back in the youth group in Seattle.

There was a piano in a back room, and sometimes I would tinker around on it between classes. It was an old school piano, light wood, on wheels, and surprisingly not terribly out of tune. I would play around with some chords, experimenting with a melody line to go with some lyrics I had penned. In essence, I was trying to write a song. Sometimes I would give up and just start playing one of the praise songs we sang on Thursday nights. I guess people in the lounge could hear me, but I didn't care. This was really just between me and God.

It wasn't long before the guitarist asked me if I would like to join him on Thursday nights to lead the singing. "Can you read guitar chords?" He showed me a page of handwritten chords and lyrics.

"Yeah, I think I can do that." I wasn't great at it, but I knew how to finger the chords in my right hand and play an octave bass note in my left.

The next Thursday evening we wheeled the piano into the lounge, and I did my best to stay on beat with the guitarist. If I dared to take my eyes off my notes I could glance over the top of the piano at the crowd of students as they sang out:

Turn your eyes upon Jesus
Look full in his wonderful face
And the things of earth will grow strangely dim
In the light of his glory and grace.

One Thursday night there was a young man sitting on the floor in the front row, singing sincerely. I had not seen—or at least not noticed—him before. He had blonde, curly hair, cut short around his ears, and was wearing a preppy V-neck sweater with his faded jeans. In the socializing that always happened after TNT, he introduced himself to me. His name was Kevin, and he was a freshman, like me. He was living in the dorm on campus, was from a small town in Southern Missouri, and had grown up attending a Baptist church there.

"Hey, you should come hang out here between classes," someone invited him from over my shoulder.

And he did. Kevin joined in our card games; in fact, he and I became successful Spades partners, sitting across from each other, bidding on tricks and reading each other's faces. We could beat just about anybody, including Tamera and her sister, Christy, when they agreed to a game.

Tamera was often in the lounge between classes at the same time as I was, even though she was much more diligent about actually studying there. She had gone to a different Springfield high school than me, but she and her sister, Christy, like Serena and me, were both living at home and commuting to SMSU. They drove to campus each day and parked in the same lot as Serena and me behind the BSU. They sometimes performed a duet at our Thursday Night Thing, leaving us all stunned by their gorgeous harmonies. And they were both beautiful. Everyone agreed on that. While Christy was blonde, Tamera had long, sandy brown hair, with bangs teased and curled perfectly above her fawn-brown eyes. She was about an inch shorter than I was, with a similar small frame and a glowing smile that would greet me as I came into the BSU after a morning class. She was majoring in piano performance, and when she invited me over to her house one day and played for me on the big white grand piano in her living room, I was floored.

"Tamera, why aren't *you* playing on Thursday nights instead of me?"

"Oh, no—you're doing great. I don't need to do that. I have so much to practice."

Indeed, she was preparing for an audition, hoping to get into the St. Louis Music Conservatory after she had completed two years of general studies at SMSU.

She opened a book of classical music that had been lying on the piano. "Do you ever play this?" she asked. "I love relaxing with this one after a stressful day." Her graceful fingers began gently playing through Bach's Prelude No. 1. I was mesmerized.

I had played it before, but not like that. The turn of every phrase was expressive and beautiful.

A few days later, in the back room of the BSU where the piano lived during the week, I sat again playing around with chords and a tune, trying to remember the chord progression that I had worked out before. My fingers would probably never play as skillfully as Tamera's, but I wanted to have the same emotion, the same depth of feeling that her fingers had produced. I was trying to mix block chords with arpeggios now and then. *A* major, *D* major, *A* over *E*, *C* sharp minor . . .

Kevin came into the room and sat on the piano bench next to me. "Whatcha playin'?"

"Oh, I'm just making something up."

"Really? That's pretty good."

"Mmmm, there's something not quite right."

"Start from the beginning again."

I played through the chords, humming the tune that was in my head.

"Oh yeah, that's good. Then where do you go from there?"

"I'm not really sure. Maybe something minor again." I tried an *F* sharp minor. No, that wasn't right.

"Hmm . . . I think it needs to be something new," Kevin suggested.

I bit my lower lip. *Something new . . . ?* "I like the *F* sharp in the melody line, though."

"Yeah . . . What else could you put with it?"

I tried a few things until my hands fell upon a *B* minor chord. That was it. From there, going back to *A* major created a lovely, tender sound.

"Do you have words?" Kevin asked.

"Um, I'm still working on the lyrics." I blushed a little.

"I would love to hear them."

Now I blushed even more. "Maybe sometime," I shrugged.

Kevin stood. "Hey, I've got to go grab a book from my dorm room before my next class. Want to walk with me?"

"Sure."

It was halfway across campus, and the sidewalks were strewn with fallen yellow leaves. We kicked them up in front of us as we strolled past the columned, white stone buildings. I had never been inside the dorms before and was curious to see what the rooms were like. The hallway was quiet as we came through the door.

"Is it okay for me to be here?" I asked shyly.

"Oh yeah, it's open floor until seven," he answered confidently, "and as long as you're with me you're fine."

About halfway down the carpeted hall he stopped to unlock his door. It was a small room, with two desks over by a window, a bookshelf, and a sink with a mirror above it.

"Oh, this isn't bad." I looked around. "But where are your beds?"

Kevin showed me how they folded down out of the wall. But he quickly pushed his Murphy bed back up. "That's a mess. Don't look at that." Actually, I thought that for two college guys the room was surprisingly neat.

While Kevin went to his desk to grab his book, I glanced in the mirror over the sink. I had recently gotten my hair trimmed in short layers over my ears, but long enough in back to fall over my shoulders. "Do you think my hair is too short?"

Kevin was standing behind me now. "I think it's pretty."

I turned around to go, but he put a hand on my shoulder, stopping me, and before I knew what was happening he kissed me. Not a long, drawn-out ordeal—just a quick peck on the lips, but enough to put me in a daze as we walked back across campus.

He ran up the steps of the science building, calling, "See you later!" And I wandered back to the BSU, where I sank down on the couch next to Tamera, who had her nose in a textbook.

"Kevin just kissed me," I whispered.

At a Thursday Night Thing a couple of weeks before Christmas break, we passed around a basket with little scraps of paper. Serena stood in front of the group, announcing, "If you'd like to participate in the Secret Santa gift exchange, put your name on one of the scraps. Then we'll pass it around again, and you can draw a name. We're talking small gifts, 'cause none of us has any money." There were a few chuckles from around the room. "... So something less than five dollars—you know."

I drew the name of Teresa, a girl who often played cards with us between classes. Kevin, mysteriously, drew my name, but, of course, I didn't know that.

I decided to cross-stitch a bookmark for Teresa. I had some aida cloth and several colors of floss left over from a wall hanging I had worked on for my grandma last Christmas. I cut a strip of the cloth, about the right size for a bookmark, and sketched out a pattern for myself on some graph paper. I could make a fancy capital *T* at the top, for Teresa, with some roses and leaves behind it. Then I chose a verse from the book of James to stitch below that in calligraphy lettering: *"Draw near to God, and He will draw near to you.*" It took several evenings to finish it, sitting in the window seat up in my bedroom listening to Amy Grant on my record player. When finally I pulled my needle under the stitches on the back, hiding the end of my last thread, I looked at my little creation with pride. I hoped she would love it.

I asked my mother for a Christmas card from one of the boxes of cards she was addressing to her long list of friends and family members around the country. I signed the card and carefully folded it around the bookmark before sliding it into the envelope and writing Teresa's name on the outside in my best penmanship.

Teresa hugged me when she opened it on that last Thursday night before finals. "Did you make this? It's beautiful," she exclaimed as she admired it.

And then Kevin placed a small box in my hand. "I'm your Secret Santa!" He was smiling that magazine-model smile of his. "Open it."

I unwrapped the little box and lifted the lid. It was a necklace. A single pearl on a delicate gold chain.

I wore that necklace every day for the next few weeks, fondling it through finals as I struggled through timed essays and made educated guesses at multiple choice questions. Then, during the school break, while Kevin was back in his hometown celebrating Christmas with his family, I often found myself staring at my reflection in the mirror above my dresser, admiring the way the pearl fell just over the collar of my charcoal gray crew neck sweater.

As the days drew closer to the end of the break, I grew more and more nervous about seeing Kevin again. I had not heard from him in the three weeks since he had left, but, of course, I knew he didn't have any money for a long-distance phone call.

On the Sunday evening before the start of January classes, several of the BSU kids gathered in a home to celebrate our last night without homework. We were at a house near campus, the family home of Alan, one of Kevin's best friends. There was lots of soda (no alcohol; we were all good Baptists), chips, and cookies. Somebody was playing the upright piano in the living room, and a crowd of people were chatting and playing cards in the kitchen. I was anxious, knowing that Kevin should be coming back into town that night.

Occasionally the front door would open, and rounds of "Hey!" would be heard as different people came in. I wandered into the living room with my cup of Pepsi and leaned against the piano where Alan's brother was pounding out a song. The door opened, and in walked Kevin, bundled up against the cold.

"Hey!" everyone shouted as he peeled off his gloves and unzipped his jacket. I caught his eye, and we exchanged a smile. Right away he was surrounded by friends and sucked into the kitchen, where the food was. I sat down on the couch, resting my plastic cup on the coffee table to wait. My hand went to the pearl necklace at my collar as I looked around the room, wondering whether he would join me soon.

Sure enough, he came back into the living room and plopped down next to me, nonchalant but quiet. Finally, after a few minutes, when everyone else seemed busy with their own conversations, he turned to me. "Hey, um—we need to talk." He ran his hand through the blonde curls above his forehead. "I'm not really sure where we stand." Now he was looking nervous.

He wiped his palms on the thighs of his jeans. "Over break . . ." He cleared his throat. "I got back together with my girlfriend from high school."

He looked at me with the sincerest blue eyes as I tried to process what he was saying.

I didn't realize I had been holding my breath, but I exhaled an audible sigh. "Oh."

"I hope we can still be friends," he offered. "Good friends."

"Sure, yeah," I nodded. "Of course."

Someone walked into the room with a deck of cards. "Hey, who's up for a game of Spades?"

Kevin looked at me with his eyebrows raised. "You in?"

I took a long sip of Pepsi and set my empty cup back down on the coffee table with a determined *plunk*. "Aren't we the reigning champs?" I asked. "Deal the cards."

CHAPTER 26

TAKING A WALK

These cloudy, dreary Vermont November days have an effect on my mood. Becky suggested I try to get out in the morning sun for at least twenty minutes a day. Easier said than done. As my mother would say, "The sun is playing peek-a-boo." If I notice that the sun is out, by the time I zip up my jacket sometimes it is already gone.

Today, Saturday, as I am rinsing off my breakfast dishes I notice out the kitchen window that there is bright sunlight shining through the leafless trees in our backyard. I should seize the moment. I call to my husband, who is reading in the living room. "Wanna try to catch the sun with me?"

"Yes!" he says with excitement in his voice, "I'll meet you out there." I throw on a sweater and my zip-up vest and head down the ramp in our garage. I push the button to open the overhead door, and as it goes up I notice a great pile of leaves that the wind has swirled up to the sloping entrance of our garage. I grab my walking stick, which is leaning in the corner there, but am unsure about stepping into the leaves, trying to recall exactly how far down my foot will go before it hits the pavement of the driveway. I take a breath and crunch down into the pile. My foot disappears into the leaves, but it lands securely.

Then I am off into the beautiful sunlight, down the sidewalk, toward my garden.

My hubby comes out the door and is quickly at my side. I pause to admire the green leaves and colorful blooms of my snapdragons and pansies that have survived the first frost. I stoop down to pull out some papery oak leaves that are caught among them. I gasp at the sight of some tiny sprouts where I spread poppy seeds a couple of weeks ago. I didn't expect them to sprout until spring. We walk along our fence, noting that the leaves on the rose bushes are turning gold and red.

"Want to walk around the block?" he suggests.

I pause. The wind might be too much for my ears. But then the sun breaks out again, and I feel the warmth on my face. "Okay." We walk about twenty steps before I pull my hand from my jacket pocket and tuck it into the crook of his elbow. This gives me a little better balance, and we can go a little faster. About halfway down the street I need to stop to catch my breath. Am I really this out of shape?

As we start walking again my mind goes to an article my cousin sent to me earlier this week. It was a story of a young girl born with CMT who was already having trouble breathing because her diaphragm was affected by the disease. I had heard of extreme cases in which a person with CMT could struggle with breathing in the last stages, but never in a young child. Our family is suspicious that my Aunt Pat's death, just before her seventieth birthday, could have been attributed to her weakening diaphragm. She spent her last days in the hospital, struggling to breathe on her own.

People have always told me that I look like my Aunt Pat. Even at my grandmother's funeral people kept saying that we were so much alike. We shared facial features, like the dark eyes and long nose that run in that side of the family. But more than that, our mannerisms and voice inflections were alike. She was a lovely lady, and I was honored to be compared to her.

One summer when I was a teenager, she and my Uncle Don and their two kids came to visit us at our home in Missouri. We laughed so much that week. One evening we took them to an outdoor theater to see *The Shepherd of the Hills*, a play based on a legend in that part of the Ozarks. The walkway to and from our theater seats was a winding, paved pathway up the side of a hill. I remember her laughter as her husband and kids pushed and pulled her up that walkway. It was only then that I realized that she, too, had inherited the CMT gene.

When my husband and I first moved to Vermont, Aunt Pat and Uncle Don came to see us on their way to visit some friends in Maine. We had just closed on our house, so after dinner at a local restaurant we invited them to take a tour of our new home with us. The rooms were empty, and there were countless repairs to be done, but we were anxious to show it to them. Uncle Don helped Aunt Pat go up the stairs to see the second floor. She held the railing with one hand and his arm with the other. One step at a time, she would lift her right foot to the next step, followed by her left.

As the years went by I would occasionally see Aunt Pat again when the family would gather for the holidays. I'll have to confess that in her later years this would be really hard for me. She could no longer use the front door because of the steps but came through the garage, where my dad had built a ramp. At the dinner table I pretended not to notice as she struggled to cut up her meat. Often she would lay down her fork, and Uncle Don would reach over and do it for her. She had to use both hands to raise her glass of iced tea to her mouth. After the meal, when we all retired to the back porch, she hung onto Uncle Don's arm for enough balance to take the shallow step down, where my mother offered her the wicker arm chair, knowing it would be easier for her to push herself up and out of it than the hanging porch swing or the rocking chair.

Watching her decline as the years went by was difficult for any family member. We all loved her. But for me it was a look into my own future. How long before I would be just like her?

I got to see Aunt Pat in the hospital just before she died. She had fallen at home and hit her head and was having difficulty breathing. She spent several weeks in the hospital, first with a breathing tube and later a tracheotomy, leaving her unable to speak. My sister and I went to see her, and as we walked into her room Uncle Don asked me, "Didn't you have trouble walking all that way from the parking lot?"

"No, it was fine," I answered. But I was moved at his level of understanding that it might be difficult for me. How many times had he walked long distances with his wife, holding her arm in his?

We reach the end of the block, where my husband stops to turn around in the crosswalk. He refers to this as the "kissing zone" and teasingly always requests a kiss from me before we head back. But I am really out of breath, and it takes me a moment before I can look up to meet his face. On our way back I know that I am hanging heavily onto his arm and putting extra weight on the walking stick. We pause a couple of times so I can catch my breath. He asks me about something, but I can't answer; I am concentrating so hard on just walking and breathing. "Ask me later," I manage to get out, and we finish the walk in silence.

CHAPTER 27

KEVIN AGAIN

Kevin and I remained good friends for the rest of our freshman year. We continued hanging out either at the BSU, my house, or wherever our group of friends congregated. We finished writing that song together and bravely performed it one Thursday night, with Kevin standing next to the piano adding his bass voice in harmony with my alto on the choruses.

> *When the walls around me come crumbling down*
> *Upon all the dreams I've stacked up against them*
> *And all I do is sit and pout*
> *Seeking a way to rebuild them*
> *Then suddenly a strong hand reaches down*
> *And with His gentle palm, cups my chin*
> *Bringing my sight away from this world*
> *And toward Him.*
>
> *Love streams down upon me*
> *That never-ending love is what He gives to me*
> *And I wonder why I ever looked away*
> *Because in spite of my mistakes He keeps on loving me*
> *This is peace.*

Kevin and I had signed up for a music theory class together, and we were partners on a big project writing a hymn and voicing it in four-part harmony. This had us sitting at the piano together again in that back room at the BSU, or in the living room at my house, scribbling out notes on lined staff paper, erasing and filling in block chords and rewriting lyrics to fit the meter.

My mother loved Kevin. Occasionally he would be at our house when dinnertime rolled around, and she was so happy to set an extra place at the table. She got used to keeping the jar of honey in the center of the kitchen table, because Kevin loved to finish off his meal with biscuits and honey. She must have known that I honestly liked him as more than just a friend. But I knew he had a commitment to his girlfriend back home, and that semester he never even attempted to hold my hand, let alone kiss me again.

When spring classes ended I got a summer job at the Chick-fil-A in the mall, where several of my BSU pals worked. My friend Tuesday was working in a department store in the same mall, and I would often go and visit her during my break. She looked so professional when I would find her arranging blouses on a rack in the women's department, with her nametag pinned to a light rayon dress, hemmed just below the knee, the ensemble finished off with high heels. Her long, wavy blonde hair would fall over her shoulder so perfectly. She would always be happy to see me in my red and brown striped polyester Chick-fil-A uniform.

It was often my job to stand in the mall just outside the entrance to Chick-fil-A and hold a plate of chicken nuggets, each stuck with a toothpick. "Would you like to try one?" I offered every person walking by. They usually went fast. If I wasn't doing that, I might be at the cash register, taking orders, handling money, and filling endless paper cups with soda or lemonade, while a "runner" behind me filled the customer's tray with the requested sandwich and fries.

Tamera was working as a hostess in a restaurant nearby and often came to visit me at Chick-fil-A. I would be taking orders from a long line of customers, when suddenly the next person in line would be Tamera, with her adorable smile beaming at me. If I had a break we would walk to the other part of the food court, where a French bakery sold the most amazing baklava. If either of us could afford the expense we would share a piece, along with a cup of hot tea.

It was Tamera who introduced me to the joy of a proper cup of tea. We were at her house one afternoon when she set out a china teapot and placed two teabags inside it before filling it with boiling water. "You should try this orange spice tea," she invited. "It's so yummy." Now, I had tried hot tea before, and I liked it all right, but Tamera had a way of making this feel like a special occasion. "We have to let it steep for a few minutes to get the full flavor," she coached as she brought out two dainty china teacups with saucers from the china cabinet. Two spoons, two cloth napkins, the sugar bowl, and a few shortbread cookies on a cut-glass plate turned our ordinary little afternoon snack into a regal celebration.

"What's happening with you and Kevin?" she asked as we stirred sugar into our tea.

"Oh, you know, he's home for the summer, and his girlfriend is there."

She looked at me over her teacup. She knew how I really felt about him.

Near the end of the summer, several of us BSU students, including Kevin and myself, had agreed to be counselors for a week of discipleship training with high school students from around the state. We all met one hot afternoon in the BSU parking lot to carpool to Southwest Baptist University in Bolivar. Kevin and I acted cool as we stuffed our sleeping bags and suitcases into the trunk of Alan's car, and we didn't even sit together on the drive up to Super Summer.

Once there, we were assigned partners to lead the small groups, and I was paired with an endearing college girl named Beth, who was attending the University of Missouri in Columbia. In fact, many of the SMSU students were paired with "Mizzou" students, creating a unified leadership team that grew to love each other like family as we prayed together, ate together, and studied together that week.

I was walking out of the dining hall with Beth after lunch one day when I noticed Kevin sitting with some friends in the lobby, where couches and chairs formed a comfortable conversation area. I naturally slid onto the couch next to him, and he threw an arm up around me with a smile. Beth looked at both of us suspiciously.

"Are you guys dating?"

We answered in unison: "No!"

I moved a little farther away, and he took his arm back.

But we exchanged a sideways glance at each other, and he smiled at me.

A few weeks later, as we began the fall semester of our sophomore year, the rules of our relationship changed. On the first day of classes, Kevin found me in the BSU parking lot. A few fallen leaves blew across the pavement in the sunny breeze.

"Hi, Beautiful!"

"Hey there!" I answered, trying to sound nonchalant. I had just finished classes for the day and was about to head home before reporting for duty at Chick-fil-A. I stood at my car door as Kevin reached the passenger side and got in. I was driving my mom and dad's old, light blue Ford Galaxie 500, and the door creaked as he pulled it shut.

"What are you doing?" I climbed into the driver's seat, wondering why he was getting into my car.

"I want to talk."

"Okay. What about?" I closed my car door.

He took a deep breath. "I broke up with her." He let that sink in.

"What?"

"We're done." He looked at me with those deep blue eyes. "I want to date you," he said. "I can see a future for you and me. We make a good team. I mean, musically . . . and spiritually. I think we work great together, and . . . Well, what do you think?"

I could hardly believe my ears. My heart was about to burst. I reached over across the seat and hugged him. "Yes!"

I couldn't keep my mind on work at Chick-fil-A that evening. I watched the clock tick down the minutes until closing time at 9:00. Kevin said he would meet me at my house after work.

This became our regular routine. We would hang out between classes, of course, at the BSU, and then when I got done at Chick-fil-A I would come home to find Kevin there. Since my dad was traveling almost every week for his job, and Serena was working long hours as a manager at McDonald's, my mother was more than happy to keep company with Kevin until I got home. We studied together, or played the piano, or just sat on the couch and watched TV until Kevin would yawn and stretch. "I guess I should go back to my dorm room and get some sleep." I would walk him to our front door, and he would pull me close to kiss me goodnight before heading down our brick steps to his car as I watched and waved from the doorway.

On Sunday mornings he would meet us at church. As my family walked in from the parking lot Kevin would be standing in the foyer waiting. "Hi, Gorgeous," he would wink at me as he took my hand, and we would walk into the sanctuary together.

I don't know which one of us said it first, but by October we began to casually use the clause "When we get married . . . ." We would be driving by an apartment building, and Kevin would say, "When we get married, I want to live somewhere like that." We would be helping with the dishes after supper, and I might say "When we get married, I am going to make all your favorite meals." Or Kevin would tease me: "When we get married, I'm never going to let you drive my car."

In late October Kevin invited me to come home with him for a weekend to meet his family. It was a four-hour drive, so we left Saturday morning early and got to his house in time for lunch. His parents were cordial and kind to me. I think we were equally nervous to meet each other, sitting at the kitchen table eating sandwiches. Kevin gave me a tour of the house and proudly showed me his room. It was small—just big enough for a twin bed pushed up against one wall, a desk with a shelf full of books, and a chest of drawers. There were photos tacked up against the striped wallpaper: Little League teams, school dances, high school friends.

"You'll sleep in here," Kevin told me. "I'll sleep on the couch."

I peered more closely at the photos while he went out to the car to get our bags. I tried to find his face among the little boys on the baseball team. Then I looked at the classic prom pictures—Kevin wearing a tux with a bright yellow bow tie to match the girl's dress. Then a classy light blue suit to go with the blue corsage pinned onto the shoulder of her pink lace dress. My eyes fell upon the girl's face. It was the same girl in both photos. *Oh,* I suddenly realized. *That's* her.

Kevin came back in with my bag and set it down on the bed. "Come on, I'll show you the rest of the house." He took me through the living room and into the dining room, where a piano stood against one wall.

"Oh! Here's your piano!"

There was a stack of music books on top of it. Kevin fumbled through the books until he found what he was looking for, then pulled out the bench and sat down. He opened up the book and creased back the pages. It was Beethoven's Moonlight Sonata.

"This is what I was working on with my piano teacher in high school." And then he played for me. It wasn't perfect. Obviously he was out of practice. But it was impressive, nonetheless.

"You've been holding out on me." I reached around his shoulders from behind, crossing my arms over his chest and resting my chin against the top of his blonde curls while he played through the rest of the first movement. "That's really good."

His mom came into the room. "It's nice to hear you play again," she said, leaning against the back of a dining room chair. "Hey, I forgot to get cheese at the grocery store for our burgers tonight. Would you two mind running to the store for me?"

"Oh, sure."

We took our time driving around town, past his old high school and past his church, before turning in to the grocery store parking lot.

We were holding hands in the dairy aisle, looking for sliced American cheese, when a girl walked up behind us. "Hi, Kevin."

Kevin looked around and immediately dropped my hand. "Oh, hi."

"I didn't know you were in town."

"Oh, just for the weekend."

She looked familiar. Kevin stammered. "Uh, Julie, this is Sue."

"Hi. Nice to meet you." And then I understood. *This is the girl in the prom pictures.*

"Yeah, you too." She turned and walked away.

Kevin picked up the package of cheese, and we walked to the cash register without saying anything. We paid for the cheese, walked out to his car, and drove back to his house in awkward silence. By the time we pulled into his driveway Kevin looked as though he were about to cry.

"Are you okay?" I finally asked.

"Yeah," he sighed, and got out of the car.

His dad cooked burgers out on the grill, and his brother and sister-in-law came to join us for dinner with their new baby. I cooed and played with his tiny fingers while the table was being set and the burgers brought in. Kevin's mom bounced her little grandson in her lap all through dinner, and the conversation was mostly about baby things.

I helped clean up the kitchen, trying to make polite conversation with Kevin's family.

"So you're a sophomore? Same as Kevin?" his sister-in-law asked me.

"Yeah, we met last year at the Baptist Student Union."

"And what's your major?"

"Elementary ed," I answered, as though in response to an interview question. "I was thinking about minoring in music."

"Oh yeah, Kevin says you're very musical."

Finally, when Kevin's brother and his wife had the baby all packed up and were headed out the door, I set down my dishtowel to shake their hands. "It was really nice meeting you all."

"We'll see you at church tomorrow," they reminded me.

"Oh, yeah."

By now it was getting dark outside. Kevin and his mom and dad and I gathered in the living room to watch TV. Kevin sat in an easy chair by himself, and his parents sat on the couch together. I took a rocking chair across the room from Kevin. There was a movie on. Something about World War II. I watched for a while, but after about an hour, during a commercial break, I excused myself. "I guess I'll get some sleep," I said. "See you all in the morning. Thanks so much for those delicious burgers tonight."

I had just crawled into the bed, with Kevin's navy-blue bedspread pulled up over my shoulders, when there was a tap at the door. "Sue? May I come in?"

I sat up and made sure I was decent. "Yeah. It's okay."

Kevin came in quietly and sat down on the edge of the bed.

"I'm sorry," he began. "I'm a huge jerk. It's really rotten for me to do this here." He looked down, shaking his head. "I'm so sorry to put you through this."

"I don't understand."

"I realized today, when we saw Julie . . ." He could hardly get the words out. "I still love her. This just . . . isn't right. It's not going to work." He sat, staring down at the bedspread for a few more minutes before getting up and walking out, closing the door softly behind him.

I lay back down on the pillow, feeling the tears at the corners of my eyes. I stared at the photos on the wall across the room. I couldn't really see them in the dark, but I knew they were there. *She* was there. Standing and smiling, with his arm around her. The pillow under my head was damp now, as I turned over and faced the wall.

The next morning I was in a fog. We went to Kevin's church, and I tried to look my best in my maroon plaid skirt and light pink blouse, but my eyes were puffy, and no amount of eyeliner and mascara could hide it. Kevin introduced me to the people sitting in the pew in front of us as his *friend* from college. I forced a smile and shook their hands.

The four-hour drive back to Springfield seemed like an eternity. Kevin hardly said a word. I looked out the window on my side and cried.

I had to be up early and drive to campus for an eight o'clock class the next day. It was Music Theory 201, on the first floor of the music building, in a classroom with large windows that looked out over the quad. It was hard to pay attention. I kept staring out the window at the sidewalks that were littered with brown, dry leaves. The professor was droning on. "Can you name some composers from the Romantic period?" I glanced out the window again. There was Kevin, hurrying quickly down the walk. He was late for class. I could hardly breathe.

That was the day I started thinking about transferring to Mizzou.

CHAPTER 28

PITY PARTY

It's part of my morning routine. I make myself a cup of English breakfast tea and sit down at the kitchen table, grab my phone, check my email, and scroll through Facebook and Instagram. But maybe I shouldn't.

There's a post from Ligia, who reached her running goal yesterday. I haven't been able to run since I was twenty-three. There's an invitation to join an exercise class with a group of friends. Not going to happen in my leg braces. There are stunning photos from Annette, who climbed another one of our scenic Vermont mountains this week. These days I need assistance just to walk out to my garden.

I know I'm not the only one who deals with this kind of devastation. What about the lonely, heartbroken single person who scrolls past those engagement photos? What about the friend who has struggled with infertility and opens up Facebook this morning to see someone else's adorable new baby? What about the recovering bulimic who is faced with all those scrumptious recipes with oozing cheese?

And yet we keep coming back. Like slaves to the screen, we keep scrolling. Because, after all, there are some delightful aspects of social media. Lois or John may have posted a new photo. I can read about my sister's crazy travel adventures. Or there may be a story from my sister-in-law with pictures of my nephew and nieces.

But this all comes with a price. A price that, evidently, I am willing to pay: the risk of stepping off the path of true friendship and falling into the mire of self-pity.

My favorite Christian author and speaker, the late Elisabeth Elliot, once said, "Self-pity is a sinkhole from which no rescuing hand can drag you because YOU HAVE CHOSEN to sink. Refuse self-pity. Refuse it absolutely. It is a deadly thing with power to destroy you. Turn your thoughts to Christ who has already carried your griefs and your sorrows."

In an attempt to turn my thoughts to Christ, I set my phone facedown on the kitchen table and reach for my Bible. I open it to the passage I have been memorizing from 1 Corinthians 12:30—13:8 and begin to read:

And yet I will show you the most excellent way.

If I speak in the tongues of men or of angels, but do not have love, I am only a resounding gong or a clanging cymbal. If I have the gift of prophecy and can fathom all mysteries and all knowledge, and if I have a faith that can move mountains, but do not have love, I am nothing. If I give all I possess to the poor and give over my body to hardship that I may boast, but do not have love, I gain nothing.

Love is patient, love is kind. It does not envy . . .

Stop right there. *IT DOES NOT ENVY.*

Do I envy my friend who is training for a marathon? Yes. Do I envy that group of fun ladies who are exercising together? I do indeed. Do I envy the mountain climber who was able to capture those spectacular views on her camera? Most definitely.

I would like to submit to you that self-pity and envy are two sides of the same coin. When I am envious of my friend's athletic abilities, I lapse into self-pity. And when I throw myself a pity party, I can't help but be envious of all those who are, at least from my perspective, better off than me. It is a bottomless slope I start rolling down, snowballing into a long list of things I wish I could do—things that other people *are* doing . . . but that I can't do.

There's a scene that I have replayed over in my mind in moments like this. I was middle-school age, having a self-absorbed pity party in my bedroom when my mother came in with a stack of clean laundry for me. "Why are you feeling so sorry for yourself?" she asked, and I told her about being the slowest runner in my gym class. I was always the last one picked when we chose teams. Everyone knew I was the worst.

Without hesitation she offered, "But have you ever challenged any of them to writing a poem or playing the piano?" That was a shining moment of motherhood. She assured me that there *were* a few things I was good at.

But I still couldn't run very fast.

So what is the way out of this slimy pit of envy and self-pity? *"And yet I will show you the most excellent way . . ."* I believe—*I know*—the solution is LOVE.

Love accepts who I am and gets past the preoccupation with myself to enable me to rejoice with others. Love reaches out, despite the twinge of hurt in my heart, and congratulates the friend who ran ten miles yesterday. Because I have my own blessings, abilities, and achievements to be thankful for.

I have a roof over my head and food in my refrigerator. I have a sweet husband, talented children, a lovely home, and a great job. For that matter, I have probably posted photos in the past that have made *others* envious. But that's not the point, either. The idea of social media (I hope) is not that we should just be posting things to make each other jealous.

We could lay the blame for our sorrowful wallowing on social media itself, but I believe the real issue lies in my heart. Look with me again at this definition of love, listed on the pages of my Bible, spread out here on my breakfast table with my phone lying next to it: *"Love is patient, love is kind. It does not envy, it does not boast, it is not proud, it does not dishonor others, it is not self-seeking . . ."* (gulp).

I'll stop for the time being, there in verse 5. There is much more to the list, but I can only handle so much at a time.

There's an equally challenging passage in Romans 12: *"Love must be sincere. . . . Be devoted to one another in love. Honor one another above yourselves. . . . Rejoice with those who rejoice; mourn with those who mourn"* (verses 9–10, 15).

The bottom line is that there is no room for envy in genuine love. And self-pity, along with the envy, must be eradicated from my heart in order to be free to love as Jesus taught.

I pick up my phone again and scroll up to Ligia's post about running yesterday. I open a comment box and take a sip of tea as I think of what to type. Finally, I just write "You go, girl!" with a heart emoji.

Later in the day she sends me a private message: "Here's a little known fact. When I am running, and I don't feel like doing it anymore, I think of you and I run for you, and I pray God will strengthen the muscles you have, and I think of your new body in heaven and how you are going to run and leap everywhere."

You bet I am.

CHAPTER 29

JAMES

There was no avoiding Kevin. If I went to the BSU between classes, he was there. At our Thursday Night Thing he was there. When I went to church with my parents on Sunday mornings he was there. We were polite to each other, of course. And since we traveled in the same circles, eventually we even managed to have cordial conversations about our families, or music, or school.

During the spring semester I was assigned to a kindergarten classroom in a nearby elementary school, where I spent three afternoons a week observing, assisting, and writing about my experiences. I loved being in Mrs. Wiser's classroom. The smell of chalk and pencils, the voices of children counting together, the look of determination on the face of a little boy trying to tie his own shoe—I soaked it all in. I cut shapes out of construction paper and helped little fingers zip up coats. I made copies of letters to parents and walked a line of children through the hallway. That classroom was a balm for my soul.

I drove up to Columbia a couple of times that semester to visit the Mizzou campus (University of Missouri, in case you've forgotten). The first time I went by myself and stayed with Beth, my leadership partner from Super Summer. She showed me around the dormitories and gave me the grand tour of the red campus, the white campus, and the library. We walked past the historic columns in the quad, where the first academic building had once stood, and ate lunch at the McDonald's under the bookstore. This campus was so much larger, so much grander than SMSU, and I had a fluttery feeling of anticipation as we walked through the archway underneath the clock tower.

Later in the spring I drove up again, this time with my mom, to fill out the paperwork and transfer my credits. In a stuffy office in Jesse Hall, my mother watched over my shoulder as I filled in the spaces on the registration form. If I continued with my degree in elementary education I could graduate on time, but there was no more room in my course schedule for music classes. That was disappointing, but the desire to step out away from Kevin and SMSU was a greater impetus for my decision.

"Are you sure you want to do this?" my mother asked as we got back in the car to drive home to Springfield.

I was asking myself the same question, but there was a part of me that just had to move forward. "I think it will be fun to live in the dorm," I assured myself and my mother.

"Well," she agreed, "you're probably ready to live away from home."

At home in Springfield I was church hopping. I missed those Sunday nights going to Lori's church with her, but she had gone away somewhere to college, and I had honestly lost track of her. My membership was still at the church my parents attended, and some Sunday mornings I went with them, even though Kevin would be there. Sometimes I met Tamera at her church, which Tuesday also attended. The congregation there was a little freer about raising hands in worship, and I liked that. Some Sundays I drove across town to another Baptist church that several of my BSU friends attended. There was a Sunday morning class there for college students that felt welcoming. We sat in a large circle of chairs and usually had a good, open discussion.

I was looking around that circle on a Sunday morning in June. There was Scott, who worked with me at Chick-fil-A, and his girlfriend, Debbie, and some other acquaintances from the BSU, but there were also several new faces. Many of the college students from out of town had gone home for the summer, while others were back in town after having attended college away. It was the first time some of them had seen each other in a while, and someone suggested they drive down to Branson for the afternoon and go to Silver Dollar City.

"Sue, you should come, too," Debbie invited.

"Well, I'd have to go home and change first."

"That's fine. We'll pick you up."

An hour later I found myself in the backseat of Scott's car, wearing my white shorts and a cute sailor top, seated next to a young man named James. He told me he had been attending Vanderbilt but was thinking about transferring to SMSU. He missed being at home in Springfield, where his family was.

"What are you studying?" I asked, curious.

"Well, I've been studying pre-law, but I'm thinking about changing that to education. Maybe something geared toward children's ministries, eventually."

"Oh, I'm elementary ed, myself."

James and I ended up spending the whole afternoon together, getting soaked on the log flume, laughing at each other trying to climb the rope ladder at "Tom Sawyer's Landing," walking like drunkards across the swinging bridge, exploring the cave, and waiting in the long line to ride "Fire in the Hole." He was tall, with a thick, dark swath of hair and deep-set eyes that hid behind plastic-rimmed glasses. He spoke with a bit of a Southern drawl, which he claimed he had picked up at college in Tennessee.

On the way back to my house that night, seated once again in the backseat together, I asked James if he would be interested in coming to a Bible study with me on Wednesday night. Tamera had invited me. Some of her friends from her church were starting one for the summer.

"Sure, that sounds good," he agreed. "I know Tamera."

"You do?"

"Sure. I went to high school with her."

"Oh!"

"What time should I pick you up?"

"Pick me up?"

"Yeah, for the Bible study."

"Oh . . . well, it starts at 7:00. I'm not sure whose house it's at, but I can find out."

"Why don't I come get you at 6:45?" he smiled.

"Okay." I couldn't wait to call Tamera and ask her what she thought of James.

On Wednesday evening James pulled into my circle driveway in a pale-blue Bonneville and knocked on my door, as though he were picking me up for a date. He even opened the car door for me to get in. The Bible study was at the home of a guy named Tim. I had never met him before, but James knew him from high school. We sat in a circle on the carpet in Tim's living room, and he led us in a short prayer before explaining his thoughts on how this study would work. Anyone could lead it, he suggested, and it could be on any passage. The idea was to take turns each week, encouraging one another in our personal study of the Bible, and to have good conversations about what we were each learning in our own walk with God.

He asked for volunteers for the first few weeks, and to my surprise James, sitting next to me, raised his hand. "I'll do two weeks from now," he offered.

"Okay, great." Tim jotted down some names in his notebook and then invited us to open our Bibles to Philippians 2, a passage that describes the humility of Jesus. After reading the first eleven verses, Tim shared for a while about his own struggle with humility. Then Tamera talked about a chapter in the book she was reading by Elisabeth Elliot. Others turned to different verses in their Bibles that reiterated the same idea and read the passage out loud. I sat with my ankles crossed, hugging my knees, loving every minute of this discussion.

When James brought me home that evening, as we pulled into my driveway he asked me a strange question: "Do you like opera?"

"Opera?" I chuckled, "I don't know. Why?"

"I have two tickets to an opera Friday night. Want to go?"

"Seriously?" My eyebrows raised as I looked over at him.

He laughed. "Well, it's the Mostly Mozart festival, and they are actually performing this one in a barn, and it's in English. It's *The Marriage of Figaro*."

I had never been to an opera before. Wow. "Sure," I said. "But what do I wear to an opera in a barn?"

He smiled, "Well, I'm wearing shorts."

Friday night when he came to the door I was wearing my plum-colored capris with my little white flats and a loose-knit, short-sleeved sweater. We drove to a large green field where men in fluorescent orange vests directed us to a parking place among rows of other cars. And as we got out and started to walk through the fresh-cut grass toward the barn, James naturally reached for my hand.

You could hear the orchestra warming up as we found our seats near the front. There was a wooden stage, obviously built for this event, and rows and rows of metal folding chairs on the swept cement floor. As we sat down James didn't let go of my hand. And I didn't want him to.

The opera was absolutely amazing. The costumes, the voices, the orchestra, the comedy—it was all so perfect. We laughed and applauded and stood with the rest of the audience for the ovation. As we walked back to his car through the field hand-in-hand, the night sky was filled with countless bright stars. The tree frogs sang a chorus from the edge of the field, and the headlights from the other cars lit a pathway for our steps.

When we pulled into my driveway, James stopped the car and said, "Wait right there." He got out and ran around to open my car door for me.

"Why, thank you." I smiled and took his hand as he walked me up the brick steps to my front door. We paused on the landing, in the glow of the porch light my parents had left on for me. He bent down to look into my eyes.

"May I kiss you?" he asked.

And I nodded.

On Sunday morning James picked me up for church, and we went back to that Sunday school class where we had met only the week before. On Wednesday evening he picked me up for Bible study again. Some evenings he would meet me at Chick-fil-A, just as I was getting off work, and walk me out to my car. He had a summer job at the hospital, as an orderly—a job no doubt arranged by his father, who was an obstetrician/gynecologist. So sometimes James showed up wearing scrubs.

I would laugh at him, "I hope there's not something gross on those," as I took his hand.

"Just a little blood," he would tease.

On one of these evenings he met me after work holding a gift bag. Inside was a snuggly, white stuffed lamb, and a card in which he had written a poem:

For Sue –

God Made the Children

God made the children
A special message to everyone
And though some curse the little ones
I think what He made was right.

God made the children
To teach the old and not so
That innocence in the spirit
Is a lesson long to be remembered

That what we once were
Never becomes what we cannot be
Yes, God made the children
I think what He made was right.

To some, children are but blank pages
Ready for the ink of growing up
They are incomplete
And need to be taught
Nothing is complete
Until the pages are full.

But children are novels
They are symphonies and paintings
Each one is different
A teacher to the old and not so
The time spent to read, listen, and gaze
Nourishes the body and ignites the soul
For it is the children who teach us.

Yes, God made the children
What He made was right.

I knew that James loved children. When one of my dad's coworkers had a backyard barbecue, inviting all the office personnel and their families, my dad insisted I should go with him and my mom. I asked whether James could come, too. It was a good thing my dad agreed, because James saved the party that afternoon. There were about a dozen kids who came with their parents but, once there, had nothing to do. As soon as James assessed the situation, he started a game of hide-and-seek with the kids, running through the yard, hiding behind trees, and letting them tackle him to the ground. While the rest of the grownups chatted, standing around holding paper plates, I watched in amazement as James entertained those kids for over two hours.

His parents had recently separated. He had to tell me this before bringing me over to his house to meet his mom and sister. It was a large modern home in a wooded area outside of town. Tall pine trees shaded the driveway and the walkway up to the front door. It reminded me so much of our home in Seattle.

As we walked up the front steps I could hear the excited yipping of two Yorkshire terriers. They were the first to greet us as we came through the door, but James's mom was right behind them, scooping one of them up into her arms.

"Oh, it's so nice to meet you!" she beamed. "Do come in!" Sharon was heavyset, with short, dark hair and the same deep-set eyes as James. We followed her into the living room, a large, open room with a high ceiling and a stone fireplace at one end. The sun poured in through sliding glass doors that looked out onto a deck, and beyond that a dense grove of trees bordered their backyard. Sharon explained that she had just gotten a new couch and loveseat. They were cherry rattan, with floral cushions, and had come with a matching coffee table with a glass top. We settled into them comfortably with the dogs crawling into our laps. James sat next to me on the love seat and threw his arm up behind me.

"When your father came by today, he was surprised at what I had picked out for new furniture," Sharon said to James.

"He asked me if I really liked this style." She stroked the ears of the little dog that was licking her hand.

"Oh, I think it's lovely," I interjected.

James's sister Cindy came through the living room to say hello before heading out the door to meet some friends. If James hadn't told me she was going to be a senior in high school, I would have guessed she was twenty-one. She was tall and beautiful, with long, flowing dark hair that she was gathering into a ponytail as she greeted us. "I should be home by ten-thirty or so," she announced to her mom. "So nice to meet you, Sue," she called over her shoulder as she went out the door with car keys jingling in her hand.

"So, tell me all about yourself." Sharon turned to me, smiling. "James says you're going to be a teacher. I loved teaching!"

"You were a teacher?"

"Yes, kindergarten. Oh, such fun!"

I knew from that moment that Sharon and I would be good friends.

A few days later, on a lazy sunny afternoon, James and I were cuddled up in the hammock in my backyard. "Do you think your parents will ever get back together?" I asked him.

James sighed, "No."

"Why do you say that?"

He paused, looking up at the sunlight dancing between the leaves above us, and exhaled a long breath. "My dad has a girlfriend. Let's change the subject. How was Chick-fil-A yesterday?"

I gazed up at the clouds. "Well, I gave a woman a piece of plastic pie."

"You what!?"

I giggled. "Well, we have these slices of key lime pie in the display case, you know. They are in those clear plastic boxes. Well, one of them is fake. I don't know why. I guess it's just for looks, when we run out. Or maybe for advertising. Anyway, it looks *exactly* like the real ones, and I accidently gave it to a lady when she bought a slice of pie."

"How did you know?"

"She brought it back," I laughed. "She came up to my register and said, 'I can't eat this.' Oh, I was so embarrassed. I gave her a new one and apologized profusely. Scott gave her a coupon for a free meal. And as soon as she left, he burst out laughing. He wouldn't stop laughing at me for the rest of the day. I don't think I will ever live that down."

James was smiling from ear to ear. But I knew there was a deeper pain somewhere behind those eyes.

I finally met his dad that summer when James wanted to take their boat out on the lake. James picked me up early one morning, and we went by his dad's apartment to get the boat key. I was surprised at how much his dad looked like an older version of James. He was of a similar height, with the same dark hair and the same nose and chin. He seemed happy to meet me, but he spent most of the conversation giving James serious instructions about driving the boat.

"I'll be careful," James promised.

We had invited Cindy, along with Scott and Debbie, and they met us in James's driveway to carpool up to the lake. Sharon had packed a whole cooler of food and drinks for us. I squeezed into the middle seat in the front of the car next to James, and Cindy hopped in next to me.

It was a glorious day. The sun was bright, and the blue sky reflected off the waves in sparkles of silver and gold. We all climbed in off the dock, and James drove the boat out into the middle of the lake, where he and Scott took turns driving and waterskiing. They convinced Debbie and Cindy to each take a turn on the water skis, too, but I said it was just as much fun to watch.

When the sun was high in the sky James cut the motor, and we opened up the cooler. The lake became quiet as we popped open cans of soda and handed around the sandwiches.

As soon as James had swallowed his last bite, he suddenly jumped over the side of the boat.

"Come on, Sue!" He flipped his wet hair back over his forehead.

Debbie and Cindy were sunbathing, stretched out in the back.

He splashed water up over the side of the boat. "Come on!"

I was hesitant. I could swim, all right, but I wasn't sure I could tread water for very long. "I'm not the best swimmer," I acknowledged.

"Grab a life jacket!"

Scott handed me an orange vest. "Here you go."

I pulled it over my shoulders and tied it into place, then eased myself over the side of the boat. To my delight the water was fairly warm and surprisingly clear. With the life vest holding me up, I glided over to James. "Oh, this is wonderful!" I cried. I relaxed and let my body float, leaning my head back to take in the warmth of the sun on my face.

We stayed out on the lake until it was nearly sunset, when the water became so tranquil and silent that I understood why people say it gets as still as glass. The sky turned pink and orange, and it was time to bring the boat in, James said. But I didn't want this day to end. I didn't want this summer to end.

James came with my parents to take me to Mizzou. We packed the trunk of my dad's car with my stuff: a suitcase, a steamer trunk containing my bedding and winter clothes, and a milk crate full of books. I also had a box that contained a new desk lamp, framed photos of my family and James, and my little stuffed lamb, along with a basket Sharon had given me with four mugs—two gold and two black (Mizzou colors). There was no more space in the trunk, so the overflow had to fit in the backseat with James and me for the three-hour drive.

I was assigned a room in Smith Hall, on the third floor. James and my dad carried my trunk up the stairs, while I grabbed the box and my mom took the suitcase. We walked up the stairs into a stark, shadowy room with a green tile floor. My roommate had not yet arrived, apparently. There were two steel bedframes, two barren desks with chairs, and two small closets with metal folding doors that screeched when you opened them. There was one window between the beds that looked out over the parking lot and a busy street.

My mom went to work making up my bed, while my dad and James went back to the car for the rest of my stuff. She pulled the sheets tightly across the mattress and fluffed my pillow before spreading out my quilt and tucking it in at the foot. She had pieced that quilt herself in bright, primary colors and had hand-sewn every stitch in the pattern of wavy lines that held all the layers securely together. The red, yellow, and blue patchwork design stood out in contrast to the empty, drab walls as the only cheery thing in the room. Dad and James came back in and set things down on the desk.

"All right." My dad hugged me, saying, "Call us if you need anything."

Then my mom hugged me, for longer than usual, and I could feel my throat getting tight.

"Let's go, Pat." My dad put a hand on her shoulder. "Let's give them a moment to say goodbye."

And then it was just me and James. We stood in the middle of the room and held onto each other for a long time. I was fighting back tears as he kissed the top of my head. "I better go. Your parents are waiting for me."

I nodded, and he quietly left the room. I watched out the window as he got into the car with my mom and dad, and they all looked up and waved to me as they pulled out of the parking lot. I sat down on the bed with my hands over my face and sobbed.

CHAPTER 30

THE EMPATHY
OF CHRIST

J esus must have had some pretty muscular legs. He walked
back and forth from Galilee to Jerusalem over and over
again. He climbed those temple steps and walked up and down
all those hilly streets. He even walked on water! His legs were
strong, and I imagine his carpenter's hands were strong, too.

When Jesus was being tempted in the desert, Satan reminded
him of the promise God had given him from Psalm 91:11: *"He
will command his angels concerning you, to guard you in all your
ways; they will lift you up in their hands, so that you will not
strike your foot against a stone."*

Did Jesus ever stub his toe? Until he went to the cross at
age thirty-three, did he ever know the pain or frustration of
illness? We are told he was hungry at times. Certainly during
those forty days of fasting in the desert. And he was hungry
again when he disappointedly came across a fig tree that had
borne no fruit.

But in his life here on earth, he never dealt with a long-term
illness. He never went through cancer treatments. He never lived

with chronic pain. He never struggled daily to hear, or see, or walk. For that matter, let's get really personal. He never passed a kidney stone. Never went through labor. Never experienced the exasperation of a heavy menstrual period, or a migraine, or a urinary tract infection.

So I sometimes wonder at verses 15–16 of Hebrews 4:

> *For we do not have a high priest who is unable to empathize with our weaknesses, but we have one who has been tempted in every way, just as we are—yet he did not sin. Let us then approach God's throne of grace with confidence, so that we may receive mercy and find grace to help us in our time of need.*

Really? Does Jesus have any idea of what I'm going through? Is he truly able to empathize with me? Does he really know what it's like to live day after day with an illness? When I pray to him, cry out to him in pain and frustration, does he understand?

Yes.

Yes indeed.

In the upper room, at their last meal together before he went to the cross, Jesus gave His disciples a promise. It is recorded in John's Gospel, chapter 14:

> *"I will ask the Father, and he will give you another Helper, to be with you forever, even the Spirit of truth, whom the world cannot receive, because it neither sees him nor knows him. You know him, for he dwells with you and will be in you. . . . Because I*

live, you also will live. In that day you will know that
I am in my Father, and you in me, and I in you."
(verses 16–17, 19–20 ESV)

As a believer and follower of Jesus, I am indwelt by the Holy Spirit. He is *in* me. And the unity I have with Christ, with His Spirit living inside me, means that everything I experience He experiences *from within me*. Not only is He right by my side through every step of my day, but He is actually taking every one of those difficult steps with me.

Every morning when I am strapping on those leg braces He is strapping them on as well. When my knees are shaking from exhaustion, He feels it. When I am irritated that my fingers will not grasp a pencil firmly, He experiences that.

God with us.

As the angel told Mary, her child, Jesus, would be called *Immanuel,* which means *God with us.* Jesus—God Himself—in the flesh, walking around with us on earth. And then, as Jesus prepares to return to the Father, He reiterates the idea to His disciples in the upper room. He is sending the Holy Spirit to be with us. Actually, to be *in* us, living every moment of every day with us. With*in* us.

I find great comfort in this.

I don't want pity from other people. I don't want anyone to feel sorry for me. Somehow I feel that this lowers me in their eyes and causes me to lose their respect. I am not looking for sympathy from people. But empathy from Christ, my Creator, my Savior—I'll take it.

CHAPTER 31

MIZZOU

My roommate, Rebecca, was also a transfer student. She had spent her first two years at a college in St. Louis, and, like me, this was her first time living away from home. But that was pretty much all we had in common. She wasn't interested in going to church anywhere, and she wasn't really interested in studying, either. Mostly she was interested in the fraternity parties, and there were some weekends when she didn't come home at night.

There was a girl on my floor, Laura, who was an outspoken Christian, and we often ate meals together in the cafeteria, but she had a boyfriend she was usually hanging out with when she wasn't studying.

Beth (my friend from Super Summer) had moved into one of the sorority houses, and I hardly ever saw her, except for Sundays. There was a bus that came to pick up students from her church, Calvary Baptist, and if I was diligent to get myself up and ready on time I could catch the bus at the street corner near my dorm. The college-age Sunday school class there was huge. We sat at round tables in a gymnasium, and after someone led a few songs with a microphone and guitar we commenced a friendly discussion with those seated at our table. A leader at each table would read the Bible passage for the day, and we would answer questions that were typed out on half-sheets of paper. Sometimes Beth would be at my table, sometimes not.

There was a Baptist Student Union, but it didn't have its own building yet. While they were having a new building constructed, the group was renting a small office space on the north edge of campus. My dorm was on the south end, and to get there I had to walk a full mile through the entire campus, which just wasn't feasible between classes. Occasionally I made the trek, but there would be only a few students there, kicking back on the couch and chairs with the part-time BSU volunteer minister. I made a few friends there, but it was nothing like my experience at the BSU in Springfield.

Mostly, I went back to my dorm room between classes or to the library to study. One day after lunch I decided to explore the rooms on the floor above the cafeteria. There was a lounge area, with a few deserted couches, a couple of vending machines in the hallway—and then, in a back room, I found an old piano. It was a tall upright, a forlorn-looking creature made of dark wood. It smelled musty, and some of the ivory had chipped away from the keys. The lid on the very top was warped, and you could look down into it and see its inner workings. A few hammers were missing, and maybe a few strings. I fingered a G chord. It sounded terrible. But my fingers ached to play. There was no bench, so I stood, with my backpack of books slung over one shoulder, and played through some chords with both hands. Twang, doink, plonk. If I concentrated hard, I could imagine what the chords should have sounded like.

I must have stood and played for nearly an hour. By the time I left I had the beginning of a song in my head, and I promised myself I would come back and finish writing it another day.

There was a bulletin board outside the cafeteria where people sometimes posted an index card saying they would be driving to Springfield or St. Louis or Kansas City. There would be a phone number, and if you were willing to help pay for gas you could ride with them. I checked these postings often, looking for a chance to go home, even for a quick weekend.

I missed James like crazy. We wrote letters back and forth constantly, and he called me every Friday night. I stretched the phone cord to its full length from the wall over to my bed, where I could sit cross-legged or lie on my quilt while I listened to his Southern accent telling me how much he missed me.

"So, what's happening at Smith Hall?"

"Well, let's see. There's a mystery dance coming up."

"What's a mystery dance?"

"Well, your roommate is supposed to arrange a date for you to go to this dance," I explained. "And you're not supposed to tell them who it is until they come to pick you up."

"Oh, so are you getting a date for Rebecca?"

I sighed. "It's not easy. She wants to go with this guy she has a crush on, Damien. But I have to find out his phone number, which means I have to ask around."

"And what about you?" James asked. "Are you going?"

"Nah."

"Why not?"

"Well, who would I go with?"

"Isn't there some guy you are friends with? Somebody at church or the BSU?"

"Mmm, maybe . . ."

"I think you should go."

I was surprised. "Really?"

"Yeah, it's okay. I think you should do something fun with friends."

"Hmm. I'll think about it."

The next week Rebecca told me she had arranged a date for me. I was dreading it. I thought maybe it would be one of the guys from the church. I felt sick thinking about going to a dance with some guy other than James.

I finally got a phone number for Damien, and he said he would be glad to take Rebecca. So that Saturday night Rebecca and I got dressed up together.

"Should I wear my blue dress or my pink one?" I asked.

"Definitely the blue. What do you think? Should I wear my hair up?" Rebecca had shoulder length, wavy red hair.

"Oh, it's so pretty when you wear it down."

We were both primping in the mirror when there was a knock on our door.

"You answer it," Rebecca said, "I'm too nervous."

I opened the door, and there stood James, holding a dozen roses. I think I screamed. Other girls peeked out of their rooms to see what was going on. They saw me, off my feet, in James's arms.

The dance was at a hotel conference room in town. It was dark as we walked in, except for the flashing colored lights. The DJ was playing vinyl records on a turntable, and there were several couples out on the dance floor. There was a side table with punch and finger foods where we lingered for a few minutes, trying to talk over the loud music, but then an irresistible beat started to play—"That's What I Like About You" by the Romantics. James set down his cup of punch and took both of my hands. "Come on!" We jumped around, holding hands, shouting the words to each other and laughing.

James slept on the floor of our dorm room that night, in a sleeping bag he had brought with him. That was against all the rules—those of the university as well as of my parents, but he rolled it out on the tile floor between my bed and Rebecca's. And the next day we had a very teary goodbye in the parking lot before he drove that blue Bonneville three hours back to Springfield.

By Thanksgiving Rebecca had decided she was moving back to St. Louis. She wasn't passing all of her classes. I wasn't surprised by that, since I never saw her studying. At any rate, I knew I would have a new roommate after Christmas, so I took the opportunity to put in a request to move to a different residence hall. I really wanted to move to Johnston. It was closer to my classes and practically next door to where the new BSU building was soon to be completed. By the first week of December I received a notice in my mailbox that I would indeed be placed in Johnston Hall. That was an answer to prayer. Still, I was taking my chances once again with a complete stranger for a roommate.

During finals week the new BSU was finished, and the doors were open. I couldn't wait to investigate, so I walked over during a study break. A convivial foyer had couches and chairs where students could hang out together. There was a large meeting room with a full kitchen. And there was a smaller conference room with a table and several chairs. A fulltime secretary had her own office, and so did a fulltime minister. Everything smelled of new carpet and paint as I wandered through. There was a bulletin board outside the secretary's office. I thought for a minute, then pulled out a scrap of paper and a pen from my backpack. "Can anyone help a girl move from Smith to Johnston Hall? —Sue Butler [along with my phone number]." I stuck it on the fresh corkboard before heading back to my doleful room to study.

I was back in Springfield for three wonderful weeks over Christmas break. James and I went Christmas shopping through the mall hand-in-hand, watched football games with my family, and decorated the tree with Sharon and Cindy. He invited me to come to his grandmother's house for dinner (his dad's mother's), saying they would be having their gift exchange with his dad. I didn't know what to bring, so I baked my grandma's molasses spice cookies and brought them in big quart canning jars for Cindy and for James's dad and his grandmother.

Later that week the two of us exchanged our own gifts in my living room. James gave me a beautiful porcelain music box that played *Fur Elise;* it had a dainty white lamb that turned round and round as the music played. I gave him a vinyl album of the Romantics. And then I had one more gift. I went to my piano and played a song for him—the song I had written on that old, banged-up piano in the back room above the cafeteria at school. I had titled it "Beyond Me."

Teacher
You have taught me the true meaning of love
I must have never known love before
Until you loved me
Then you taught me a love far beyond me.

Giver
You have given me a heart full of joy
I must have never smiled before
Then you smiled at me
And you gave me a joy far beyond me.

I can't explain all this love in my heart, you know
It's beyond me
And I've never felt so much joy in my heart, my friend
I've never been so in love.

Helper
You helped me when I needed a friend
I must have never had one before
Then you took me in
And you showed me a friend far beyond me.

I can't explain all this love in my heart, you know
It's beyond me
And I've never felt so much joy in my heart, my friend
I've never been so in love.

James was sitting back on the couch, beaming at me. "I have to show you something," he announced, standing up. "I have to take you somewhere."

"Where?"

"I'm not going to tell you. Just come with me." He started throwing on his coat.

We went out to his car, and he pulled a bandana out of his glove box and tied it around my eyes so I couldn't see.

"What are you doing?"

"Shhhh. You'll see when we get there."

He drove across town, through stoplights and traffic, until finally we turned down a quiet street and into a driveway. He stopped the car.

"Okay, now you can look."

I pulled off the blindfold. We were sitting in the driveway of a duplex. There were two front doors, one to the left of the driveway and the other to the right, with two garage bays between them.

"Where are we?" I was confused.

"This is my new place. Mine is the one on the left."

"What?" I peered through the windshield at the front door. "How can you afford this?"

"Well, technically, I'm renting it from my dad." He unbuckled his seatbelt and opened his car door. "Come on!"

We walked up the steps, and he unlocked the front door. There was a small entryway with some carpeted stairs to the left. Half of the stairs went down, and the other half went up. Straight through the entryway was a kitchen with an open area for a table. Down the stairs were a living room with a fireplace and a laundry room where a washer and dryer were already hooked up. Up the stairs was a hallway with a bathroom and two bedrooms. The rooms were all empty, waiting for James to bring over a twin bed and dresser.

"And my dad said he found a couch for me, and a used kitchen table," he was telling me as we wandered back into the kitchen area.

"This is so nice," I admired.

"I have to get a roommate to split the rent with me. But it's a lot closer to school than my mom's house." Then he turned to look straight into my eyes. "And maybe someday you and I will live here."

CROSSING THE STREET

This is the kind of thing God does for me.

My parking spot is taken. MY personal parking spot. Well, okay, it doesn't have my name on it, but it's the only handicap parking spot on the same side of the street as the cafe on Main Street. I need it. I need that spot because it is near the ramp up to the cafe entrance. From any other spot on the block I would have to step up onto the curb (no easy task) and then walk a distance down the sidewalk to the ramp.

I am supposed to be meeting a friend here for lunch. She is probably already inside, waiting. I drive by the parking spot slowly, peering through the windows of the obstructing vehicle. *Does it have a handicap placard? Is it parked there legally?* Yes, actually it is. The tag is hanging from the mirror.

I turn at the corner and go around the block again. The car is still there. Ugh. Where am I going to park? Now all the other spots are taken as well. I take one more loop around the block. I'm going to have to park *somewhere*.

Then I notice a spot across the street. It is a handicap spot, the only other one on the block, and it's open, but if I park there

I will have to cross the street. I turn my car around in a driveway and head back toward it. It's my only option. As I maneuver my car back and forth to parallel park, I am wondering whether I can walk across the street safely. There is a crosswalk nearby, and it leads right to the ramp for the cafe, but I am nervous about the cars. Will they stop for me? It might take me a long time to cross. Will the drivers be impatient?

After I turn off the engine, I sit looking out my car window at the front door of the cafe. I wonder whether my friend is inside. I text her and wait. Maybe she could come and walk me across the street. She doesn't answer my text. I wait a few more minutes, but she still doesn't answer. Sigh. I guess I'll have to do this on my own.

I look back at the street and wait until no cars are coming before I step out of my vehicle. As my feet hit the pavement I can feel my knees shaking. With my cane to steady me, I go to the edge of the crosswalk. One car approaches slowly, then stops. I've got to cross now. They are waiting. No time to get up my courage. I take a step out into the street.

"Hey, Suzanne!" A familiar, deep voice startles me from behind. I can't look back because I am afraid I will lose my balance now that I have started across. "Hey, Suzanne!" I know this voice. And my anxious heart relaxes now as I realize who it is. It's my pastor, Travis. He is crossing the street right behind me. I know without a doubt that if I fall right here in the middle of the street he will pick me up.

But I don't fall. Just having someone there has given me the confidence to cross. When I reach the other side, at the bottom of the ramp, I finally look up at his friendly face. "Hey, Travis!"

He doesn't know the magnitude of what his simple greeting has just done for me. He doesn't know that God placed him there at that street corner at exactly the right time today. We chat for a little bit before walking into the cafe together, and I greet my friend, who is sitting at a table waiting for me.

Yep. That's the kind of thing God does for me.

CHAPTER 33

JOHNSTON HALL

I had to be back at school on the Saturday before classes began in January to move all of my stuff out of Smith Hall and into Johnston. I don't think anyone ever answered my note on the BSU bulletin board, but my parents drove me up to Columbia, and, once again, James came with them to help.

We found my new room on the second floor of the dorm, right across the hall from a study lounge. That study lounge itself was a thing of beauty. There were floral print couches in the carpeted room with wide, sunny windows, a table with chairs, and on one wall a sink and a countertop with a microwave. My new roommate, Carol, greeted us at the door to our room and welcomed us.

"Can I help you carry some stuff in?" She was tall and graceful, with dark hair that curled under at her shoulders and thoughtful, big brown eyes.

She had brought a royal blue rug that covered most of the tile floor in our room, and her bedspread had a print of red, yellow, and blue tulips. She had a little fridge, just inside the door, and a red director's chair next to the phone. When we spread my quilt out over my bed, it seemed to complete the theme of primary colors in perfect harmony. We each had a desk and a dresser of solid maple, and deep closets with paneled wooden doors. There was an old heat radiator under the windowsill, and the doublewide window looked out into a courtyard, where benches surrounded a large tree. I could have cried.

Saying goodbye to my parents and James was a little easier this time, although it was still torturous to let go of James's hand in the parking lot and watch them drive away.

I came back up the stairs to my new room and started unpacking, while chatting with Carol. I found out that she was a junior, like me, and that her former roommate had graduated in December. She was from St. Louis and majoring in journalism— advertising, to be specific. And then, as I was stuffing socks into a dresser drawer, Carol asked me a question.

"Would you like to come to church with me tomorrow?"

I looked up, excited. "What church do you go to?"

"Calvary Baptist."

I set the socks down. "Calvary Baptist?" I couldn't believe it. "You're kidding me! That's where *I* go!"

"What? I haven't seen you there."

"Well, it's a big class. Wait . . . you're a Christian?"

"Yes!" she answered emphatically.

What an amazing thing God had done for me.

(Years later Carol told me that she had seen my posting on the bulletin board at the BSU when she had wandered in, like me, to check out the new building. She had gone directly to the front desk at Johnston Hall and requested me as a roommate. Even though she had never met me, she said, she thought anyone at the BSU would be "good odds." Praise God for that bulletin board!)

The girl who lived in the room next to us, C.C., was also a Christian who went to the same church, along with a fellow named Joe who lived in the guys' dorm on the other side of the courtyard. Joe had a car, and the next morning he drove the four of us to church together.

We became a little family: Carol, C.C., Joe, and me. We ate most of our meals together in the cafeteria. We watched old movies together on Carol's little black-and-white TV in our room. We walked to the library together after dark. And on Sunday nights, when the cafeteria was closed, we ordered pizza together and ate it on the blue rug in our room.

C.C. was African-American, my height, and had short black hair. She called it "memory hair" because it would stay perfectly in place however you styled it. She was a music major, studying voice, and had the smoothest, richest vocal tone. I once asked her to sing "We Shall Overcome" for me. She stood in the middle of our dorm room and belted it out with such emotion that I was moved to tears.

But she could also be hilarious. She might burst into our dorm room while Carol and I were putting on our makeup in the morning, singing like Elmer Fudd: "Oh bwoom Hilda, you're so wuvweee . . ."

Carol would sing back in a Bugs Bunny voice, "Yes I know it, I can't help it." They had a whole repertoire of silly songs from cartoons and musicals that they often sang to each other.

Joe was also studying journalism and often had stories of people he was interviewing for articles he was writing. Medium built, he had sandy brown hair and a big, toothy smile that seemed permanently stuck onto his face. Maybe that's because he was so constantly amused by the three of us girls.

Carol and I grew especially close. We would climb into our beds at night and turn out the light, then talk in the dark for a long time. Of course I talked about James, and she divulged which guys she liked. I told her about CMT and about how I was starting to feel clumsy. She said she had noticed that I always held the railing on the stairway. We told each other stories from our childhood, and what we wanted to do in our futures.

"Someday," she said, "I'll see you in the grocery store, and we'll both have a toddler in the front of the cart and grape jelly stains on our shirts."

One afternoon we found a flyer under our door about a Bible study that was going to meet in the Georgian Room, on the main floor of our residence hall. "What's the Georgian Room?" I asked Carol.

"You know, that room with the fireplace and the piano."

"What!? There's a room with a piano?"

"Yeah, on the main floor, to the right as you come in the front door. You can sign it out. There's a key for it at the front desk. Anyone can reserve the room if they live here."

Life was just getting better every day.

At my first opportunity I asked at the front desk if I could use the room, and the desk attendant gave me the key. As I slowly opened the door, like Dorothy in the *Wizard of Oz*, I couldn't believe my eyes. It was an elegantly furnished room with a white-mantled colonial fireplace, soft gray carpet, and Victorian sofas. The windows were dressed in grand draperies, and opposite them, against the wall, there was indeed a piano. It was a shiny black upright, and there were music books stacked on top of it. I sat down on the bench and fingered a few chords.

It was in tune! I looked through the books and chose a book of sonatinas. I opened it, creasing the pages back gently, and played through three or four pieces. It was heavenly. Then I played some of my own songs, the one Kevin and I had written together and the one I had written for James. I tried to remember the chords to some of my favorite praise songs, and then I fumbled around with a new melody that was taking shape in my head.

It was a glorious hour in a blissful place, and throughout that semester I would repeat it as often as my schedule would allow. The front desk attendant would grant me the key, and I could sneak into this euphoric room for an hour alone. Just me and God—and the piano.

CHAPTER 34

PIANO LESSONS

I hear a car door outside in my driveway and open the front door in time to see eight-year-old April skipping across the asphalt, her dark braids bouncing against her shoulders. She is followed by her mother, who is carrying her piano books. I open the storm door to welcome them in.

"Hi, guys! How are you this week?"

April is breathless. "Good! I practiced six days!"

"Six days! You must be really good at your songs!"

She unzips her coat and wriggles her shoulders out of it as it drops behind her. "Yeah, and I played my song for Grandma when she was at our house for Thanksgiving!"

I reach down for her coat and hang it by its hood over one of the hooks on the wall. "Oh, I bet your grandma loved that!"

She takes her books from her mom and rushes to the piano, planting herself on the bench with a thud.

Her mother comes into the living room and settles herself on the couch. "April, take a deep breath."

I sit beside the bench in my teacher's chair and set the Circle of fifths chart on the piano in front of us. "Okay, let's warm up your fingers."

April starts right in on her *C* scale. She knows the drill. Both hands together, fingers curved, wrists up off the wood. I hear her making a funny sound in her throat with each note of the scale, like a whine. Next, she poises her fingers to begin the *G* scale. She strikes the first note and then looks up at me. "What animal starts with *G*?"

I am confused. "What *animal*?"

"Yes. *C* is for cat . . . What is *G* for?"

It suddenly dawns on me that she was meowing during the *C* scale.

"Oh! Well, let me think. Ummm . . . *giraffe*?"

She plays the first couple of notes and then pauses. "What sound does a giraffe make?

"Oh . . ." I am stumped.

April rescues me. "I know! He bites the leaves off of the tops of the trees!"

She plays the entire scale, including the *F* sharp, making a munching sound with each note. I join in. This is brilliant.

"*D* for *Dog*!" she practically shouts. We bark through the *D* scale. Then we chomp our teeth like an alligator for the *A* scale, and "caw" like an eagle through the *E* scale. I now have a new strategy for reviewing scales that I never would have thought up on my own.

I open April's book to the song we are working on, a simplified arrangement of Verdi's La Donna e Mobil, and her fingers fly through it.

"Wow! You really did practice a lot this week! That was amazing!" I pick up my pencil. "Can I hear you play through this phrase here, one more time?" There was a half note that wasn't being given its full value. She plays it again, repeating the mistake she made before. "Okay. I'm going to be picky about this note right here." I circle it on the page. "Let's make sure we give it the two beats that it is asking for."

She plays the phrase again, and I count out loud, emphasizing those beats as her fingers try to rush the tempo. "Stay with me," I politely request. We repeat the phrase until she plays it to my satisfaction. "All right, let's take it from the top, and don't forget that crazy accented staccato at the end."

I sit back and watch her little fingers play. I am always amazed that such tiny hands can accomplish such music. We turn the page to a new song, and I ask her to tell me what key it is in. It has one sharp.

"*G!*" She knows her stuff. Her hands go right to a *G* scale position, and we sight-read through the first few phrases. This is more difficult. She has a hard time naming the notes, even though we have drilled the flashcards and talked numerous times about strategies for identifying them. There's the classic "Every Good Boy Deserves Fudge" for the lines, and "FACE" for the spaces, or you can think about that curly treble clef circling the *G* line and go up or down from there, but so far these mnemonics haven't helped. After struggling through the first couple of lines, she drops her hands to her lap with a dramatic sigh.

"Can you show me how it goes?"

"Sure." I join her on the piano bench and play through the first page. I know that there are some piano teachers who would cringe at this. But with April it works. If she has the tune in her head, it is so much easier for her to figure out the notes on the page. And I trust that as she plays the song and watches the sheet music the connections between the notes on the page and the keys under her fingers are being made.

We are just about out of time when she remembers something she wanted to show me. "Oh! I've been figuring out how to play a Christmas song!"

"You mean you have the sheet music, or you are figuring it out by yourself?"

"No, I was just playing around until it sounded right." She begins playing "Angels We Have Heard on High," and not just with the melody in the right hand. She adds left hand harmonies at every measure.

I sit in wonder, watching her as she plays the whole song, absolutely beaming with pride. "That is beautiful, April. I can't believe you even found left-hand notes to go with it."

Her big blue eyes smile over at me, and she giggles, "Well, I just tried different ones."

I nod, and catch hold of her braid, placing it over her shoulder. "That was awesome."

Margaret bursts through the front door, trying to catch her breath. "Whew! It's starting to snow out there!" Her little brother, Matthew, isn't far behind her. They have walked over from the elementary school, a few blocks away from my house. We all look outside my living room windows and see big, fluffy white flakes drifting down and disappearing in the grass.

April and her mom start gathering up their stuff while Margaret and Matthew drop their backpacks on the floor in my front hall and shed their coats. I remain in my teacher's chair, aware that if I get mixed up among the boots, coats, and backpacks strewn about my front hall I might trip and end up on the floor with them.

"I was trying to catch a snowflake on my tongue," Margaret reports as she unzips her backpack and searches for her piano books, "But it's so hard to get one! You look up into the sky and try to follow one as it comes down, but then you have to aim for it!"

I can only imagine how this looked, Margaret walking down the sidewalk with her tongue sticking out, looking up, occasionally running haphazardly with her backpack bouncing on her shoulders.

She comes to the piano bench and plops down, plunking her books roughly on the rack above the keys. Matthew goes quietly to the couch and opens a book to read.

April's mom smiles at me as she zips up her coat and waves as she and April turn to exit. "Thank you, Suzanne."

"Thank *you*!" I give a little wave. "See you next week!"

Margaret charges into her scales. Her sock feet are swinging back and forth from the bench in a totally different tempo from the irregular beat her fingers are playing. She hits a sour note and then bangs repeatedly on the key she meant to strike.

"Let's try that again," I encourage.

We plug through the rest of her scales, her thumb persistently trying to go under at the wrong time. Each time she misses a note, she voices an audible "Ugh."

"You'll get it, Margaret. Don't worry." I pat her back. "Let's try again. "

We get through it, and then she opens her book to "Silent Night." "Okay, this one I'm pretty good at," she reassures herself.

"All right. Try to make it sound like a lullaby. Very light and slow."

She takes it a little faster than I would prefer, but I am pleased that she is playing it fairly softly. I know this takes great control for her. Halfway through the page she suddenly stops.

"What the heck is ''round yon'?"

"Oh, that's like . . . around that thing over yonder. Over there." I point off to some imaginary thing in the distance. "It's actually part of the sentence that we started on the line before." I point to the words on the page. "'All is calm, all is bright' around that virgin mother over yonder."

"Why would it be bright around her?"

"Well, because she is Jesus' mother, and she has just given birth to baby Jesus."

A light seems to come on in Margaret's head. "Oh! I didn't realize this song was about baby Jesus!"

"Yes!" I gleam at her, leaning forward and seeing the fresh wonder in her hazel eyes. "That's why it is a silent and *holy* night. The night Jesus was born."

She swings around, facing me, and brings her sock feet up onto the bench. "I don't get why, if Joseph and Mary were His parents, how could God be His father?" She hugs her knees.

"Ahhh. Yes," I nod slowly. "Joseph wasn't really his father, was he? Mary was pregnant by God's Holy Spirit. She wasn't actually married to Joseph yet. They hadn't . . ." I suddenly realize I am venturing into territory that Margaret's parents may not have covered yet.

She looks up at me. "That's like the only time in history that God ever did that, right?"

"Yes!" I am relieved that she didn't ask me to finish. "That's why it's so amazing!"

She drops her feet back down off the bench and places her hands on the keys. "But why does it say 'Holy infant so tender'? Isn't tender like chicken?"

Now Matthew hops off the couch and comes over to us. "I love chicken tenders!"

I am trying to keep a straight face. "I think it means like fragile. Breakable. You know, like when chicken is cooked so well it almost falls apart. And babies are really fragile when they are first born. You have to be really careful when you hold them."

Margaret puts her hands back on the keys and we start once again at the beginning of "Silent Night." Matthew goes over to the rocking chair near the bookshelf and sits down again. He rocks the chair with his feet off the ground, waiting for his turn.

When he finally comes to the piano, his small hands run through his scales easily. I wonder about trying April's idea of making animal noises but decide to save it for another day. It's time to introduce the next scale on our Circle of fifths chart, the *E* Major scale, with four sharps. First I demonstrate with my right hand, to show him which four black notes to use.

I know my hand looks funny. My technique is not what it used to be. My wrist comes up too far and the knuckles where my fingers meet my hand bend downward. I have told my students that it's because I have a muscle disease, and not to worry, that they won't catch it from me. I can hold my left hand in the proper position lightly on the keys to show them what it *should* look like, but when I actually press down on the notes, it doesn't look so good.

Matthew tries the *E* scale. "Want to play it once without the black notes, just to hear how bad it sounds?" I ask, smiling.

He giggles and plays through it with just white notes, then wrinkles his nose and looks up at me, shaking his head.

"Okay, so let's play it again now with all the sharps. That's right—one, two, three, thumb." I am watching closely to make sure his little thumb goes under at the right time. He has wriggled off of the piano bench and is standing, leaning back against it. But I don't mind. It's the same height for him whether he is standing or sitting.

"Would you like me to move the bench up for you?" I scoot it forward, and he climbs back onto it, but I won't be surprised if he ends up standing again.

We open his book and his fingers glide through his first song comfortably. "Good job!" We turn the page in the book to learn the next song. I point to the right-hand notes with my pencil as he names each one. This comes so naturally for him. Occasionally he has to play the note before he tells me its name, but I'm thrilled that he seems to instinctively know where it is on the keys. We play through each hand's part separately, then together.

Before long a car pulls into my driveway, and their mother comes quietly through the door. As Matthew and I finish working our way through the new song, his mother motions to Margaret to start getting her things together. I ask Matthew to play through it once again on his own while I find both of their assignment sheets and jot down what I'd like them to practice this week. They know by now that this means playing through their assigned scale and songs five times a day.

Matthew strikes the last note passionately and hops off the bench. His mother takes his coat from the hook in the front hall and holds it out for him. Still seated in my chair, I clip their assignment sheets to the front of their books and lay them on top of the piano.

Margaret sits down on the floor in the hall to pull on her boots while her mother zips up Matthew's coat. "What do you say, guys?"

"Thank you!" they chime.

"The pleasure is all mine." I push myself up from my teacher's chair and stand for the first time in ninety minutes. I brace myself against the piano, catching my balance. With my hip leaning against it, I hand their mom the books.

"Did you have a good Thanksgiving?" she asks politely, handing me a check.

"Oh, it's always so good to have my kids home. How about you?"

"It was great. We all converged on my mom and dad's house."

Margaret interrupts as she pulls her backpack over her shoulder, "There were twenty-three people at our Thanksgiving dinner!"

"Wow!" I laugh.

Their mom smiles and opens the storm door as they file out. "See you next Tuesday!"

The snowflakes are starting to stick to the grass along the edges of my walkway. As I watch through the doorway, Margaret leans her head back and sticks out her tongue. "Mom, have you ever caught a snowflake?"

"Get in the car, silly!" She holds the car door open.

Margaret turns back to wave at me as she climbs into the car. And I wave back, grinning with joy.

CHAPTER 35

FISHING

Some of my friends spent their spring break lying on a beach in the sun. I spent it standing on a chair, stenciling mallard ducks above the cabinets and around the top of the walls in James's kitchen. He would drag another chair behind me, standing on it with a tiny brush of white paint to clean up the places where I had smudged my green paint out of the lines. We sang along to Lionel Richie and Mr. Mister on the radio, or James would play one of his Beach Boys albums while we dabbed paint and took every opportunity to brush up against each other. I thought this kitchen might be mine someday, but for now we could make it masculine. I can always paint over the ducks later. And doing this project with James, I thought, was a glimpse into household projects we might do together in years to come. I was more than happy to spend that week by his side.

I had been back at Mizzou for a couple of weeks after that when James called, as usual, on a Friday night. I sat in Carol's red director's chair to talk with him, twirling the phone cord around my fingers.

"I've had a job offer," he told me, "for the summer. It's at a kids' camp I worked at before, when I was at Vanderbilt. They asked if I would be the Camp Director this year." I could hear the excitement in his voice. "It's up in the mountains, in Tennessee."

"Oh."

"It means I would be away for the summer . . . while you're home."

"The whole summer?"

He sighed. "Pretty much. I'd have to be there by the end of May, and I won't get back until the middle of August."

I wrapped the phone cord around and around my index finger. "You really want to do it, don't you?"

"Well, it would be a lot of fun. But I'd have to leave the week before Cindy's graduation, right after you get home."

I swallowed hard, knowing he really wanted to go. "James, if you want the job, you should take it."

My parents let James come to get me by himself in May, as soon as my final exams were over. Carol had finished her finals the day before me, and she had already packed up her stuff, rolled up her blue rug, hugged me goodbye, and headed home to St. Louis for the summer. I took my last exam and then came back to my empty dorm room to wait for James. Everything was down from the walls, my bedding was packed up inside my footlocker, and my suitcase was bulging with clothes. I sat on the edge of the bare mattress, waiting. The framed photos of James and my family were packed inside a box with all the letters he had written to me that year. My beautiful music box was wrapped inside one of James's sweatshirts, sharing a crate with my fluffy stuffed lamb and my desk lamp.

I must have fallen asleep on the mattress. I woke to the familiar sensation of James kissing my cheek and threw my arms around his neck. And then James and I carried out to his blue Bonneville those same boxes of stuff he had helped us carry into Smith Hall that fall.

"My dad wants to take us on a fishing trip," he told me as he was driving, "when I get back, in August. He wants to take the three of us—you, me, and Cindy."

"That's nice of him."

"This is a big trip, Sue. He wants to take us to a fishing camp in Saskatchewan."

"Are you kidding me?"

He chuckled. "No." He looked over at me. "Have you ever been fishing before?"

"Oh, maybe when I was a kid. I think my grandfather took us once or twice."

"Well, my dad is getting you a fishing pole, so you can practice casting this summer before we go. And I think he's ordering a rain suit for you, too."

"What's a rain suit?"

"You know, like a raincoat and matching pants."

"Are you serious?"

He laughed. "Totally."

Before James left that week for Tennessee, he brought over my fishing pole and taught me how to cast. We stood in my backyard, out away from the trees, and he showed me how to hold it back over my shoulder, then fling it forward, letting the line out. It took me a few tries before I got the hang of it. Then I had to reel it back in, dragging the orange float through the grass.

"Oh, you caught a big one!" James teased.

We had an awful good-bye in my driveway, with tears and hugs and kisses.

"I don't know if there will be a phone there that I can use very often," he warned, "but you know I'll write to you."

I nodded, not wanting to let go of him.

"Promise me you'll practice fishing." He winked at me as he got into his car.

A few days after he left I received a package in the mail with a blue rain suit—drawstring pants and a jacket with a hood. When I put it all on, my dad said it "swallowed me whole."

James had been gone about a week when his mother, Sharon, called and invited me to go with her to Cindy's graduation. Of course I was happy to go, and she said she would pick me up at my house. I was up in my bedroom, just getting my shoes on, when my mother called up the stairs, "She's here." I looked out my upstairs window and saw her car in our driveway, just coming to a stop. Then the driver got out, but it wasn't Sharon. . . . It was James! He was smiling and holding a huge bouquet of daisies. I got down the stairs as fast as I could, out the door, and into his arms. He swung me around, nearly dropping the flowers.

"James! How can you be here?"

He laughed, "I wouldn't miss my sister's graduation!"

We found Sharon saving seats for us in the crowd of parents and grandparents at the basketball arena. She was waving wildly to us as we came in.

"You tricked me!" I hugged her as we slid into the row.

We all stood together as the graduating seniors marched in, and Sharon wiped away tears. James and I held hands through the entire ceremony, just as we had during the opera on our first date. When Cindy's name was called, we shouted and clapped as loudly as we could, and after the recessional we went to find her in the lobby. In a sea of white caps and gowns, I spied her long, dark hair waving lustrously down her back. She was hugging her dad.

She looked over at us and squealed, then pulled me into a tight hug. "Let me see your hand!"

"What?"

Out of the corner of my eye I could see James quickly shaking his head at her.

"Congratulations!" I shouted, over the noise of the crowd.

She turned to hug James, and he whispered something in her ear. Then, as Sharon was hugging Cindy, James put an arm around my shoulder. "Let's go," he said.

"Don't party too hard tonight," he teased and winked at his sister, as we made our way toward the door.

It was dark outside now, as we walked through the parking lot, my hand in his. When we got into the car I slid over in the front seat, so I could sit close and rest my head on his shoulder as we drove through town to his duplex. "Come inside for a little bit?" he asked, as we pulled into his driveway.

We walked into the kitchen, where the ducks on the walls were now hidden in the evening shadows. But instead of turning on the light, James pulled me close in the dark and kissed me. He reached for my hand, and I thought he was being playful with my fingers. I couldn't see in the darkness, but suddenly I realized he was slipping a ring onto my finger.

He kissed me again. "Marry me?" he whispered.

I giggled. "Mmm hmm."

It was a beautiful, large, round diamond in a classic solitaire setting.

"It was my mom's diamond," he told me as we turned on the light to see it, "but I had it reset. Do you like it?"

It shimmered on my hand, under the light. "It's absolutely beautiful," I breathed. "I love it."

By the time James brought me home, my parents were already asleep in bed. I kissed him goodnight on our brick steps and came in the front door quietly. The bouquet of daisies was in a vase on the hall table, thanks to my thoughtful mother. I stood for a moment and smiled at them in the silent shadows, before softly climbing the stairs to my room.

I got a summer job at a toy and gift shop in the mall. We sold little bouncy balls; cat-shaped erasers; tiger-print sunglasses; miniature magnetic fishing games; and hanging mobiles of whales, swans, and butterflies. I worked the cash register, dusted shelves, rearranged displays, or stared at my diamond ring.

On my days off my mother and I made a couple of trips to fabric shops to look at dress patterns and get ideas for bridesmaids' dresses. I hadn't asked anyone officially yet, but I was thinking at least Serena and Cindy would be in the wedding. I had plenty of time to decide. James and I were thinking we would get married the following summer, probably in June.

One day my mother pulled her wedding dress out of the back of her closet, and I tried it on. She had made it herself back in 1961. It was sewn entirely of lace, tea-length, with an under-dress of satin. Once very white, it was now more ivory in color, but that looked beautiful with my brown eyes. The sleeves were long, and made of the same lace, coming to a point just above my hand, with a row of lace-covered buttons at my wrist. A long row of the same lace-covered buttons went down my back, ending in a little bustle. It fit my figure perfectly. The delicate edges of the lace came to the middle of my calves, but as we looked at my reflection in the full-length mirror in my parents' room my mother showed me how we could add layers underneath it if I wanted it to be longer.

James wrote letters to me, as promised. One was written by a mountain stream, where he was sitting on a rock with his feet in the water thinking of me. I would write to him before going to bed at night, sitting on my bed with my little stuffed lamb.

I wrote to him that summer about an appointment I had at the muscular dystrophy clinic. My mother went with me. Serena and my dad must have had similar appointments to which she also tagged along. A team of doctors met with my mom and me in an exam room. I sat on a table while they all looked at my hands and feet, arms, elbows, and lower legs. One of them banged on my knees and elbows with the reflex hammer. Another took a sewing pin out of his pocket and gently poked my toes, then my foot, then my ankle, asking me where the sensation changed. On my toes and foot it was a dull tap-tap-tap, and then just above my ankle it suddenly felt very sharp. They made a note in a file folder. Then they had me walk down the hallway in my bare feet as they all watched. They asked me to stand on a chair and watched as I climbed up onto it and then back down. At the end of our appointment, as I was putting my socks back on, one of the doctors sat on a stool to chat with me. He asked me about my life—what I was studying in school and what other activities I was involved with. I told him I had one more year of college, I was going to be a teacher, I played the piano, and I was engaged. He wrote all this down, smiling, and said he had noticed my ring. He told me I was a bright young lady and shook my hand.

In July Sharon invited me to drive out to Tennessee one weekend with her and Cindy to visit James. I quickly asked for the weekend off from work. We left early on a Friday morning and took the interstate east. We drove all day, each taking a turn at the wheel before finally arriving at the camp in the mountains around sunset.

James saw his mom's car pulling in to the campground and ran over to meet us. He had a bandana tied loosely around his neck and a whistle hanging down below that. After hugging us all, he proudly showed us around the camp, walking us through the mess hall, the chapel, and his office. The kids from that week had already left, but he introduced us to the other staff members as we crossed paths—the cooks; the nurse; counselors; and his assistant director, Janice, who was a cute, spunky girl my age with bouncy, short curls. She seemed eager to meet me. "James talks about you all the time."

He walked us back to the car in the twilight, where he helped us gather the sleeping bags and pillows we had brought. Then he led us down a short pathway through the trees to an empty cabin where he said we could bunk for the night. We unrolled our sleeping bags on the meager mattresses and said goodnight to James before changing into our pajamas.

The three of us had just crawled into our sleeping bags, lying in the dark and wondering whether there were any mice in the cabin, when something nearly scared us to death. Someone was dragging a stick across our window. Then they creaked open the door and let out a ghoulish moan.

"It's only James," Cindy laughed.

He was carrying his own pillow and sleeping bag, which he unrolled on a mattress near me. After stretching out on it, he reached over and took my hand in the darkness. By the pale moonlight coming through the window I could just make out his profile. I watched as he breathed deeply. I knew he was exhausted.

Our plan was to take James away in the morning. We would drive into Nashville and find a decent hotel, so he could get at least one good night's sleep. We drove down the mountain roads, passing dense woods and an occasional house. Some had a sign out by the road: "Quilts for Sale" or "Handmade Baskets." Then finally, as we got closer to the city, more houses, gas stations, and restaurants started to appear.

Sharon checked us in at a hotel, and when she came back to the car she said she had gotten two adjacent rooms with a door between them. They each had two double beds, so we could each have our own bed. James said that sounded wonderful. We brought in our suitcases, and James lay down on one of the beds. Within minutes he was asleep. Sharon and Cindy and I hung out in the other room, watching TV and occasionally going for walks. There was a McDonald's just across the parking lot, and I decided to get James some food. I brought back a quarter-pounder with fries, some ice cream, and a box of McDonaldland cookies. He was sitting up when I came back, and he devoured them, scooping up ice cream with the cookies, one by one. Then he lay back down and went to sleep again. As the rest of us were getting ready for bed that night, he was mumbling something about getting Janice to take out the garbage. I stroked his hair and reassured him that someone would take care of it.

When we took James back to camp the next day, he seemed rejuvenated and energized, but I was still worried about him. We walked through the camp to his office with him, where he grabbed a clipboard and immediately stepped back into his role as director. A new group of kids would be coming that afternoon, he told us.

I was hugging him goodbye when Janice came in. I turned to her and hugged her, too. "Take care of James," I whispered.

We hadn't been back in Springfield for more than a week when Sharon called to tell me she was going into the hospital. "I have to have surgery," she said. She had been having some stomach pain on our trip but didn't think much about it until we got back and it became much worse.

I met Cindy in the hospital waiting room and hung out during Sharon's surgery, until the nurses let us in to see her. They had removed her spleen, the doctor told us. She would be in the hospital for a few days, recovering.

Cindy and I took shifts staying with Sharon. There was a recliner in her hospital room that I slept in one night so she wouldn't be alone. I read magazine articles out loud to her when she was sick of watching TV, and she told me stories of James as a child. Although she was the one lying in a hospital bed, she was clearly worried about her son. "When you are off at a camp like that," she said, "it's like living in an alternate universe. It's like a separate life, and then you have to come back home to reality."

There were just a few weeks before James would be home, but our reality was going to be the same as that of the last school year, with me off at Mizzou and James in Springfield at SMSU. I worked most days at the toy shop and continued to practice my fishing skills in the backyard, casting the line out into the grass and slowly reeling it in, as James had taught me. At least we would have that time together on the fishing trip before parting ways again.

I came over to Sharon's house to wait for James on the night he arrived home. Cindy and Sharon and I sat in her living room, watching and listening for that blue Bonneville pulling into the driveway. My bags were packed for the fishing trip, since we would be leaving the next morning. A couple pair of jeans; a sweatshirt; flannel shirt; boots; socks; and of course, my rain suit were all stuffed into a suitcase, waiting. Finally we heard his car and all ran to the door to greet him. He came bearing gifts: a quilt for his mother from one of those roadside houses we had passed on our Tennessee trip and baskets for Cindy and me, large and square, with hinged lids. Inside mine was another quilt.

Sharon had baked his favorite cookies, and we all sat around the kitchen table and talked. James looked tired. Occasionally he would seem far away in thought, and then he'd come back to the conversation.

"What time do we leave in the morning?" he asked.

"Your dad said he would pick me up at six-thirty," I told him. "I think our flight is at eight-something."

The next morning we flew to Chicago and then on to Regina, and finally to some small airport where we boarded a little seaplane that landed on the water of a picture-perfect lake in Saskatchewan. We stepped out of the floating plane onto a dock, and James held my hand as we walked up a pathway to a log-frame lodge. As we walked in the creaky door, carrying our suitcases and gear, we could see a dining area with several tables and a front desk where James's dad went to check in. The man at the desk gave us keys to a cabin, which was a short walk away, near the lake.

We trudged back outside and down another trail to a little brown cabin, rustic and homey. We unlocked the door to a small living room—just enough space for a couch and a wood stove. James's dad went right to work building a fire with some wood that was stacked just outside our door. There were two bedrooms, each with two twin beds, made up with sheets and blankets. And there was a small bathroom between them, with a shower and toilet and a little sink. It wasn't the Holiday Inn, but James and his dad were so excited to settle in. As Cindy and I claimed our beds in the "girls'" room, James's dad explained to us that we had to be at the lodge for breakfast at six, after which our Indian guides would meet us at the docks to take us out in the rowboats.

Our first day of fishing was sunny but cold. We went out into the lake in two boats. James and I went with one guide and Cindy and her dad with another. They rowed us out into the middle of the lake, where everything was quiet and still. Ducks floated blissfully on the water, and occasionally a fish would jump. I showed off my skill at casting, and James was impressed. We caught several fish the first morning—northern pike and walleye. When we had reeled them in close to the boat, the guide would scoop them out of the water with a net.

At lunchtime we rowed to shore, and our guides built a campfire. They didn't speak much English but talked to each other in their native tongue. They cleaned and filleted the fish we had just caught, dredged them in cornmeal, and cooked them in a frying pan over the open fire with potatoes and onions. It was the most delicious fish I had ever eaten.

Cindy and I walked up into the woods to use the "toilet" while the men packed up the cooler and put out our campfire. Then we rowed out into the lake again for more fishing. In the late afternoon the guides brought us back to the docks, and we all went to shower and change before dinner at the lodge. James and his dad built a fire in our woodstove, and we sat around it, warming our toes while waiting for our turn to shower. The temperature was dropping as we walked to the lodge for dinner. Afterward we huddled around the fire again, sharing fish stories until Cindy and I buried ourselves under the blankets and said goodnight.

The second day was my twenty-first birthday. My mother had stashed a card in my suitcase, and I opened it that morning before breakfast. It was so precious to read the message in her handwriting—simply that she loved me and was proud of me. Our guides took us out in the rowboats again, repeating the same process as the day before. We fished all morning, made a campfire at lunchtime and cooked what we had caught, and then fished all afternoon.

That night at dinner, to celebrate my birthday, James's dad ordered steaks for all of us, with big slices of chocolate cake for dessert. The waitress brought mine out with a candle, and everyone sang to me. Then we came back to our cabin, and

James stoked the fire while his dad went into their room and brought out a gift for me. It was all wrapped up in birthday paper—a tin full of butter mints and an envelope with a picture of a blanket that he said he had ordered for me. It was navy blue with rows of white lambs and yellow ducks. I don't know whether he knew the significance of lambs and ducks but wondered whether James had given him a hint.

"That's so nice of you—thank you!" I beamed. "And really, this whole trip has been so wonderful!"

Cindy yawned and announced that she was hitting the sack. Their dad said he was sleepy, too.

James and I sat in front of the woodstove, keeping warm, while they got ready for bed.

The night grew quiet, except for the crackling of the fire and the crickets outside. I was resting my head against his shoulder when he cleared his throat and said he was going for a walk. He tied his shoes back on and slipped out the cabin door quietly. I sat in front of the fire, with my knees to my chest, and waited for him.

He was gone for quite a while. I poked the fire now and then to keep the flame going, then sat back and watched the coals glowing yellow and orange.

Finally, James came back in and sat down on the floor next to me.

"Hey," I whispered, "What's up?"

"Oh, just thinking about stuff."

I looked up at his face and realized he had been crying.

I put a hand on his cheek. "I love you."

Now he was fighting back tears. "I love you, too." Then the tears spilled over. "I will always love you." His eyes were closed tightly. He took off his glasses.

"Hey," I rubbed his arm. "What's wrong?"

He shook his head slowly, and more tears came. I felt a twinge in the pit of my stomach. My heart started beating rapidly, and suddenly I knew.

I knew.

"What happened with you and Janice?" I asked quietly.

A sob abruptly escaped his throat. "We fell in love." He was fully sobbing now. He could hardly breathe. He buried his face in the sleeve of his flannel shirt. "She thought . . . she thought she was pregnant." He took in a labored breath.

"She . . . you . . ." I couldn't finish.

"Yes." He didn't look up.

I stared down at my hand, resting on his arm. The diamond glimmered in the flickering light from the fire. I pulled my hand back into my lap. I felt sick. I started shaking all over. I was nauseous. I turned toward the bathroom door and began crawling toward it. I reached the toilet just in time. James crawled after me and held back my hair, crying, while I vomited. I lost the steak dinner and the chocolate cake. James sat with me on the bathroom floor, moaning and wiping his eyes.

I stayed in front of the toilet until I was sure there was no more. Then James helped me stand up and walked me to my bed. He pulled the blankets up over my shoulder without saying a word and left the room.

The next morning I stayed in bed while they all went to breakfast. I got dressed alone, washed my face in the sink, and gathered my hair into a ponytail. It was raining, so I pulled my rain pants on over my jeans and zipped up the jacket over my flannel shirt and sweatshirt.

I met them out by the dock. James and I didn't talk much. He held my hand to help me into the boat, and then our guide rowed us out into the middle of the lake. I stared out into the water. When we came to a stop, I cast my line out a few times, unsuccessfully. I slowly reeled in the orange float and cast it out again. After a long silence I turned to James. I wanted to be clear about one thing.

"Is she pregnant?" I asked in a hushed voice.

He looked down at his reel. "No."

I stared off into the distance. My eyes became blurry with tears. I wiped my cheek.

Our guide looked up at me. "No worry," he said. "You catch fish."

The rain was falling harder now. I pulled my hood up over my head. There must be some way we could work this out. I could forgive him. We could forget it. No one would ever have to know. Then I looked over at James casting out his line and thought of the meanest thing I could say to him. "You are just like your father." Before I could catch myself, it was out.

He looked so hurt.

And then there was a tug on my line. It nearly pulled me out of the boat. James had to help me reel it in, which took some coaching from our guide. When he finally caught it up in his net, he laughed. "Big one! See? Northern pike!"

Later that afternoon when we weighed it, James's dad congratulated me. It was ten pounds. James showed me how to hold it up by its eye-sockets, which grossed me out, but I managed to stand on the dock and hold it long enough for Cindy to snap my picture.

James and I didn't say a word to Cindy or his dad about our relationship. I held his hand tightly walking back to our cabin, and we snuggled up in front of the fire as though everything were fine. He was the only person in the world who knew what I was going through that day. And I was the only one who knew what he was struggling with.

We sat close and held hands throughout our flights back to Springfield, and then James drove me home, for the last time, in his blue Bonneville. We took the back roads to my house, the way we had driven many times before, past a couple of farms and over the creek. Now and then James would wipe his eyes. At one point he pulled the car over to the side of the road. He bent his head down to the steering wheel and wept. I put a hand on his shoulder. It shook with each breath.

"James," I said, "I forgive you. I will forgive you, and we can stay together."

He shook his head. "No. You don't deserve this. I can't . . . " He took a deep breath. "I love her."

He wiped the tears from his face and pulled the car back onto the road. We pulled into my driveway, and he got out to open the trunk and carry my suitcase up the brick steps to my door. I walked up the steps behind him, and we stood for a moment, looking at each other. Then I slipped the ring off my finger and handed it back to him. Silently he got back into his car and drove away.

CHAPTER 36

DECEMBER

Today I am feeling defeated.

My suitcase is lying on my bed, packed for me to fly down to my parents' retirement house in Florida. It is overflowing with not only my clothes but also Christmas presents, my laptop, my address book, Christmas cards to write, and some of my husband's clothes, since he will be joining me down there in a week.

This is not how we planned our Christmas: Lois was coming home after finals to spend a week here at home in Vermont before flying with us down to Florida, where we would meet John and Serena at my parents' house.

But plans changed when my mom fell Thanksgiving weekend in the middle of the night. She got up to use the restroom, and as she was getting back into bed she stumbled and fell back against her nightstand, breaking a rib and cracking three vertebrae.

My dad called me the next day, after they had gotten home from the hospital. At first, when I offered to come early to help with the cooking and laundry, not to mention the Christmas shopping and decorating, he said, "No, just come when you were planning to come." But the next morning he called and asked, "How soon can you come?" We agreed that I could fly

262

down as soon as my Christmas concerts with the gospel choir were over, the second week of December.

We had our last performance last night. My group of twenty-eight smiling singers, dressed in black and white, stood on the platform in a local church and filled the sanctuary with a cappella harmonies that spoke of the joy and peace of the Christmas season.

But now I am feeling neither of those. Up before dawn, I am walking back and forth from my closet to my suitcase. Exhausted. Worried. Wobbly. Teary.

Finally, I zip up my suitcase and go to the top of the stairs to holler down to my husband that I am all packed. I sit down on the top step, thinking I will scoot down the stairs on my bottom since I am feeling the lack of sleep in my joints—instead of my usual tedious method of grasping the rails on both sides and stepping down one foot at a time.

I pause and rest my chin in my hands, my elbows against my knees. I have been grumpy this morning. Really grumpy. Angry at my kind husband when he asked me which one of his shirts he should add to my suitcase for the Christmas Eve service at my parents' church. I was in the middle of a thought about packing my makeup, and I snapped at him, "What else are you going to spring on me? I can't think about that right now!"

He had held up two shirts on hangers for me to choose from. "We have to put it in your suitcase, because there won't be enough room in the little one I'm taking next week."

I groaned. I already had his khakis and a couple of his shirts in my large suitcase. "Why don't we just buy another big suitcase?"

"Suzanne, we already talked about this. How would I pull two big suitcases through the airport?" I imagine the scene, with me clinging to his elbow as I always do in airports, keeping a wary eye out for running children or hurried, oblivious travelers who might bump into me. He's right, of course. That makes me even grumpier.

Now, sitting on the top step, the tears come. At first it is just a single tear that I brush away. I hear him shuffling papers downstairs at his desk. I sniffle hard to see whether he will notice that I am crying. No response. More shuffling papers.

Now the tears really come. I can feel my face wrinkle up as I bury my eyes in my hands. He comes to the bottom of the stairs and clears his throat.

"When Eva knocks, let's just pretend we're not here," he says.

"What?" I look up. "Eva's coming over?" Eva has been my neighbor for nearly two decades, but I don't know if I want to greet even the dearest of friends at this moment.

"She just texted to say she has a Christmas gift for you and wanted to catch you before you left."

I catch my breath and wipe my hands on my jeans. "Can I have a Kleenex? There's a box on the piano."

He walks over to the piano and back, then hands them up the stairs to me.

I blow my nose. "I can't let anyone see me like this."

He lets me cry for a minute in silence. "If she knocks, we won't answer."

In the car on the way to the airport, I am still grumpy. We argue about whether it's okay to be grumpy. I dig for Kleenex in my purse and dab my eyes. At least Eva never came by, so I don't feel deceitful.

He tries to sound matter-of-fact. "I don't know if they will have a jet bridge from the terminal to the airplane. They might have to wheel you up a ramp from the tarmac to the door of the plane."

I drop my hand to my lap. "Oh, you are kidding me!"

"No. I think that's what they do on these smaller planes."

I ride the rest of the way to the airport in silence because I know that anything I say will sound like complaining, and we've already had that argument.

Sometimes I just want to be angry. Let me be angry! I want to be angry at this disease. I want to be angry that my parents live so far away. I want to be angry that the world is not accessible. I want to be angry at those stupid terrorists for making all of our lives more complicated with the added security in airports. I want to be angry that I cannot walk through the metal detector without my shoes on because of these awkward leg braces, so I have to tell the agent that I need assistance and explain my whole situation. I want to be angry at the woman who therefore has to pat me down. I want to be angry at strangers for staring at me or pretending to look away. I want to be angry at other travelers who don't pay attention to the path of the suitcase on wheels that they are dragging behind them.

By the time we get through security (they gave my husband a pass so he could walk me to the gate), I am a total wreck. The waiting area at my gate is pretty crowded. The only two available seats next to each other are near the desk, facing the rest of the crowd. I would really like to sneak off to a corner somewhere and finish my crying jag. I spy the wheelchair they have brought out for me. It is waiting near the door that will lead out onto the icy tarmac and up a snowy ramp to the plane. We sit, not speaking, facing the rest of the crowd.

After a few minutes he tells me he is going to walk around. I nod. He meanders over to the window to look outside at the planes.

I am nervous about what will happen at the other end of this flying adventure today. Apparently they will have an attendant with a wheelchair to get me off the plane and push me through the crowd, help me get my luggage, and then wheel me out to the curb, where my eighty-year-old Daddy will drive up in his SUV to collect me. *Oh, Lord.*

My thoughts are suddenly interrupted. A sweet, familiar voice surprises me like a tiny burst of sunlight breaking through the storm clouds. "Suzanne!"

I look up to see my housekeeper, Lisa's, friendly smile. "Oh, Lisa! What are you doing here?"

She bends down and wraps me in a tight hug. I wonder if she can tell I've been crying.

"I'm headed down to see my daughter this week," she reminds me.

"Oh, that's right!

She sits down on the seat beside me. "Are you on your way to your mom and dad's? You told me you were going early."

I nod. "Are we on the same flight?"

"No, I'm going to Tampa. I'm a few gates over, but I saw you and your husband walk by. I just wanted to come say 'Hi and have a great trip.' I've been thinking about your mom."

I suddenly feel very egocentric.

"Lisa, you are so sweet. Thank you."

She hugs me again before she walks away.

My husband returns moments later and sits down next to me. "Was that Lisa?"

"Well . . ." I take a deep breath and look off in her direction. "That . . . that was an angel sent from God."

CHAPTER 37

SENIOR YEAR

I'll have to say that my senior year at Mizzou was academically my best but emotionally my worst. I dove into my studies and challenged myself to make straight As, which I did. Carol would sometimes return to our dorm room after her classes and find me sitting cross-legged on my bed, with books and papers spread out, presumably studying. But often I was choking back tears. "Your eyes are leaking again," she would tease, sitting down next to me. How many times did she listen to the same heartbreaking story that semester? And how many times did she remind me of her favorite Bible verse? *"Trust in the LORD with all your heart and do not lean on your own understanding. In all your ways acknowledge Him, and He will make your paths straight" (Proverbs 3:5 NASB).*

C.C. and Joe would meet us for dinner in the cafeteria, and we would laugh together, but inside I was aching. I felt lost. I didn't even know who I was. For the past year I had been James's girlfriend. Now I had to get used to the idea that I was not going to be his wife. But who was I?

I don't know whether I trusted in the Lord with all my heart. I went to church on Sundays. I went to Bible study at the Baptist Student Union. I read my Bible and said prayers. But I was just numbly going through motions, like fingers playing through scales using muscle memory, not thinking about individual notes. It was what I had always done, and it is what I continued to do automatically.

For the final stretch of my senior year I was assigned to an elementary school about four miles from campus for my student teaching. My dad found a used company car for me, so I could drive from the dorm to the elementary school and back; it was a white Chevrolet Celebrity. I would wake early and go by myself to the cafeteria for a quick breakfast in my teacher clothes (as Carol called them). There were readymade sack lunches I would grab for my school day. And then I would drive myself to Mrs. Lou Thompson's second-grade classroom, where I would be cheerfully greeted each morning by a mix of black, white, and brown faces belonging to youngsters who knew me as "Miss Butler."

I sat in on reading circles, helped little fingers hold their pencils correctly, and listened to countless tattles during recess. I opened nearly every child's bottle of glue, so they could glue dried beans onto popsicle sticks, ten to a stick, for our math lesson. I sat on a stool in the front of the classroom and read aloud chapters of *Stuart Little* after lunch. I walked children to the drinking fountain when a tooth was coming out and watched as Mrs. Thompson deposited the tooth in a special envelope for the child to take home.

And after school Mrs. Thompson and I would chat. We were concerned about certain children—some who were struggling to read, some who needed to be challenged, some who were acting out aggressively, and still others who came to school filthy. It didn't take long for me to realize that her heart was knit to that of each child in her classroom, and as the weeks went by I found that mine was, too.

Before the term was over Mrs. Thompson invited me over to her house for dinner, and I got to meet her husband and five-year-old son. I sat on the floor of her living room and built airplanes out of Legos with her little boy. It was a small house, but it was full of love. Her husband had just planted a tree in the front yard and was eager to show it to her. We had a delicious spaghetti dinner, and afterward we baked chocolate chip cookies for our kids. Her life was what I dreamed of.

On my last day the children wrote sweet notes to me, featuring crayon drawings of me along with lots of hearts and rainbows. I brought the notes back to the dorm room, where C.C. and Carol and I read through each one, chuckling at the caricatures of me and "aww-ing" over their sugary sentiments.

God had answered my identity quandary with the simplicity of handwritten love notes from children. Who was I? I was Miss Butler. I was loved by children. And I was going to be a teacher.

CHAPTER 38

CHRISTMAS GIFTS

"What shall we do for dinner tonight?" my mom asks. She is lying on the couch, supported by an extra pillow under her broken back, with her feet in my lap. I am taking a minute to rest my knees. The breakfast dishes are all cleaned up, and I've already folded one load of laundry, with a second in the dryer now. The house is quiet, except for the Christmas music that is playing from the CD player on the bookshelf across the room. My silver-headed daddy has just wandered outside for his daily stroll around the neighborhood.

"Well," I answer, "we have some chicken left over from last night. I could chop it up with some rice and onion. Throw some cheese and breadcrumbs on top."

"That sounds good," she sighs.

"I'll see if we still have some salad. If not, we'll send Dad to the store."

"We might need lunch meat, anyway."

I rub her feet gently. "Want us to put the tree up today? If Dad can get it out of the closet, I'll hang the ornaments on it."

"Well, see what he thinks when he gets back."

She is getting sleepy now from the pain medication, so I go back to reading the funny papers while she closes her eyes.

She opens them again briefly when she hears my dad coming back inside. He plops down in his red leather easy chair across from the couch and removes his shoes and leg braces. Just like mine, they are white plastic with Velcro straps. But he doesn't bother disguising them with tan-colored nylons, as I do. His knee-high white socks, worn daily underneath them, create enough of a camouflage, while also providing a little bit of cushion where they rub against his aging skin. He stands the braces up inside his shoes, next to his chair, and leans back. The footrest comes up as he reclines, and he is ready for his morning nap.

An instrumental version of "Deck the Halls" plays softly while I look out the window at the bright sunlight reflecting off the concrete driveway. My dad's roses are blooming plump and red out there, on five separate bushes that he started from cuttings he snipped (with permission) from a bush outside the post office in town. He refers to them as his "post office roses." The bushes are at least four feet tall now, thick and green with abundant blooms he has to cut back every couple of months. I wish I could grow roses like that. But then again, this is Florida, where, as he puts it, "stuff just cain't help but grow."

I lean my head back and take advantage of this quiet moment to shut my own eyes for a while. The music plays on: *"O come, let us adore him . . ."*

"Ah, me." My dad yawns as he sits up in his chair.

"Charles, would you get me an ice pack?" My mother's eyes are open now, and wet with tears.

"Sure, Darlin.'" He reaches over to grab his braces and fumbles with the straps.

"I can get it, Mom," I offer.

She pulls her feet back off my lap, and I push myself up, using the arm of the couch to lean on. I grab my cane and head off in the direction of the kitchen.

I find her ice pack in the freezer door and lay it on the counter. Better get a towel to wrap it in. I go to the drawer where she always keeps her dishtowels and take out the one on top. The apples printed on it are faded from years of machine washings, and the edges are frayed. As I fold it around the ice pack, it brings back countless memories of cooking and doing dishes with her.

Dad comes into the kitchen now. "You want a water bottle, Miss Patricia?" he speaks loudly in her direction.

"Yeah. What time is it?" she answers weakly.

"Quarter to eleven," he calls back.

She is trying to swing her feet around to sit up now. "What time am I supposed to take my pill?"

"Let me look." I hand Dad the wrapped ice pack, and he carries it over to her with the bottle of water. We have been keeping a log of her medications on a little pad of paper on the kitchen counter. "This says you took your pain pill at 8:05 this morning."

"Alright." She breathes out as she leans forward. My dad is helping her get the ice pack in the right spot between her back and the couch. She leans back against it.

"Is that alright?" he asks.

She sighs deeply. "Yeah, that's good."

I grab my cane from where I've leaned it next to the refrigerator and head to the laundry room to check on the clothes.

Dad and I are the "kitchen crew" for lunch. I get out the bread and the plates, and he gets out the deli meat, cheese, mustard, mayonnaise, and lettuce. Oh, and don't forget the pickles. I place a slice of bread on each plate and cut them each in half.

"Pat, you want turkey or ham?" Dad calls to Mom, who is lying down again on the couch.

"Oh, turkey, I guess."

Dad will have mustard on both halves of his bread. Mom will have mayo. I'll have some of both. That's the routine. I'll finish making the sandwiches while he puts ice in glasses. I'll have water, and he will have cranberry juice.

My mother bravely pushes herself up from the couch and comes to the kitchen table.

"Mom, you can eat it in there, if you want. You're allowed," I offer, as I carry a plate to the table.

She chuckles, but that quickly turns into a wince of pain. "No, I need to get up."

She slowly sits down into her chair, and I adjust a small throw pillow behind her back. We have stolen it from the family room, and it looks out of place here in the kitchen, but it has a new home here in her chair for the time being.

When we are all seated, my dad takes her hand and reaches across the table for mine. I reach over and take my mother's trembling fingers. We bow our heads.

"Lord, we just thank You and praise You for another day," my dad begins. *"Thank You for all the good things You provide for us. We thank You that Sue could be here with us. And we just continue to ask You to heal Pat, Lord. Help her back to get better and take away her pain. We ask in Jesus' name, Amen."*

I am putting our plates into the dishwasher when I see my dad dragging the Christmas tree, in its box, out into the family room. From the couch my mom is giving him instructions. "Pull that chair over closer to the bookshelf." She wants the tree to be centered in front of the window. "Be careful, Charles." It is in two pieces, with lights already strung around each branch, and when you slide the top half into its place in the trunk the whole thing stands about six feet tall.

It takes Dad a few minutes to find the end of the cord. "Well, it's all hung up in the branches," he sighs. Finally, he plugs it into the outlet under the window. There are little green fake pine needles strewn all over the carpet, and the furniture is somewhat displaced, but as the lights come on we are distracted from that. It suddenly feels like Christmas.

Dad drags the empty box back to the closet, leaving a trail of green needles behind him.

"We'll vacuum that up later," I promise my mother, not quite sure how I am actually going to accomplish that, since I don't have the balance required to vacuum my own house. I suppose I could get down on my knees and manage vacuuming like that.

"Might's well wait until you put the ornaments on it," she says. "Those needles will just keep falling." And then, as though she can read my mind, "I'm so sorry you have to do all that. You don't have to . . . ." She takes a staggered breath, and I can tell she is fighting back tears.

"Mom, I don't mind," I reassure her. "Remember all the times you took care of me when I was sick?"

I rest my cane against the arm of the wingback chair next to the tree and lean against the chair for balance as I begin straightening the branches. They have been crammed into a box all year, and some of them look a little sad.

Dad sits down in his easy chair and picks up his library book to read.

"Whatcha reading, Dad?"

He looks up. "Oh, this is a thriller! A murder mystery."

I smile. Typical.

I pick up my cane and walk around the tree to straighten the branches on the other side. There isn't a chair to lean on here, so I steady myself with the cane and do the job one-handed.

My mom shifts on the couch, trying to get comfortable.

"Do you need another ice pack?" I ask.

"No, I think I'm alright." She watches me as I lean over to fiddle with a bough near the bottom.

After a long silence she clears her throat. "I've set aside some of my old jewelry for Lois, but I'll have to get you to wrap it for me."

"Sure." I uncurl the end of a prickly branch, and a few more pine needles flutter down to the carpet.

She continues, "And somewhere in one of my desk drawers over there I have my dad's old pocket watch." She pauses, thoughtfully. "It doesn't have a chain anymore. I don't even know if it still runs. But I was thinking I could give it to John for Christmas."

I stand upright and look over at her. "Oh, Mom." I know this is one of her treasures.

"We could put a little note in the box, saying, 'This used to be your great grandfather's.'"

I pause. Her eyes are closed again. I can tell she is getting sleepy from the medicine.

"I'm sure he would really love that," I assure her.

CHAPTER 39

JOB HUNT

My parents drove the three hours to Columbia to watch me walk across the stage in my cap and gown. Then we packed up my belongings; I tearfully hugged Carol, C.C., and Joe good-bye; and we drove back to Springfield.

Everything I owned fit easily into my bedroom at home: my clothes and linens, a small turntable stereo with a few vinyl albums, a typewriter, and the few books I had not sold back to the university bookstore for cash.

But I knew I couldn't stay long under my parents' roof. They would be moving to Chicago in August. Once again, French's was relocating my father.

While I sent off my résumé to various school districts across Missouri, I also looked for a summer job. Through some referrals at my church, I found a position directing a Christian day camp for underprivileged kids. It didn't pay a whole lot, but I knew I would love it.

It was across town, on the "other side of the tracks," in what used to be a church building. I was in charge of four college-aged, underpaid staff members who herded, played with, and loved on the campers all week. We held a chapel service every morning, fed the kids lunch, and then played games and did crafts in the afternoon. The former church office became my workspace, where I called local pastors and asked them to come and speak and then typed thank you letters for those who did. The fellowship hall and church kitchen served as our lunchroom. Ladies from local churches came each week and made hot lunches for the kids. I had to arrange for that, too. Then there were outdoor games and crafts to organize. The youth pastor from my church gave me a book of crazy outdoor games. We tried them all. We also strung a lot of macaroni necklaces and used any leftover craft supplies from area churches that donated them to us when their vacation Bible school weeks were over. I typed up thank-you letters for those as well.

We began every morning by greeting the thirty or so kids outside in the sunshine (unless it was raining, in which case we pushed the tables aside in the fellowship hall). We gathered in a circle and sang the "Hokey Pokey," complete with every required dance move.

> . . . *You put your left foot in*
> *You put your left foot out*
> *You put your left foot in and you shake it all about*
> *You do the Hokey Pokey and you turn yourself around*
> *That's what it's all about! . . .*

Then it was on to "I'm Gonna Stand Up, Sit Down, Clap My Hands and Shout Hallelujah." You can imagine the scene. I kept an ear out for any new songs that involved hand motions, although I had several in my memory bank from my own days at church camp.

Little cabin in the wood
Little man by the window stood
Saw a rabbit hopping by
Frightened as could be
"Help me, help me, help!" he said
"Lest the hunter shoot me dead!"
Little rabbit, come inside
Safely to abide.

Then, of course, it was "Tiny Cabin in the Wood," in which our hand motions were miniscule and our voices high and squeaky, followed by "GIANT CABIN IN THE WOOD," which required huge, sweeping hand motions and low, husky voices.

When we filed in for chapel (hopefully ready to be quiet and listen), we passed the food pantry and clothes closet in what had formerly been Sunday school rooms. Here the mothers and fathers of these youngsters were met by volunteers from local churches and were allowed once a week to rummage through what was available. I shared my office space with these volunteers as well, with their stacks of paperwork and bags of unsorted clothing.

I was on the phone in the office one afternoon, trying to line up a chapel speaker, when one of the counselors, Steve, came in with a crying boy. They had been outside playing kickball, and the boy had fallen down in the grass. There was no obvious injury, and suspicious that this was an attention-getting ploy, Steve brought him inside to find the first aid kit, which was in my desk drawer. He set the child down on my chair, the only clear spot in the room.

"Where does it hurt?"

"On my foot," the youngster sniffled.

"Where on your foot?"

"On the bottom."

Steve removed the child's shoe and, seeing nothing, dug around in the first aid kit. "Let's see. . . . This might help." He held up a tube of generic first aid cream.

"What is it?" The boy's eyes lit up.

"It says, 'Sore Foot Medicine.'" Steve applied some of it to the child's foot and helped him get his shoe back on.

"That's much better!" the little cheater smiled.

The two ran back outside together.

At the end of each day, when the kids had all been picked up by their parents or legal guardians, the counselors and I would all collapse in Sig's office. Sig was the director of this ministry, and it was his fulltime job to keep tabs on all of its various aspects: the food pantry, the clothes closet, and the five of us. It was Sig who had interviewed and hired each of us, and now he provided comic relief at the end of every long, hot day. Sig's office had also been a Sunday school room at one time, but now it was decorated with photos of his wife and kids and posters of the Georgia Bulldogs.

"The natives were restless today," he chuckled as we filed in and sprawled ourselves on the worn carpeted floor. Sig had confiscated an entire carton of outdated chocolate-covered graham crackers from the food pantry and kept the boxes in the kitchen freezer for these daily "unload" sessions. We passed around the deliciously cold box of cookies while moaning, sighing, and telling stories about the day. Then we hashed out the next day's plans, and Sig would lead us in prayer.

The summer was flying by, and I still didn't have a teaching job.

I was determined to find one in St. Louis to be near Carol and Tamera. Carol had landed a job with an advertising agency in St. Louis and had decided to live with her folks in the nearby suburbs to save money. Tamera had one more year to finish her degree in piano performance, and she needed a roommate in her little apartment next door to the St. Louis Music Conservatory. I was hoping to be that roommate.

In mid-August, after the last day of camp, when every stinky, sweaty child had hugged me goodbye and we'd had our last celebrative box of frozen cookies in Sig's office, I knew I had to hunt down a job in St. Louis. Carol's parents had graciously invited me to stay with them for a week while I desperately prayed and searched for a teaching position. As Carol went off to work in the mornings, I sat at the desk in their living room calling school districts. Most of the positions had already been filled.

I did go downtown for one job interview, wearing my light blue business suit. I thought I looked smart but pretty. My skirt was hemmed just below the knee, and my pale pink blouse was buttoned up with a floppy bow at my neck.

When I walked into the principal's office he asked me to sit in a hard wooden chair across from his desk. Everything in that office smelled old. The institutional tile floor, the wood paneled walls, the ominous desk, the shelves of dusty volumes—all made me feel young and small. I handed my résumé across the desk, and as the middle-aged man took it and sat down he looked at me sternly and asked, "How much experience do you have with inner-city kids?"

I stammered something about my summer job, but it seemed lame. The question itself told me that I was not right for this position at all. The rest of the interview was just niceties, and I left knowing I would never hear back from him.

The next morning I began thumbing through the yellow pages and calling Christian schools. One asked me to come in that afternoon. As soon as I walked in and saw the tiny chairs and tables, along with the bulletin boards displaying big letters and numbers, I realized this was a preschool. The very kind woman who showed me around told me they had very specific lesson plans and offered to let me look through the thick binder of each day's drills, but she was sorry to say they could pay me only minimum wage. I thanked her and left.

I had one last strand of hope. Another Christian school, on the south side of St. Louis, had answered my phone call and asked whether I could come for an interview the following day. The next morning I woke in Carol's parents' guest room, donned my light blue business suit, and drove down the interstate, following the directions I had scribbled on scrap paper.

I pulled into the parking lot of a beautiful, newly built school adjoining a large church. Catching my reflection in the large glass doors as I entered the building, I adjusted my collar and took a deep breath. I found my way to the school office and greeted an official-looking secretary. She rose from her chair and kindly introduced me to the principal, who invited me into his office. The walls were lined with bookshelves sporting trophies alongside Bible commentaries. I handed him my résumé, and he looked it over as he sat behind his desk, noting my recent graduation. Then, motioning politely for me to sit, he asked me about my faith. Was I a baptized believer in Jesus Christ? Yes. Would I be comfortable teaching Bible stories? Definitely! He leaned back in his chair, commenting, "I think you are an answer to prayer."

He invited me to walk down the school hallway with him and look into the classrooms. He pointed out the one that would be mine, should I take the job. There were rows of clean desks. A chalkboard covered one wall. A large bulletin board hung between windows that looked out over a soccer field. The carpet smelled new.

I suddenly realized that he was offering me the job. "I wouldn't normally hire someone on the spot, but school starts in two weeks and we need a first grade teacher. You would have sixteen students." We walked back to the office, and he asked the secretary for a copy of a teacher contract. He sighed as he handed me the paper. "Unfortunately, our salary scale is low. You would be starting at $11,200. I realize that doesn't compete with public schools. Take the weekend and pray about it. Can you let me know on Monday?"

"Yes, of course." I shook his hand and walked out to my car calmly, even though my heart was pounding. I had a classroom.

CHAPTER 40

GROCERIES

There is nothing scarier to me than a wet tile floor. When I walk into the grocery store and see that familiar yellow plastic sign set up on a glistening, slippery floor, warning, "Caution, Wet Floor," my knees begin quaking and I imagine that the stick figure falling onto his patootie is me. When my son was younger he would point to the stick figure and laugh: "Look, Mom, they have break dancing here!" But break dancing is not what I have in mind now when I see that sign.

Winter is worse, not just because of the ice but because the floor of the grocery store is almost always wet. The melting snow makes little streams and unavoidable puddles in the parking lot, so that everyone's wet shoes make the first ten feet inside the store a veritable ice rink. Add to that the snow or slush that is caught in the treads of every shopper's shoes (including my own) and is constantly melting as we walk around the store. I grab onto the grocery cart to steady myself, even if I am picking up only a few items. If I am by myself, I will probably have to ask a kind stranger to help me get that heavy bag of flour from the bottom shelf into my cart.

Actually, I have come to the conclusion that I just can't do the big grocery shopping trips by myself any longer. It isn't just the wet tile floors that make it difficult, but the amount of time on my feet. By the time I walk every aisle, make it through the checkout line, load the bags into the car, carry the groceries into the house one bag at a time, and unpack the bags and put everything away, my knees are screaming at me, and I am wiped out.

When I mentioned this to my friend and prayer partner, Corinne, last Tuesday during our biweekly prayer and teatime at my kitchen table, she offered to go to the store for me. "How about Friday morning?" she asked.

I was astonished. "Oh, Corinne, are you sure? It's a huge job, and I'm so picky about which brands I get."

"Well, let's give it a try," she offered. "I'll come to your house first, and we can go through the list in detail."

There are few friends as charitable as Corinne. I don't remember exactly when I met her. I first knew of her because our little church was supporting her parents as missionaries in Africa. She had spent most of her childhood there. But her mother had grown up in our church, and her grandmother was still a prominent member, so her family would visit whenever they were back in Vermont. After college Corinne worked as a missionary with inner-city kids, and once again our church supported her financially. Then she moved to Vermont more permanently, settling in to live with her aging grandmother. We saw her every Sunday during that time. And so did a kind-hearted farmer at our church who had lost his first wife to cancer. He soon fell in love with Corinne, and she became a farmer's wife, just as her grandmother had been.

At my kitchen table every other Tuesday morning we sip tea and talk easily for an hour or so. Then we join hands across the table and praise God for His mercy and power, ask Him to bless our church and our families, and beg Him to move mountains.

I have made a very specific grocery list. I tried to place the items in the order she would find them while walking through the store. Produce first, then canned items, meat, frozen foods, dairy, and finally bread and eggs.

Corinne knocks politely on my door, and when I yell "Come on in!" she steps happily into my front hall, bundled up against the cold. Hat and mittens, coat, scarf, and boots. "Good morning!" She slips out of her boots and leaves her mittens on my hall table, then glides over to my kitchen table in her sock feet.

"You think you've written everything on here?" She sits, her long, wavy light brown hair falling down to her elbow as she picks up my list and the pencil. She reads through the list out loud.

"I usually get the big can of whole peeled tomatoes," I explain. "I think it's twenty-eight ounces. It's on the bottom shelf in that aisle."

She makes a note. "And what kind of ground beef do you usually get?"

"Oh, eighty-five percent lean. Or ninety if they don't have it."

"Okay. And oh, what about potatoes? How many?"

"Oh, a small bag of those medium-size red potatoes."

She scribbles that down and studies the list once again.

I hand her a wad of cash. "I think this should be enough."

"If it's not, we can settle up when I get back," she smiles.

She is gone for about an hour. I try to keep myself busy by playing the piano and folding some laundry. At one point she texts me, "They are out of the bread you wanted. Do you want me to get the store brand?"

"No, I'll just wait. Thanks."

Finally I see her car pulling into my driveway, and I push the button to open my garage door so she can bring the bags up the ramp into my kitchen. The snow swirls around in my driveway as she opens her trunk and then clomps up the ramp in her boots. She sets two bags on my kitchen counter, then goes back for more. I start unpacking the bags, thankful for each item as I reach in and pull out a package of meat, a bag of frozen peas, and a can of tuna. When she comes back inside with the last bag, I offer her a cup of tea while I put things away. "Don't you want to sit down for a bit?"

"I'm sorry. I can't stay," she apologizes. "I've got to go pick up my son."

"Oh, Corinne, I can't thank you enough." I am genuinely humbled.

"I wasn't sure if this was the kind of lettuce you wanted," she says, pulling it out of a bag.

"Yes, yes. It's perfect," I assure her.

"Oh, and your change is in this bag, I think," she says, pointing with her mitten.

"Thank you so much." I hug her tightly.

"I'm happy to do it!" She waves as she walks back out my door and down the ramp into the cold. "Anything for you, Suzanny!"

CHAPTER 41

TEACHING

Back at my parents' house in Springfield, I sat at the kitchen table with my dad as he read through the teacher's contract with me. He got out a yellow legal pad and we drew up a budget. If I didn't buy anything other than groceries, I could probably afford to pay rent, utilities, gas, and a small car payment each month. My mom and dad had paid in full for that used, white, four-door Chevy Celebrity I was driving but asked me to start making payments to them each month. On paper my budget looked doable. In reality, there would be many months when I would have to call my dad and tell him I would be late with the car payment.

I moved my clothes, books, and typewriter into Tamera's one bedroom apartment in St. Louis. Not wanting to crowd into her small bedroom, I converted a large storage closet into my room. There was just enough space for a twin bed, which I got by chance from a college student who was moving out of a nearby apartment, and a small metal shelving unit that had been left by the former occupant. It doubled as my nightstand and a place to stack my clean laundry. With one side of the bed pushed up against the wall, there was just enough room for me to stand and dress. There was a light fixture on the ceiling above my bed, but no window in my tiny sleeping space.

I lived off cornflakes, rice, pasta, a little chicken, cheap white bread, and peanut butter, with an occasional guilty run through the McDonald's drive-through on my way home from school. For lunch I packed myself a bagel and an apple. Sometimes Tamera's boyfriend, Tom, would come over to our apartment and cook up something amazing, like steamed artichokes or stir-fry Chinese vegetables, and as I walked in the door the aroma would waft through our apartment like a summer breeze.

I lived and breathed first grade, staying until five or six o'clock most days, writing lesson plans and cutting shapes out of construction paper for bulletin boards. At my apartment in the evenings I sat at our little kitchen table and graded papers with my red ballpoint pen, tracing over lowercase *b*s that were meant to be *d*s and guessing at the handwriting of a math page with no name. I knew their handwriting. I knew how each of them gripped their pencils. I saw their faces when I closed my eyes at night. I prayed for their little hearts and for their families. One child had just moved in with grandparents because his parents were getting divorced. One had a father in prison.

Every morning we began with Bible time. The children would gather on the carpeted floor in the front corner of the room as I told stories from the book of Genesis, from Adam to Joseph, and then the stories of Jesus. We sang simple praise songs together: Terrye Coelho's "Father I Adore You," Ronald Krisman's "Jesus in the Morning," and Kurt Kaiser's "Oh How He Loves You and Me." Then we had share time, when they could ask me to pray about whatever was on their minds. That is when I became attached to their precious hearts. We prayed about ailing dogs and hospitalized grandparents, about scraped knees and scary things they had heard on the news.

At recess some of the girls would sit on my lap as I watched the others play on the swings and monkey bars. After school I often found little love notes on my desk, written in crayon on scraps of construction paper.

On Saturdays I would sleep in, waking slowly to the sounds of conservatory students practicing their instruments. Tamera would walk next door to the conservatory to spend hours at a piano preparing for her senior recital. Tom would meet her there and practice his French horn. In the apartment above us another student would tune up her cello. And from the third floor of the conservatory, drifting across the alleyway to our apartment building, came the sound of a percussionist refining his skills on the marimba.

I visited Carol's church on most Sundays. It was a large church, with a thousand or more in the congregation, and a Sunday school class designated for "young singles." There were twenty or more of us attending the class, seated in a circle of metal folding chairs around the room, reading a passage of the Bible together and discussing it while secretly eyeing the crowd for any potential mates.

Carol's kind parents would always invite me over for lunch afterward. There would be a pot roast, with potatoes and gravy, carrots and peas. We would talk and laugh around their dining room table until Carol's mom would stand and pick up a serving bowl. "Sue, clean up those peas" (which meant, "Eat the rest of them"), and I would oblige. This was my family away from home, and Carol and I could relax in their living room to watch classic movies or play through a stack of sheet music on their piano. Carol's dad loved to sing Stephen Adams's "The Holy City," and if I would play it he would stand next to the piano and belt it out in his strong tenor voice.

Jerusalem, Jerusalem
Hark, how the angels sing,
Hosanna in the highest!
Hosanna to your King!

Carol's family also had a player piano with paper rolls of music to choose from. I could never quite get the hang of it, but Carol would sit on the bench and get the foot pumps going, and we would watch and laugh as the invisible fingers played Scott Joplin's "Maple Leaf Rag."

Some Sundays I would visit a church with Tamera and Tom. We tried Assembly of God churches, Anglican churches, Baptist churches, and extremely charismatic churches. Then we would have intriguing, lengthy theological discussions over cheap burritos at the little Mexican restaurant down the street from our apartment.

One Sunday afternoon Tom's landlady asked him to invite us all over to the boardinghouse where he lived so we could listen to her new CD player. This was brand new technology, and as we sat around the formal living room listening and staring at the new black box, she and Tom discussed whether the digital sound was anywhere nearly as good as that of a vinyl record album. I couldn't tell any difference, but she insisted that it "sounded digital." I was more spellbound by the song we were listening to. It was one of the most beautiful pieces I had ever heard. When I asked what it was, Tom looked surprised. "Why, it's Pachelbel's Canon in D."

Near the end of the school year Tamera had her senior recital. Her mother came and took over the tiny kitchen in our apartment, stuffing mushrooms and wrapping bacon around crackers before toasting them in our gas oven. Tamera dressed in a full-length, flowing red gown and spent an hour in front of our bathroom mirror pinning her hair up. Her mother and I arranged the hors d'oeuvres on fancy trays and carried them across the alley to the conservatory, where we set them on white tablecloths in the foyer, along with a punchbowl filled with a mixture of fruit juice and ginger ale. Taking our seats in the concert hall, we all applauded enthusiastically as Tamera floated across the stage to the piano bench, where she paused for a moment in silence to collect herself before placing her hands gently on the keys. Then the piano came alive as she played Prokofiev and Chopin, sweeping across the keys confidently and flawlessly. She was magnificent.

The last day of my own school year was heart-wrenching as I stood by the classroom door, hugging each of my precious children good-bye. I would see them the following year at school, of course, but they would no longer be in my classroom. They would no longer share secrets with me or call me "Mommy" by accident. They had learned to read and add three-digit numbers. They could write a paragraph about George Washington or Abraham Lincoln. They could tell you the names of the planets in our solar system. But most of all, I hoped they knew that Jesus loved them.

CHAPTER 42

PUBLIC
RESTROOMS

Stores with wet tile floors, as I've mentioned, are certainly intimidating to me. But public restrooms can be equally worrisome. Even in carpeted restaurants wet, slippery floors are pretty common in the restroom. I'd much rather use my own bathroom in my own house if I can, so I always go before I leave the house. But sometimes you just gotta go.

When we are on a road trip or at a new restaurant my husband often asks, "How was it?" when I return from the ladies' room. So I have started to rate restrooms according to my own criteria. You might rate restrooms on their cleanliness, or on whether there was enough toilet paper, and I would join you in that. But the following five criteria cover areas the average able-bodied person might not necessarily notice:

1. Was the floor wet when I walked in? This is often dependent upon where the paper towel dispenser or hand dryer is located. If it is all the way across the room from the sink, you can bet on a wet floor as people drip water from their freshly washed hands while they walk across the room to the dryer.

2. Did I have to walk a long way across this wet floor to get to a stall? Often the handicap stall is the farthest from the entrance. I don't necessarily need to use the handicap stall at this point in my life, but if it is available, and not too difficult to get to, I will use it because the toilet is taller and easier for me. But can I get to it safely?

3. Could I close the stall door? Believe it or not, doors to handicap stalls do not often have a handle to grab from the inside to pull the door closed. And since most handicap stall doors open outward instead of inward, I am not sure how anyone in a wheelchair would be able to close the door behind them. I can grab the top edge of the door and pull it shut, but how will I do this someday when I am permanently seated? A related question is whether or not the lock works. Will the door swing open while I am in the middle of things? If the door opened inward, one could push it shut, but since it swings outward. . . . Let's just hope the lock actually works.

4. Was there a good place for me to lean my cane while washing my hands? This comes up especially at an airport or other large facility that has a long row of sinks along a countertop. Sometimes I have leaned my cane against the counter, and as I've soaped up my hands I have watched it slide down and crash to the floor. If I can lean it into a corner, or any nook in the countertop, I won't have to worry about that.

5. Was the towel dispenser or hand dryer near the
    sink, or did I have to cross a wet floor holding
    my cane with a wet hand to reach it? (Again, this
    refers back to #1.) I used to have a cane with a
    wooden handle, painted black. This was especially
    slippery in a wet hand. If the floor was also wet, the
    combination could have spelled disaster. The cane
    I use now has a spongy black handle, much easier
    for me to grip in a situation like that.

    I made the mistake once of posting this
    complaint on Facebook. A distant friend chimed in
    that I should assess the paper towel situation before
    I wash my hands and, if necessary, grab the paper
    towels first and tuck them under my arm while
    washing up. I was so embarrassed that I had not
    thought of this myself that I deleted the conversation.
    But I have taken the advice, nonetheless.

There you have it. Given the five benchmarks above, I can
rate any restroom fairly against any other. The ladies' room at
my favorite restaurant gets five stars. The one at my parents'
church gets four. Many rest stops along the interstates get one
or two stars, tops.

Recently, while traveling to a friend's wedding in another
state, my husband and I had to stop at a rest area. Here's what
happened:

As I walk into the ladies' room, a worker is mopping the
floor. I stop dead in my tracks. "Oh!" The mopping woman

looks up at me, and I stammer, "I'm . . . I'm afraid to walk across the wet floor. Um . . . Would you mind giving me your elbow?"

She nervously comes to my side, and I take this stranger's arm as she walks me to the first available stall.

"Thank you so much."

She doesn't speak.

Halfway through my business, I hear a strange voice outside my door. "Are you alright?"

Is she talking to me?

Again the voice, this time with a knock on my door. "Are you alright in there?"

"Yes, I'm fine!" *I haven't even been in here for a full minute.*

"Okay, I'll tell your friend."

What?

When I come out of the ladies' room into the lobby of the rest area, my husband is leaning against a wall, looking at a map. I sidle up to him with my cane. He looks over at me, puzzled.

"Some lady just came up to me and told me you were 'doing just fine.'"

"What? Was she an employee?"

"I don't think so." He glances out the window. "I think I saw her leave and get into a car. She wasn't wearing a uniform or anything."

I sigh. "She must have been the one who knocked on my door to see if I was okay."

"What? Why would she have done that?"

"She must have seen me when I came in. I had to ask the employee who was mopping to help me across the wet floor."

"Oh . . ." he begins folding up the map. "But how would she have known I was your husband?"

"I don't know. . . . Maybe she saw us when we came in."

"That's creepy." We start walking out to the car together.

"I guess she thought she was being helpful." She didn't realize she was making me feel help*less*. I take his elbow as we walk outside and down the slope of the sidewalk near the handicap parking space. He opens the car door for me, and I look up at him as I settle into my seat.

"One star."

CHAPTER 43

THE FUNNY BONE

I was sitting next to Carol in a circle of metal folding chairs in our Sunday school classroom at the First Baptist Church of Ferguson. He was sitting across the room, wearing a peel-and-stick name tag that said RICH ROOD in all caps, the last name printed directly under the first, each letter lined up with the one above it. He was tall and thin, with a dark brown beard, neatly trimmed just under his chin line, and thick dark hair, trimmed up around his ears. He wore glasses with brown plastic frames and a smart-looking oxford shirt with a paisley tie.

I wondered if he really pronounced his last name like "rude." What a name!

He chimed in occasionally in the discussion over the Bible passage we were reading together. But that was all I noticed about him that day.

It was my second year of teaching at South Side Christian School in St. Louis, and I had settled on attending Carol's church with her almost every Sunday. I had even joined the choir, which rehearsed on Wednesday nights before the midweek service, giving Carol and me another excuse to see each other during the week. And I had signed up to help out in a children's Sunday school class. I was assigned to a third-grade classroom that met during the second of three services. This meant that I had to get up early on Sunday mornings to attend the 8:00 worship service, then meet with the third-graders at 9:15, and finally attend the "single young adult" Sunday school class at 10:30.

One of those Sundays I went to grab a donut in the fellowship hall before heading up the stairs to the third-grade classroom. As usual, a pile of nametags was lying next to the coffee pot. I grabbed a marker and printed out my name in my best teacher's handwriting: "Miss Butler." I peeled off the backing and stuck it to my shoulder. I noticed that a few sprinkles of powdered sugar from my jelly doughnut had dusted the front of my favorite dress. It was black crepe, with a white Peter Pan collar and white ribbon that ran in a rectangle across my chest. It was fitted at the waist and capped off in puffy sleeves that were gathered into narrow white cuffs just above my elbows.

"Miss Butler?" a voice laughed. "Is that what you prefer to be called?"

I looked up to see Rich Rood from the young adult class. I smiled. "Well, that's what the kids call me." I explained that I was on my way to teach. He smiled and nodded as I turned to go upstairs.

Like most of the young men in our single adult class, Rich was a computer engineer at McDonnell-Douglas. It made sense that the church would draw from the hundreds of engineers who worked there, nearly five miles down the road. Those mathematical and analytical minds dominated our Sunday morning discussions on Scripture. But there were a few exceptions, like Brad, a law student, who was obviously interested in Carol; and William, who worked as a docent at an old, historic home in St. Louis.

Rich was chatting with William in the hallway of the church one Sunday morning when I came walking by. They stopped talking as Rich glanced my way. "Are you limping?" he asked, concerned.

Am I? I wondered, hugging my Bible to my chest, "I guess it's just the way I walk."

"Oh, I hadn't noticed," Rich offered shyly.

The group of single adults often went out for pizza after church on Sunday nights. We looked for one another to sit together in the sanctuary on Sunday and Wednesday evenings, and potluck meals in the fellowship hall often found us gathered at one of those long tables, laughing. Occasionally someone would organize a bowling night, or a gathering at someone's apartment to play Pictionary. So it was nothing unusual when several of us were standing in the foyer of the church on a Wednesday evening in late March and Rich piped up, "Hey, does anyone want to go with me tomorrow night to a comedy club? My cousin's fiancé is coming into town. He's a comedian, and he's performing at the Funny Bone."

"Yeah, I can go," I shrugged.

I looked around at the other faces in our circle, but no one else seemed to be accepting Rich's invitation. My eyes met his, behind those dark-framed glasses as I realized it was just going to be the two of us.

"Okay," he looked as though he was just realizing this, too. "I'll pick you up. 6:30?"

"Sure." The group was dispersing now, and as we walked out to the parking lot I gave him directions to my apartment.

I had moved to an apartment closer to my school for this second year of teaching. It was farther away from the church but only a few miles from the school. Tamera had moved with me, since she had graduated from the music conservatory. Tom, now her fiancé, had helped us lug our mattresses, couch, and kitchen table up the two flights of wooden outdoor stairs. There was a large storage closet in our new place, and Tamera had teased me about sleeping in it, but indeed, I had my own room this time, with a large window that looked out over the parking lot and a line of trees that separated our apartment complex from a McDonald's drive-through.

As planned, Tamera and Tom had married in December. I was a bridesmaid in a blue velvet dress, and the sanctuary of her home church in Springfield was lined with white-painted saplings strung in elegant Christmas lights. It was a fairytale wedding. Afterward Tom and Tamera had gone to live in Cincinnati, where Tom had attained a position with the symphony orchestra.

For a couple of months I was without a roommate. My checking account was down to pennies. My dad called one Saturday morning to tell me that the check I had mailed to him for a car payment had bounced. I drove to school in the mornings praying that I would have enough gas fumes to get me there. I laughed about this in the teacher's lounge one day, and as I was walking back to my classroom a fellow teacher slipped five dollars into my hand.

But one benefit of living alone was the solitude, after spending the day with twenty rambunctious first graders. In the quiet evenings I would cook up some rice for myself with a quarter of a chicken breast, and then I would turn on the radio and listen to Chuck Swindoll preaching as I settled into the couch and worked on a cross-stitch sampler. As I climbed into bed at night I would open my Bible to Matthew 6, in the middle of Jesus' famous Sermon on the Mount. I practically had this passage memorized:

> *"For this reason I say to you, do not be worried about your life, as to what you will eat or what you will drink; nor for your body, as to what you will put on. Is not life more than food, and the body more than clothing? Look at the birds of the air, that they do not sow, nor reap nor gather into barns, and yet your heavenly Father feeds them. Are you not worth much more than they? And who of you by being worried can add a single hour to his life? And why are you worried about clothing? Observe how the lilies of the field grow; they do not toil nor do they spin, yet I say to you that not even Solomon in all his glory clothed himself like one of these. But if God so clothes the grass of the field, which is alive today and tomorrow is thrown into the furnace, will He not much more clothe you? You of little faith! Do not worry then, saying, 'What will we eat?' or 'What will we drink?' or 'What will we wear for clothing?' For the Gentiles eagerly seek all these things; for your heavenly Father knows that you need all these things. But seek first His kingdom and His righteousness, and all these things will be added to you.*

"So do not worry about tomorrow; for tomorrow will care for itself. Each day has enough trouble of its own." (verses 28–34 NASB)

And then, in February, God faithfully provided for me. My dear friend C.C. from college needed a roommate. She had recently graduated and moved to St. Louis, but the apartment where she was living on her own wasn't working out. So on a cold Saturday morning Carol and her boyfriend, Brad, helped C.C. move her waterbed, a pressed-wood entertainment center, a TV, her VHS movie collection, and her giant stuffed panda up the stairs and into my place. She set up her bed in what had earlier been Tamera's room and added her bottle of shampoo to the corner of the tub. We celebrated our first evening together as roommates by watching an old Judy Garland movie and eating popcorn on the floor of our small living room, with C.C. snuggled up against her panda bear.

C.C. had been coming to church with Carol and me, so Rich knew her, and as I gave him directions to our apartment I wondered whether she would be there when he came to pick me up the following evening. Would it be less awkward if she were there? Should we invite her to come along to the comedy club? Or did I really want this to be more like a date?

The next day at school, when my class had gone out for morning recess, I found a note in my mailbox in the school office notifying me that "Rich Rude" had called. The school secretary had carefully printed a phone number for me to call him back. I stepped into the nurse's office to use the phone. It rang only once before his familiar voice answered, "Rich Rood."

"Hi, Rich, it's Suzanne Butler—Sue." I stammered, "I go by Suzanne at school."

"Suzanne," he said slowly, thinking about it. "I just wanted to warn you. . . . I mean, you don't have to go with me tonight. It might be rather raunchy. I think the jokes could get pretty dirty, and there will be drinking and stuff."

"Oh." I bounced the curly phone cord up and down on the nurse's desk. "Well, I think it will be alright." *How bad could it be?* By now I was rather excited to go on this date, if you could call it that.

"Okay, then. Well, I'll see you at 6:30."

"You sure you'll be able to find my apartment?"

"Yeah, I already found it on a map."

"Okay. See you then."

I wanted to dress casually but fashionably. C.C. approved of my choice: a peach, loose-fitting knit tunic top, set off with shoulder pads and tapered long sleeves, and tan knit pants that were tight at the ankles. A wide, light blue band was gathered around my waist, pulling the whole outfit together with my cream-colored flats. I fluffed my short, permed hair in the mirror and held the curls up with my fingers while I gave my whole head another misting of hairspray.

Rich was precisely on time. I opened the door to find him standing with an umbrella in the light spring rain. "Ready to go?" He held the umbrella over my head as we went down the wooden stairs. I walked closely next to him to his car so we could share the umbrella, and he opened the car door for me politely.

"Matt said he would look for us. That's my cousin's fiancé," Rich explained as we drove to the club. "He said he would have a couple of tickets for us."

As we entered the place Matt was indeed waiting to greet us. "Hey, guys! I saved you a seat!" He showed us to a high table in the corner of the room. Rich introduced me as we sat down, and Matt smiled at me. "Can I get you something to drink?"

"Oh, just a Coke for me," I responded.

"Yeah, Coke for me too," Rich looked around in the dimly lit space. Most everyone else was drinking something from the bar, and many people were smoking. "Sorry." He raised his eyebrows.

He had to turn in his chair to face the stage as the first comedian came on. From where I sat I was looking over his shoulder at the man with the microphone, and I could easily tell when Rich was laughing. Sure enough, the jokes got dirtier as the night went on. Matt's jokes were a bit cleaner, but the performers who came before and after him were extremely smutty, and we were both trying not to laugh. I could see Rich's hand going up to cover his mouth from time to time, and his shoulders shaking as he tried to stifle the laughter. I was hoping he didn't hear any giggles that escaped from my throat, ashamed that I couldn't help but be amused by this type of humor.

After the show we said a polite goodbye to Matt, and Rich held the umbrella once again as we scrambled through the rain to his maroon Ford Escort. He opened my car door and waited with the umbrella as I got in, then scurried around the back. I watched as he collapsed the umbrella and set it on the floor of the backseat before sliding into the driver's seat and pulling his door closed. Then we looked at each other and burst out laughing.

"That was . . . Wow."

He put a hand to his forehead. "Oh my!"

"Want to get chocolate milkshakes?" I suggested. We had to go right past the McDonald's drive-through, after all.

"Sure."

We started driving back toward my apartment, still sighing and chuckling about the whole experience. Rich pulled up to the drive-through speaker and ordered two chocolate milkshakes. Suddenly I wasn't sure I should expect him to pay for mine. I unzipped my purse and fished out a dollar as we pulled forward to the window.

"Here ya go." I held it out to him.

He was reaching for his wallet in his back pocket. "Oh . . . um . . . okay." He pulled a dollar out of his wallet to pay for his own.

The cashier handed the shakes through the window, and Rich passed them over to me. I held them in my lap. "We could take them back to my apartment if you want."

The rain had just about stopped by the time we parked near the stairway. C.C.'s bedroom light was on. We carried our milkshakes up the wet steps, and I found my keys in my purse while Rich held the cold cups and straws.

"Come on in." I led the way to the couch and sat down at one end. Rich sat down at the far end and took a sip of his milkshake.

"I'm so sorry about those jokes tonight."

"Don't worry about it. We just can't repeat any of them to our church friends."

He smiled. "So, were you roommates with C.C. in college?"

I swallowed a mouthful of milkshake. "Mm . . . No—Carol. But C.C. was on our floor." I went on to talk about my first roommate at Mizzou and how grateful I was for Carol. Rich told me about living in the dorm at the University of Michigan. I learned that he had grown up in the suburbs of Detroit and that both of his parents were high school teachers. I told him all about the different places I had lived. The conversation went on for nearly an hour, with Rich sitting on the edge of his corner and I sitting at my end, angled toward each other but with enough space between us to exhibit the uncertainty we both felt regarding the definition of our relationship.

"Well, I guess I should go." Rich stood, towering over me.

"I'll throw that away," I offered, taking his empty cup and straw. We walked toward the door.

"I guess I won't see you Sunday," he said. "I'm going home for the weekend, since I have Monday off.

"Oh, why do you have Monday off? Is it a holiday?'

"NATO day."

I laughed. "What's that?"

"North Atlantic Treaty Organization!" he said teasingly, as though I should have known. "McDonnell-Douglas celebrates it." He shrugged.

"Well, I'll see you on Wednesday, then."

"Yeah . . ." He opened the door and stepped out onto the wooden landing, looking back over his shoulder. "See you then."

As I closed the door, thinking about his nicely trimmed beard, I suddenly felt queasy. That chocolate milkshake hadn't settled well in my stomach. Maybe it was the smoke-filled room I had sat in that night. Maybe it was the combination of the two. I made my way to the bathroom and threw up.

On Saturday Carol came over to our apartment, and C.C. cooked up some of her special African chicken with curry tomato sauce and cabbage. The flavor combination was so delicious I dragged the bits of cabbage through the sauce on my plate to get every last morsel. The three of us, with bellies full, collapsed on C.C.'s waterbed, sighing. The waves sloshed underneath us as we stared up at the ceiling lazily.

"What do you think of Rich Rood?" I asked, curious to know their impressions.

"I think he has an inner warmth about him," Carol replied thoughtfully.

"I don't think I've ever seen him without a pair of dress pants," C.C. smiled.

"Do you like him?" Carol turned to me.

"Maybe."

On Monday evening Rich called me. I sat on the floor next to my kitchen table and played with the phone cord.

"How was church yesterday?" he asked.

"Oh, fine. Nothing unusual. How was your weekend at your parents' house?"

"Great! We watched basketball. Michigan won a great game against Illinois in the final four. It was awesome. The finals are on tonight. They're playing Seton Hall, and Michigan is favored."

"Oh, wow."

"My mom said my aunt had asked Matt if I brought a boy with me to see his show."

"A boy?"

He laughed. "Yeah, that's the way she talks. Anyway, Matt told her it was a boy named Sue."

"Oh, my goodness." I chuckled. "Isn't there a Johnny Cash song about that?"

Rich knew it. "My name is Sue. How do you do?" he chanted in his best Johnny Cash voice.

I giggled.

"So anyway . . ." His voice became serious. "I had a great time on Thursday night . . . in spite of the smut."

"Yeah, me too."

"We should do something again sometime."

"Sure. When?"

"Um . . . I don't know. How about Saturday maybe? I was thinking about going to the history museum in Forest Park."

"Sure."

"Well, I'll see you Wednesday night at church. We can talk about it then."

CHAPTER 44

ACCESS

I hesitate to write this chapter, because I don't want to sound like a whiner. But I know that many people with similar or worse disabilities than mine must face this issue. So in the name of raising awareness, I humbly submit the following complaint: there are several businesses in my small town where I am not welcome—at least that's how it feels. It isn't because of my race or religion or gender or age. It's because I simply can't get in.

The florist is five steps down from the sidewalk. No other way in, as far as I can see. I often order flowers over the phone with the very kind owners there, but I've never been inside. One local restaurant has a flight of stairs just inside the front door. They told me on the phone that I could come in the back door through the kitchen if someone were to drop me off in the back alley, but we couldn't park back there. No thanks. The print shop is up five wooden steps with a railing, but I'm not sure it could withstand my yanking and pulling. The chocolate shop is a whole flight of stairs down, in the basement under the bank. I guess they don't want my business. Actually, come to think of it, perhaps I should be thankful. That has probably helped to preserve my health.

The coffee shop in a nearby town where my daughter worked for one summer as a barista has three steep cement steps up to the front door, with no railing. Not even a back door with a ramp. I went to order a latte from her only once that summer. My husband had to lift me up the steps. (I'm sure that wasn't embarrassing for her *at all.*)

When we want to go out to a new restaurant, the first question I have to ask is "Can I get in there?" It really is best to call first. Most front entrances these days are accessible, but some have a ramp in the back. At least I can get in that way. Still, I feel as though I am a second-class citizen, unable to use the front door.

Old church buildings are notorious for their less than welcoming modes of entry. When I am scheduling venues for my choir performances, I have to call and ask, "Do you have a handicap access?" Many have a ramp to a back door, and then a lift to the main floor where the sanctuary is located. Some have an open, motorized lift in the front foyer of the church. It is a humbling thing for my choir to watch me step into the metal box and noisily inch my way up.

Once we are inside the sanctuary, the platform can be another challenge. Many churches have four or five carpeted steps near the pulpit, with no railing and no alternate route. I remain on the floor and direct the choir from there. Please don't ask me to make an opening comment from the pulpit.

But of all places I cannot access, the one that saddens me most is the home of a friend. There were days, ten years ago, when I could make it up Ligia's steps and hang out in her kitchen to drink tea together and solve the world's problems. Now I rarely set foot in anyone else's home.

When one of the ladies from church has a gathering at her house, I have to ask, "How many steps?" and "Do you have a solid railing?" Then, even if I think it sounds doable, I have to enlist someone to help me up those steps. If there is snow or ice, forget it, but even if the steps are dry I certainly don't want an audience of ladies standing in the doorway watching my struggle and offering advice.

A friend asked me if I couldn't somehow keep a ramp in my car that I could set up against the steps of a home. But how would that work? Who would carry it from my car and set it up? Even if it were just a board lying over the steps, the slope would likely be too difficult for me. It would have to be long enough for the angle to work, and even then, what about a railing? Besides, how embarrassing would that be?

There's no good answer for this. I'm certainly not going to ask all of my friends to build ramps. And there are building codes already in place for businesses in America. It isn't fair for me to put a guilt trip on anyone. I'm just being honest about the way I feel.

On these wintry days, when I am feeling confined inside my house and the sidewalks and parking lots around town are too icy or slushy for me to venture out, sometimes I take myself out for a drive. From the safety of my garage, I head over to the drive-through and get myself a cup of coffee and then drive around on some of the back roads until I find a good spot to stare out at the mountains and pray. There is an old cemetery a couple of miles from my house, across the road from a dairy farm, and if the pull-off area isn't covered in snow it's a perfect place to get a panoramic view of the Adirondacks. Through my car window I can see Otter Creek winding through the valley between white fields and leafless hedgerows that mark off property lines. There is a long ridge beyond the creek that hides Lake Champlain from here, but the miles of mountains across the lake are breathtaking. There is Dix, and Giant, Mt. Marcy, and many others I can't name standing firmly and resolutely against the winter sky. In that setting my complaining suddenly seems trite. Do I not believe in the faithfulness of God? Hasn't He helped me thus far? I take a sip of coffee and gaze out my windshield at the grandeur before me.

> *I lift up my eyes to the mountains—*
>> *where does my help come from?*
> *My help comes from the LORD,*
>> *the Maker of heaven and earth.*
> *He will not let your foot slip—*
>> *he who watches over you will not slumber;*
> *indeed, he who watches over Israel*
>> *will neither slumber nor sleep.*
> *The LORD watches over you—*
>> *the LORD is your shade at your right hand;*
> *the sun will not harm you by day,*
>> *nor the moon by night.*
> *The LORD will keep you from all harm—*
>> *he will watch over your life;*
> *the LORD will watch over your coming and going*
>> *both now and forevermore. (Psalm 121)*

CHAPTER 45

"YOU'RE PRETTY INTERESTING"

I waited for Rich in the foyer on Wednesday night, and we
sat together with William during the service. Afterward, as
though he were looking for an excuse to hang out, Rich had an
idea.

"Hey, my mom sent some of her pound cake home with me.
Maybe you could come over and help me eat it."

"Sure!" William answered.

"That would be great!" I agreed, not sure whether Rich had
meant to include both of us.

I had not been to Rich's apartment before, so William and
I followed him over in our separate cars. We pulled into the
parking lot of a building that looked as though it had once been
a motel. There were three floors of doors and windows, with a
concrete walkway at each level, lined with a metal railing. Rich
bounded up the cement steps to the third floor, taking two steps
at a time. William and I followed.

It was a very small apartment. The front wall was entirely
made up of the door and a large window that looked out onto the
walkway. Drapes were drawn across the window. Rich unlocked

the door and we entered his living room, with a couch, a chair, and a TV in the corner. There was a countertop that separated the kitchen from this living room, and a tiny kitchen table was pushed against the wall. His decorating was sparse. There were only three things on his walls: a calendar hanging by the phone near the kitchen, a large map of St. Louis, and a poster of a fighter jet.

But everything was tidy. When I asked to use the restroom I had to walk through his small bedroom, where his bed was neatly made and a stack of books was straightened on his nightstand. When I returned I found Rich and William shooting baskets with a nerf ball into a small hoop that Rich had hung across his drapery rod.

"Oh!" Rich shouted as it bounced off the rim. "So close!"

"Try it from the kitchen!" William suggested. He tossed the ball to me. I flung it toward the hoop, but it bounced off of the drapes and rolled onto the carpet. Rich scooped it up and pretended to go for a layup.

"What about this pound cake you promised us?" I asked.

Rich tossed the ball to William and came into the kitchen. He unwrapped a plate on which slices of golden, unfrosted cake had carefully been placed by his mother. "Oh, I got some strawberries today." He reached into the refrigerator and took out a pint of fresh berries.

"I can cut them up if you want," I offered. "Do you have a knife?"

"Um, I have a regular knife." He opened a drawer and pulled out a table knife.

"Okay." I picked up a handful of strawberries and went to the sink to wash them off.

I set them on the counter as I reached for a paper towel.

"Oh, don't set those there. That's not clean." Rich scooped them up.

"Your counter isn't clean? It *looks* clean."

"No, I never wipe it off. Here." He set a plate on the counter and placed the berries on it.

"Okay." I proceeded to cut off the caps of the berries and slice them in half with the dull knife, while he placed slices of cake onto three plates. I decorated them with the berries, and we took our plates to the couch.

"Oh, this is delicious!" William commented.

Indeed, I thought it was just like *my* mom's. "You'll have to thank your mother for us," I enthused.

"See if you can make it from here." Rich handed me the nerf ball. I tossed it toward the hoop, but it fell short. "Oh man. Try again." In one movement he was up off the couch and had flicked the ball back to me. I squinted and threw it overhand. It was closer this time.

"Once more," Rich offered, tossing it back to me. It took several tries, but finally the ball went in. Rich's arms went straight up. "Score!" he shouted.

William picked up the ball and went to the corner of the room. "How about from here?"

"Let's play horse!" Rich suggested.

William threw it but didn't make the shot. Rich tried it from a different corner and whisked it right in. Then William attempted to make it from that spot. Nope. "You get an *H!*" Rich taunted.

"Sue, your turn!"

"No, I'm going to quit while I'm ahead," I said, pulling up my knees to sit cross-legged on the couch to watch. With lots of cheers, groans, and laughter, Rich finally won the game. William shook his hand. And then I said I should probably go, since I had to teach tomorrow. We all walked down the steps together, and William went to his car.

"Good night, guys! This was fun!" He got in and started backing out, as Rich walked me over to my car.

"So . . . Saturday." He put his hands in his pockets. "You still want to go to the history museum?"

"Sure!" I smiled, opening my car door. "What time are you thinking?"

"How about lunch?"

I leaned against the open door. "I could make us some lunch at my apartment."

"Yeah, okay." His eyes twinkled at me from behind those glasses.

I sat down in the driver's seat and pulled the car door closed, then rolled down the window. Rich stood for an extra moment next to my car, looking at me. "Noon?" I asked.

"Yeah . . ." he bent down a little to see my face. His eyes narrowed, and he clicked his tongue. "You're pretty interesting."

I started the ignition. "See you Saturday."

Friday after school I bought croissants at the grocery store bakery, along with two cans of chunk white chicken breast, an onion, some celery, grapes, and a bag of Fritos. Saturday morning I mixed up some chicken salad and sliced open the croissants. I washed off the grapes and put them in a bowl on my kitchen table.

I may have checked my reflection in the mirror a few times. I was wearing jeans and a light pink, short-sleeve blouse with a long white sweater vest. I finished off the look by tying a fringed scarf around my waist. It was plaid, in pastel colors, and I wrapped it around my waist twice, tying the knot to one side so that the fringe hung down just above the bottom of the sweater. There was little doubt in my mind that this was an actual date.

C.C. was working, so it was just the two of us for lunch. When Rich arrived he seemed right at home, and we sat at my kitchen table as though we were old friends. Rich said a quick blessing before we started eating. And then we chatted comfortably.

He told me about working at the flight ramp near the airport, where they were having test flights on the military planes. There was one character with whom he worked who had come up with the idea to have beeper races during the lulls when they were just waiting around. They laid a binder on someone's desk and lined up their beepers along the top edge. The slight slope of the binder made a perfect racetrack. On the count of three, they would reach for their phones and call their beepers. It took several seconds of anticipation as the signals went out. Then one of the beepers would start vibrating. Then another. You can imagine the excitement as each man cheered for his own beeper to be the first to make it down the slope!

Rich left a few Fritos on his plate, and as I stood to clear the table I teased him. "Eat those up! Don't be wasteful." He laughed and obediently picked them off the plate.

In his maroon Ford Escort we drove around some old neighborhoods of St. Louis on our way to Forest Park. There were side streets and cul-de-sacs of beautiful old homes with stately trees. "Oooo, look at that one!" I would point out the window. He loved the red brick houses with the gabled entranceways.

"What would be your dream home?" I asked him.

"Hmm . . . I think a penthouse suite in a high-rise in some big city like Chicago."

"Really?"

"Yeah, how about you?"

"I think I'd like to live in an old farmhouse somewhere."

We meandered through the history museum, chatting easily while looking at memorabilia from the St. Louis Browns. Then we drifted into the exhibit of dresses from the Veiled Prophet fairs. This annual St. Louis tradition, dating back to the 1870s, names a debutante queen every summer. There in the museum, each queen's dress was worn by a mannequin behind glass, attesting to the continual changes in fashion.

Then we drove over to the zoo and wandered past the apes, the giraffes, and the polar bears, who were playing happily with a beach ball on this sunny spring day.

"Should we go for dinner somewhere?" Rich asked as we walked back toward his car.

"Sure!"

"How about the Spaghetti Factory, over by the Arch?"

We drove over to Laclede's Landing and parked Rich's Escort, then walked up the steps to the Gateway Arch. You could see the Mississippi River, sparkling in the evening sunlight, and the paddleboat McDonald's docked at the riverfront. I stood on the white stone marker in the grass directly under that great monument and looked up. The sky was a brilliant blue, the same color as Rich's eyes behind those glasses.

"I have this recurring dream," I said, looking up, "that I'm driving in my car and the highway does a loop-de-loop up and around the Arch." He was smiling at me.

We ate dinner at a quiet table in the corner of the old spaghetti restaurant, and I kept thinking how easy this was, how comfortable. We talked about the kids in my classroom, we discussed what he had been reading lately in his personal Bible study, and I told him about CMT. He listened, unpretentiously.

"I'm paying this time," Rich announced when the check came. "I can't believe I let you pay for your milkshake last week." He shook his head.

"Well, I did provide lunch today," I teased.

When we got back to my apartment, Rich walked with me up the stairs. It seemed only natural to hug him goodbye in my doorway.

"I'll see you tomorrow at church."

"Good night."

CHAPTER 46

TEAM DINNER

"My knees are already shaking," I admit to my husband as I climb into the car in our garage. We are on our way to a dinner at our pastor's house.

Once a year Eric and his wife, Annette, host a dinner for the elders and deacons of our church. Part of me is really looking forward to it. Annette will have a beautiful table set, candles lit, soft music playing, and amazing food. We will laugh and pray with our dearest friends, the people with whom we serve this little church.

But first, I have to get into their house.

This January has been extremely cold. Last week we had freezing rain, which covered the sidewalks in ice. Then snow fell. Then melted. Then refroze. Our own front yard looks like a zamboni has polished it to a perfect sheen.

"Eric said he would work on his walkway," my husband reassures me.

This is the wrestling match that goes on in my head whenever I am going to someone's house: *The ground will be uneven. God will help you. There will be slippery patches of ice. You'll have your husband's elbow. How will I get up the steps? God has always made sure there was someone there to help you when you needed it. Will the steps be slippery? Annette knows your situation.*

We turn onto their road, out here in the country, and through the car windshield I look up at the half-moon shining distinctly in the dark winter sky.

"My knees are shaking." I say it again for emphasis as we pull up to their house. The lights from Annette's kitchen are shining through the windows, making long yellow rectangles on the glistening snow. I can see Eric walking around inside.

I love this house. It is more than a hundred years old. The white clapboard siding is set off with dark green shutters, now hidden in the twilight and shadowed by the old crabapple tree in the front yard. A white wrought-iron fence runs along the road out front (a summertime chore for Eric and Annette's kids to paint), and four wooden steps, painted green, lead up to the front porch off the kitchen. Those steps now await me.

My husband comes around to my door and opens it. "It doesn't look too bad," he observes. We look together down the narrow stone walkway, where Eric has obviously chipped away today at the ice.

"Okay." I step out of the car and take his hand while he closes the door behind me. My cane crunches through a layer of snow beside the walkway. He takes my free hand and wraps it into the crook of his elbow.

We are just beginning to make our way down the path when I hear another car pull up. I would like to look back and see who it is, perhaps wave and say hello, but I dare not look away from the path. Baby steps. My husband is actually walking on the snow beside me, allowing me to walk on the dry stone pathway. I hear the other couple walk up behind us, and I wonder who they are.

Then a voice speaks. "Can I give you a hand on the other side?"

"Oh, it's Vicky!" I smile. She and her husband, Frank, are new on the church leadership team. They came to our church over a year ago, full of energy and with hearts to serve. Frank started fixing doorknobs and storm windows in our old church building even before we officially voted him in as a deacon. And Vicky always adds new insights and laughter to our Bible studies. I smile in amazement that God brought them to our church.

We are at the steps now. Annette comes out to greet us. "I'm so sorry about the ice," she says. "I think the steps are fairly dry, though."

"Oh, I'm so sorry you had to worry about it." I look up at her. My husband takes my cane in his free hand as I reach over to the railing. I manage to get my left foot up on the first step and grab the railing to pull on, but I forgot how tall these steps are. I can't quite get my other foot up.

"Can I help?" Frank asks, right behind me. "What if I give you a lift?" He puts his hands on my waist and lifts me up, as I pull on my husband's arm and the railing. That works. We do the same thing for the remaining three steps, as Annette stands at her door, welcoming us.

"Ah!" We are up on the porch, and then through the door into her warm kitchen. "Thank you, Frank," I smile back at him as I unzip my coat.

"Glad to help." He nods politely.

"You can throw your coats over on the couch." Annette points to the little den just off their kitchen. It is a step down from the hardwood kitchen floor to the carpeted den. It is a welcoming space, with a woodstove and a game table all set up to play checkers. Still, I think I'll stay at the kitchen level. Vicky steps down next to the couch and slips her coat off. Then she reaches for mine. "Here, I'll take that. I'll be the coat girl," she giggles.

The door opens, and in walk our associate pastor, Travis, and his wife, Kiersten, followed by another couple. The kitchen is filling up now, with people and happy chatter. "Who is watching your kids tonight?" "What have you been up to today?" "Did you get your car fixed?"

I look around at this warm home in wonder. There are Christmas lights still strung above the kitchen cabinets, among old cracker tins and a branch of bittersweet berries. Candid photographs of Annette and Eric's four children decorate the walls. Candles are lit here and there, and the aroma of lasagna fills the air. More people come in, and Vicky, the "coat girl," takes their wraps, as people greet each other with hugs.

Before long Annette directs us to the dining room, where sixteen plates are set around a huge square table. She laughs that she borrowed a table from the church to set beside her own dining table. It isn't quite the same length, so she has improvised with another little table from their house. But with a couple of tablecloths thrown over the whole thing, a hodgepodge of antique china and silverware, candles lit, and place cards in Annette's lovely handwriting, I think it is one of the most beautiful tables I have ever seen.

There is a fire going in the woodstove in this room, and Eric warns the folks sitting on that side that they may get too warm. Lucy, the golden retriever, is lying under the table, no doubt anxious for crumbs to fall. We all find our places and gather around. The walls of this delightful room are painted dark red, and the old china cabinet at one end is a blue-green of chipped paint over old wood. I believe Annette told me she found it in the barn years ago. Now it is filled with her eclectic collection of teacups. At the other end of the room a grandfather clock, showing the incorrect time on an old, faded face, ticks away. Eric says it belonged to his dad.

When we are all seated, except for Eric and Annette, who are standing near the doorway to the kitchen, Eric asks us to bow our heads. He thanks the Lord for the food and for the people in this room. You can hear the old clock ticking, and I reach for my husband's hand beside me. As Eric finishes his prayer, a resounding "Amen" comes from several voices.

Then Annette speaks up. "There are two salads on the table; you can pass them and help yourselves. The one at the far end is a Greek salad, and the one on this end is just . . . non-Greek."

Someone chuckles, "So, this one is Gentile . . ."

Another voice chimes in, "In Christ there is neither Greek nor Jew."

Someone else speaks up: "So it's all just salad."

I hear Eric's laugh behind me. "So Annette and I are going to serve you." He gestures with his palms up. "She's going to tell you the menu, and then we will take your plate and bring it out to you."

Annette clears her throat. "We have a spinach lasagna for those of you who are vegetarian. We have a fully loaded meat lasagna with sausage and ground beef and venison. We have a sweet potato casserole that has crumbled venison on top, and then we have chili, which also has meat. Or if you would prefer to just have salad, there is plenty of that as well."

Eric leans over my shoulder and takes my plate. "What will you have, Suzanne?"

"Hmmm. I think I'll have the sweet potato dish."

"Anything else? You can have two. Or three!" he laughs.

"Oooo. Then I'll also have a very small piece of spinach lasagna."

"Alright!" He steps away with my plate.

Annette puts a hand on Kiersten's shoulder next to me. "What would you like, my dear?"

Kiersten doesn't hesitate. "Oh, I'll have the fully loaded lasagna." Annette takes her plate to the kitchen. "Lasagna is my demise," Kiersten laughs softly. "I think if it was my last meal I would choose lasagna."

"Really?" my husband raises his eyebrows. "So as they are leading you to the execution, and they offer you one last meal . . . "

"Yep, lasagna," she giggles.

Travis joins in from the other side of Kiersten. "What would be your last meal, Suzanne?"

"Oh my goodness, let me think. . . . The falafel at Three Squares Cafe is pretty amazing. How about you?"

"Ohhhh, this right here." He points with his fork down at the lasagna on his plate. "How about you, Al?" He looks across the table.

"Mmmm. Maybe a hotdog."

"What?" several voices ring out.

He laughs. "Hotdogs are hard to beat!"

Al's wife, Tia, is shaking her head at him.

"Annette, this is absolutely delicious." I look up at her as she brings in another plate.

"Oh, I'm glad. I just followed Vicky's recipe for the sweet potatoes."

"It's perfect," Vicky nods.

I take a sip from my water glass as I look around the table. What a wonderful group of people. Next to my husband sits our deacon, Bill, and his wife, Dinny, who joined our church about three years ago. Bill had a career as a head custodian for a large factory, and he naturally notices things at our church that need attention. Dinny plays the piano; she sight-reads out of the hymnal really well and is a great substitute when I have a Sunday away.

Around the corner from them sit Al and Tia. Al runs the sound system on Sunday mornings and is our go-to guy for anything involving wires. He also teaches the adult Sunday school class occasionally. Tia often sings with the worship team and really has a heart for taking care of people. If there is anyone in the hospital, or at home needing help, Tia is there.

Next to Tia are Dan and Corinne. You have already met Corinne. Farmer Dan lost his first wife to cancer twelve years ago but faithfully trusted God through all of it. He usually leads the prayer time on Sunday mornings from the pulpit, heartfelt and sincere. He also keeps tabs on some of the elderly widows, especially when they cannot make it to church in the throes of winter. Corinne teaches the teen girls' Sunday school class and keeps the other Sunday school teachers organized.

Then there are Bob and Barb. A quiet couple, they do more than one would suspect, typically behind the scenes. Bob takes care of the church flower gardens, showing up sometimes daily in the heat of July to water the flowers he planted in May. He is also not afraid to climb a ladder when starlings build a nest behind a loose clapboard. Barb is our church clerk, typing up the minutes from our business meetings and prudently covering even the most difficult of discussions. She also volunteers at the local Pregnancy Resource Center and has a very comforting way about her; she is a soothing person to confide in.

Seated next to Barb are Peter and Ligia. Peter is probably the most energetic person I know. He teaches fifth and sixth grades at one of the local elementary schools and is loved and respected by all. Right now he is organizing a variety show at church, arranging for different kids and adults to show off their talents or participate in skits. And of course, you already know Ligia. She is equally as crazy as Peter, and together they are heading up a Young Life group at the high school. I'm sure she is an excellent role model for those young girls. Her dark, curly hair is pulled back tonight in a braid that cascades around her shoulder.

Around the next corner sit Frank and Vicky, about whom I've already told you. Before joining our congregation they were part of a smaller church that disbanded a couple of years ago when their pastor retired and their meeting space was no longer available. But I have known them longer than that. Frank was recommended to me by my neighbor when I needed a handyman to build a railing for my front steps and replace a rotting threshold. Then he and Vicky replaced the vanity and flooring in my upstairs bathroom. Then we hired them to level our kitchen cabinets and replace our countertop. I was amazed by their Christ-likeness even then, commending them for the way they worked together so well as a husband/wife team.

And finally, to my right sit Travis and Kiersten, the youngest couple at the table—our miracle associate pastor and his stunningly beautiful wife. Three years ago, when our church was praying for someone to come alongside Eric as a younger pastor who could relate to the next generation and assist in shepherding our little flock, God sent us Travis. I call it a miracle because after a year of praying for someone like Travis my husband called a nearby Bible college to see whether they might have anyone they could recommend. He left a voicemail on an answering machine, and the person who listened to the message was Kiersten. She was working in that office and told her husband, Travis, about our inquiry. Travis had been praying that God would send him to some small church in the area. The following Monday night, as the elders were meeting together and praying in my dining room, Travis called our house. Now here he sits, laughing with people about their last meals. He has been subbing at the high school, and all the kids are drawn to him. He is on a first name basis with the kitchen staff at the local cafe and will always greet each of us with a huge bear hug.

Kiersten's biggest role right now is that of being a mommy to their toddler daughter, and another little one is on the way. She is also leading a women's Bible study, and her gentle voice when she is teaching is always kind but sincere. She is a natural beauty with her long blonde hair and big blue eyes. I tease her that she is a Barbie doll, and she laughs, pointing to her pregnant belly and insisting that she is a *fat* Barbie doll.

Our hosts are still serving us, clearing away empty plates and refilling water glasses. Eric works fulltime as an engineer in the same building as my husband and pastors this church in his "spare time." He loves fixing old cars and reading the latest Christian books. He is always bringing books out of his own library to share with someone at the church, and in his thought-provoking sermons he will often refer to something he has recently read from a respected Christian author.

Annette, as you know, was one of my first friends in Vermont. Together we have applauded our children through basketball games, high school musicals, and graduations. A teacher by nature, and currently teaching a fifth-grade classroom in a local public school, she has taught hundreds of Bible stories to the children of our church, including my two. She has organized numerous mission trips and countless women's events. Now she reaches around my shoulder to take away my empty plate.

Eric walks back in from the kitchen carrying a small loaf of bread and a glass of red wine. He sets them on the table and then goes back to the kitchen to retrieve stools for himself and Annette. Kiersten and I slide our chairs over slightly to make room at the corner for them. Eric opens his Bible and says he would like to read a passage—a charge, really—to us as leaders of our church. We are all quietly listening, and once again I can hear the tick of the old clock.

Eric reads from 1 Peter 5:1–5:

> *So I exhort the elders among you, as a fellow elder and a witness of the sufferings of Christ, as well as a partaker in the glory that is going to be revealed: shepherd the flock of God that is among you, exercising oversight, not under compulsion, but willingly, as God would have you; not for shameful*

gain, but eagerly; not domineering over those in your charge, but being examples to the flock. And when the chief Shepherd appears, you will receive the unfading crown of glory. Likewise, you who are younger, be subject to the elders. Clothe yourselves, all of you, with humility toward one another, for "God opposes the proud but gives grace to the humble." (ESV)

Then Eric turns to the familiar passage in Matthew 26:26–29:

Now as they were eating, Jesus took bread, and after blessing it broke it and gave it to the disciples, and said, "Take, eat; this is my body." And he took a cup, and when he had given thanks he gave it to them, saying, "Drink of it, all of you, for this is my blood of the covenant, which is poured out for many for the forgiveness of sins. I tell you I will not drink again of this fruit of the vine until that day when I drink it new with you in my Father's kingdom." (ESV)

Eric breaks apart the bread, sets it on a small plate, and hands it to me. I take a pinch of it and pass it to my husband. Then Eric offers me the glass of wine. I take a little sip and pass it on. It strikes me that we have just been joking about our last meals of choice and that this was, quite literally, Jesus' last meal. The clock ticks away as we pass the bread and the wine around this hallowed table. I unashamedly wipe away a tear as I think of the Lord Jesus, knowing it was His last meal, serving His disciples by washing their feet. It surprised the disciples that night that He would humble Himself and serve them, on His knees, one by one.

And following His divine example Eric and Annette have served us this evening in a gracious way, waiting on us at this table. Oh, but it doesn't stop there. It doesn't even begin there. How many times have they humbly served us over the years? Sermons and Sunday school lessons, meals when I was sick, occasionally watching our children when they were little, giving us a hand with a flooded basement, and even chipping away at an icy walkway today.

"This is the body of Christ," Eric's voice reminds us, "given for you."

I look around the table at the beautiful faces. Yes, this is the body of Christ. And it is still being given. Just as Jesus humbled Himself, each of us gives to one another—to our entire church family—in humility, in kindness, and in love. Each of us has his or her own acts of service that we give to each other. Yes, this is the body of Christ, given for us.

The bread and the wine have made their way around the table now, and Eric turns to me. "Suzanne, would you lead us in a song?"

I close my eyes and lift my head. *"Amazing grace, how sweet the sound..."*—The room fills with the richness of all our voices melded together, deep and high, timid and strong, melody and harmony—"... *that saved a wretch like me; I once was lost, but now am found, was blind but now I see."*

CHAPTER 47

ARCHES

Rich and I looked for each other on Sunday morning and sat together in the Sunday school circle. On Wednesday night he watched for me in the foyer, and we sat side-by-side in the pew for the service. The sleeve of his flannel shirt felt warm against the sleeve of my thin, jersey-knit turquoise top.

I invited him to come over to my apartment Friday evening to watch a movie. C.C. was going to her mom's for the weekend and said we could watch something from her collection. I looked through the shelf of VHS tapes in our living room. There were some great possibilities: *Singing in the Rain*, *The Clock*, *Pee Wee's Big Adventure*, *Places in the Heart* . . . I settled on an old black-and-white classic featuring Katherine Hepburn and Cary Grant, *Bringing Up Baby*. It was light-hearted, but kind of romantic—perfect, I determined.

Rich arrived wearing jeans and a baggy crew neck sweater. I made some popcorn and we sat a little closer together on the couch this time. But he didn't put his arm around me. Halfway through the movie I sensed he was getting bored. "We could pause it and go for a walk," I suggested.

"Yeah, okay."

"We could walk over to McDonald's and get milkshakes."

He started to stand up. "Would you mind if I got vanilla this time? I don't really like chocolate."

"What? You don't like chocolate? Why did you get chocolate before?"

"I don't know." His eyes twinkled at me. "I guess I was nervous or something." He smiled.

"You can get whatever you want." I walked toward the door and he followed. We scuttled down the wooden staircase together and crossed the parking lot toward the line of trees. The April air was fresh and cool, and the sun was just going down over my apartment building.

"You were nervous?" I asked, blushing.

"You had some kind of evil spell on me," he teased.

We reached the edge of the parking lot and had to step over the curb and onto the dirt and mulch under the trees. There were evergreens mixed in with redbuds and dogwoods. Rich bent down to avoid hitting his head on a branch, and I looked down to watch my footing among the tree roots.

I saw something move. It hopped away from my foot. "A little toad!" I followed it for a few steps, then swooped down and caught it between my hands. "I've caught him!" I could feel him wriggling around in the space between my palms. Rich stepped out from the trees onto the pavement of the McDonald's lot and looked back at me.

"I caught a toad!" I said again, emerging out of the trees. "Want to hold him?"

Rich laughed. "No."

"Aw, he's a cute little guy." I pulled a thumb back just enough to look inside the cave of my hands and see him. His little chin was quivering. "Don't you want to hold him?"

"I have no desire to touch him."

"What? Didn't you ever catch frogs when you were a kid?"

He laughed again. "No."

"Aw." I turned back toward the trees and squatted down at the curb. "Here you go, Mr. Toadie." I opened my hands and set him down in the dirt. He took one hop and then sat there, as though saying goodbye.

Rich stood on the pavement waiting for me with his hands in his pockets. When I rose, he walked with me to the door and opened it for me. "I hope you wash your hands."

"Of course."

I went right to the ladies' room and soaped them up properly before joining him at the counter to order. He got a cheeseburger and some fries. I got a chocolate shake. "Oh, I guess I'll get a vanilla shake." He took his wallet out of his back pocket and paid, narrowing his eyes and smirking at me. I smiled back, catching our silent private joke about who was paying. We sat at a table and ate, smiling at each other. I kept stealing his fries. It was darker outside when we made our way back to my apartment, and somewhere among the trees he took my hand.

The following Thursday evening found us holding hands again, in the stands at Busch Stadium, watching the Cardinals take on the Montreal Expos. It was a glorious evening, sitting back in the hard red seats, holding hands with our elbows draped over the armrest between us. The Gateway Arch, rising above the outfield, glowed pink and golden in the reflection of the setting sun. I wasn't really paying much attention to the game. During the seventh inning stretch we decided to take a stroll around the stadium. Rich held onto my hand as we walked casually around the perimeter of the upper level. We passed by vendors selling caps and shirts and a line of people waiting to buy hotdogs and nachos. The aroma of jalapenos and popcorn hung in the air. We kept walking.

As we made our way around the great circle of concrete walkway, the Arch suddenly came into view. Rich steered me over toward the railing to get a better look. The sky behind the Arch was dark now, and a placid full moon hung in the sky just behind it, perfectly round and gleaming white.

People were starting to go back to their seats now. The walkway around us grew calmer. We leaned against the railing, staring out together at the Arch and the dazzling moon. Rich turned to face me. He held my hand gently and peered into my eyes. He bent down toward me.

"I love you, Suzanne." And he kissed me.

CHAPTER 48

FALLING

Maybe it's because I didn't sleep well last night. I was worried that I wouldn't wake up in time to shower and eat a bite of toast before getting to the church by eight o'clock this morning for rehearsal with my worship team.

Maybe it's because I was mentally tired from rehearsing, then leading worship, then talking with several people after church. One woman came up to the piano after the service and confided in me that she is battling depression. The tears welled up in her eyes as she told me how alone she feels.

Maybe it's because we went to lunch at the cafe on Main Street and the sidewalks were covered in ice and snow. If we hadn't already told our friends we would meet them there, I would have bagged it and gone home for a tuna sandwich. But my husband assured me that if I stayed on the part of the sidewalk where crunchy snow covered the layer of ice, I would be okay. Still, I clung to his arm as though my life depended on it and took baby steps while the frigid wind stung the tops of my ears.

Maybe it's because the nap I had on the couch this afternoon was just enough to make me feel hazy. I woke with the sun shining in through the sliding glass door right into my eyes. My husband was sitting on the floor with his bookkeeping binder and the checkbook, watching the Steelers confront the Jaguars. The volume was turned way down, so I don't think it was that last play that woke me up.

Maybe it's because my stomach felt unsettled and I didn't feel like eating much dinner, so I just snacked on saltines and a little canned soup.

Whatever the reason, I am suddenly lying facedown on the hardwood floor of my dining room.

Let's rewind . . .

I am in the kitchen, taking my dishes to the sink. I decide to go into the dining room to look at my amaryllis bulb and see if it is sending up any new leaves. My husband gave it to me for Christmas. I have planted the bulb properly in the pot of dirt it came in, set it in the sun on my dining room table, and watered it. For two weeks I have had my doubts about it. But yesterday I thought I saw a tiny bit of green coming up out of the papery knob.

I take one step into the dining room and can feel myself losing balance. I am falling forward like a tree from its stump. Here comes the floor. By reflex, a hand goes up and I turn my head. But it is not enough to cushion the fall completely. I feel my cheekbone strike the wood floor, feel my teeth against my lip.

I lie still for a moment, catching my breath. A whimper escapes my throat. I open my eyes to a sideways view of the underside of the table.

My husband is standing over me now. "Are you hurt?" he asks quietly.

"I don't know yet. Give me a minute." I take a deep breath and turn over, pushing myself up to a sitting position, with my legs straight out in front me. "My lip . . . and my knee." I pull my pant leg up, revealing my leg brace and my bare knee, which now sports a nickel-sized red circle where the skin has been rubbed off. He goes to the kitchen drawer to find a clean dishrag and wets it at the sink.

"Did you trip on something?"

"No."

"Do you know what happened?"

"I just . . . went down."

He hands me the dishrag. I hold it to my knee, which is now starting to bleed. I feel as though I am five years old and have fallen on the sidewalk.

Now the shaking starts. This always happens after a fall. It lasts a few minutes. I think it's the adrenaline rush. At least that's what I've been told. This time, however, it comes with tears. I close my eyes tightly and clench my teeth, but the sobs are coming. I hear myself beginning to wail. He sits down on the floor next to me and wraps his arms around me. I am still holding the dishrag to my knee with both hands, but I rest my head on his shoulder and cry. He gently rubs my back while my moans get softer. I wonder if I am getting mascara on his shirt collar.

My mind goes back to the scene from earlier today when we were walking from our car to the cafe on Main Street and I was gripping his arm so tightly, walking so slowly across the hard-packed snow. I wonder who was watching us. What families of piano students drove by and saw us? What old school friends of my son or daughter were looking at us through the cafe windows? What did they think? *That poor woman.* Is this who I have become?

"Want a Kleenex or something?"

I nod and sniff.

He pops up onto his sock feet and skates across the vinyl kitchen floor to the bathroom on the other side of our house. He comes back with a Kleenex and holds it out to me. I trade him for the dishrag and blow my nose. Together we look at my knee. "Should we put a Band-Aid on it?" He squats down to get a better look.

"Yeah." I fold over the Kleenex and blow my nose again.

He goes to the kitchen cabinet and retrieves the box of Band-Aids and a tube of antibiotic ointment. He takes the lid off the tube and squirts a little gel onto my waiting finger. I spread it over my knee. Then, like my mother, he peels the backing off the Band-Aid and covers over my wound.

"Suzie, I don't know if the physical therapy is really helping you."

I nod, wiping my nose. "I know."

He gathers up the Band-Aid wrapper. "Are you ready to stand up, or do you need another minute?"

I sigh. "I think I'm ready."

He walks around me to stand behind me and puts two strong arms under mine. "Ready?" He lifts me straight up to my feet. I feel a twinge in my knee joint as I put weight on it. I am afraid to let go of his arm as he comes beside me. "Where do you want to go?" he asks, keeping a firm hold on me.

I know what he means, but I decide to be brutally honest in the moment. "Heaven would be nice."

"Awwww." He pulls me close, into a hug, and I bury my face in the pocket of his shirt. I take a deep breath and let it out slowly. The words to the hymn I led this morning in church are stuck in my head. *"All I have needed Thy hand hath provided. Great is Thy Faithfulness, Lord, unto me."* I feel his gentle kiss on the top of my head.

"What were you doing before you fell?" he asks.

I wipe away my tears and look up.

"I was coming in here to look at my amaryllis," I remember. I lean back onto my good knee and look over at the pot on the table. "I think it's growing."

He takes a step toward it, holding onto my hand as we look together. "I think you're right."

CHAPTER 49

THE SECOND TEE

It was a chilly November afternoon when I drove over to Rich's apartment after school. It had been a tiring day of dealing with some behavioral issues in my classroom, and I just wanted to see Rich's face and feel his hug. I knocked on the door of his apartment, and he opened it in surprise. "Hey, I was just about to call you!" He greeted me with a hug. "Want to go for a walk? The sun is just about to set."

"Sure!" I answered.

"Just a minute; let me grab my jacket." Rich went into his bedroom and came back with his coat. "Want to go over to the golf course?"

"Sure!"

We had walked there before. It was directly behind his apartment building, with a chain-link fence between the parking lot and the lush green grass. But there was a place you could sneak through. In a corner of the parking lot the asphalt sloped downward, and the metal fence rose up from the ground just enough to crawl under it. Rich pulled up the bottom edge of the fence as I snuck under it, and then I did the same for him.

The sunlight played in the clouds above us, painting the sky amber and violet. We walked hand-in-hand along the pathway until we reached the second tee. Then Rich turned toward me and drew me into a hug. The top of my head fit perfectly under his chin. I looked out at the trees with their brown leaves still hanging on and, just above them, a gilded sun and rosy clouds.

Rich sighed. "I love you, Suzanne," and took a step back. "I love spending time with you." He reached into his jacket pocket. "I want to spend the rest of my life with you." He took out a small box and opened it. "Will you marry me?"

I couldn't believe this was happening. "Am I dreaming?" I asked aloud. I looked down to see a stunning, brilliant marquise diamond. "Yes!" I wrapped my arms around Rich's neck, and he lifted me off the ground in embrace.

We were married in April, in the church where we had met, on the day before Easter precisely one year after we had first held hands. I wore my mother's wedding dress. Serena, Carol, Jill, and Tamera were at my side in pink satin dresses with puffy sleeves. My mother and I spent precious hours in her sewing room, cutting the fabric and stitching those dresses together.

And C.C. sang a song I had written, based on a verse that Rich had quoted to me, Song of Solomon 4:9, along with one of my favorite passages from Romans 12:

> *You stole my heart with one glance of your eyes*
> *I fell in love with you.*
> *Standing here now in the presence of Christ*
> *I pledge my life to you.*

We join our hands today
We join our hearts today
We join our lives today
We are one.

We present ourselves as a living sacrifice
Make us holy and acceptable to You
We present ourselves as a living sacrifice
Make us holy and acceptable to You.

We give our hands today
We give our hearts today
We give our lives today
We are Yours.

We present ourselves as a living sacrifice
Make us holy and acceptable to You
We present ourselves as a living sacrifice
Make us holy and acceptable to You.

CHAPTER 50

LEADING
WORSHIP

I am putting the finishing touches on my eyelashes with mascara when Rich calls to me from the kitchen.

"Are you about ready?"

"Yes, just let me brush my teeth."

I take a final look in the mirror after spitting in the sink and brush my bangs to one side with my fingers. I glance at my watch. It's 7:45. Time to drive to church.

Rich is waiting for me in his jeans and a wrinkled flannel shirt that he threw on when he got out of bed this morning. I am wearing my gray wool dress slacks and a nice black sweater with a floral scarf and my pearl earrings.

Let me explain. I have to be at the church an hour early to practice with the worship team. He is driving me to church so he can walk me in, and then he will come home to shower and get properly dressed while we practice.

He helps me on with my coat. "Do you have everything you need?" he asks.

"I just need to grab that stack of music on the dryer."

"I got it."

I walk down the ramp in our garage and around the car to the passenger side. I have to steady myself against the back of the car, and as I touch it my fingers leave a mark in the dust. I try not to let my coat brush against it as I pull open the door and get in. My legs rest against the running board as I turn to sit, and I know the back of my pant legs will have a line of dust on them. I pull my legs into the car and try to brush it off with my hands. Rich appears at his side of the car and climbs in, handing me the sheet music. "Thanks."

As we back out of the garage, the car begins to "ding" at me because I am not fast enough at buckling my seatbelt. "I hear you! I hear you!" I talk back to it as I fumble with the buckle.

We stop at the stoplight in town, and I am sorting through the music, trying to organize a pack for each of the four people on our worship team: the drummer, the bass player, the singer, and myself.

Rich is talking to me about the basketball game he watched last night, but I am not really listening. I am staring at the sheet music in my hands. I can't remember how the intro to this song goes. I am trying to hear it in my head and to picture how I would finger it on the keys.

As we turn onto the rural road heading out of town, we catch a glimpse of the Adirondacks across the lake. The morning sun is shining on them, and last night's snow has decorated every peak with powdered sugar. We drive past the mobile home park and the farm store, and then the road opens up to the fields. Little stubs that were once stalks of corn poke through the snow like Rich's whiskery face. Across the fence ten or twelve beef cattle bend their noses down into the snow, and a little calf snuggles up to its mama's hind leg. The road narrows as we cross Dead Creek, and Rich's voice breaks through my foggy mind: ". . . starting to ice over again."

I gaze longingly at the flat gray surface, remembering summer days of kayaking among those cattails, which now stand defiantly with their roots frozen into place.

Rich pulls into the driveway of our little country church and slows to a stop. "Wait here, and I'll shovel you a path." I sit tight as his boots make footprints in the half-inch of snow that covers the walkway and the ramp to the back door. He disappears into the building and comes out a moment later with the snow shovel. Setting it down in front of him like a plow, he pushes it along, creating a perfect path for his own feet as he strides easily to my car door, then leans the shovel against the car and opens my door.

"M' Lady." He offers me his hand.

I set the stack of sheet music on the dashboard and try to get out of the car without getting grime on the back of my pant legs again, but I cannot avoid it. I stand and hold onto the car door while Rich brushes off my calves. I grab my cane from its place next to my seat and hand Rich the stack of sheet music. "Carry my books?" With one hand holding my cane and the other tucked into his elbow, we walk the fresh path to the door. There's a slight catch in my bad knee, but so far it's holding me up.

I bang my shoe against the outside wall of the church, just outside the door, to knock the snow out of the treads. These are not my favorite shoes. Black running shoes are not really my personal style, but they are the practical choice for fitting over my leg braces and walking in snow. I'd much rather be wearing fashionable patent leather heels. When I bought these they had white tags on the tongues and white stripes around the upper soles. But in order to make them a little less conspicuous I have colored in the white places with a black permanent marker.

Rich leaves me standing on the rug just inside the door. "Are you okay from here?" He hands me the stack of music.

"I think so. Thank you."

I wipe my feet thoroughly on the rug before stepping timidly onto the wood floor to be sure it won't be slippery.

"Want me to walk you to the piano?"

"No, I'm good." I venture forward.

The door closes behind me.

I walk past the nursery where my own babies toddled twenty years ago, among the plastic toy stove and the big cardboard bricks. I walk past the bulletin board on the wall of the fellowship hall, where Corinne recently stapled white paper snowflakes over red wrapping paper, with construction paper letters spelling out the verse from Isaiah 1:18: *"Though your sins be as scarlet, they shall be as white as snow" (KJV)*. I walk past the kitchen, where I have stood at the sink washing countless dishes as I listen to a sister in Christ talk about the struggles in her marriage. And then I walk into the sanctuary, where Travis's booming voice greets me. "Hey, piano lady! How's Suzanne?" He sets down his bass and reaches over to wrap me in a bear hug.

"Good! How are you?"

His toddler daughter looks up from the papers she is "sorting" on the front pew and gives me a surprised smile.

"Hi, Princess!"

She patters over to me as I sit down on the piano bench and spreads out her arms to hug me around the waist. I kiss the top of her wispy blonde head, and she turns around, leaning her back against my knees. "Heavy," she says. I get it. She wants me to lift her onto my lap. I happily comply, and as soon as she is seated her fingers reach for the keys. She uses just her index fingers with both hands and pounds out a steady tempo.

"How is your beautiful wife and new son?" I ask Travis as the strange melody continues.

"Sleeping at the moment, hopefully!" he laughs.

The front door of the sanctuary opens and more members of our team trickle in, peeling off gloves and hats. Here is Jon, our drummer, who is a student at the Bible college just over the bridge in New York; and Kelsie, also a student there, whose assignment for this hour is to play with the precious little person on my lap. Here is Tia, similar in age to me, who so easily sings harmony to match my lead vocals; and her husband, Al, who strolls right over to his place at the soundboard with his hands in his pockets, looking over the knobs and wires as though they are pupils in his classroom. Little Princess squirms down and bounds toward Kelsie, who wraps her in a hug as we all exchange happy greetings. The two of them shuffle off together toward the nursery.

It takes us a while to get our act together. I plunk out notes for Travis to tune his bass strings, while Jon sits down at the electronic drum set and fiddles with the wires as he taps with his drumsticks.

"Did you have a snowy drive over?" I ask.

"It wasn't too bad," he smiles. "Actually, it was beautiful on the trees and stuff."

I lean over the piano to hand out the packets of sheet music as Tia sets her music stand in place. She and Travis are chatting about newborn babies, and I hate to interrupt, but we've got to get started.

"Travis, could you pray?"

"Sure." We all bow our heads as Travis begins: *"Father, thank You that we can come and praise You this morning. Would You help us as we practice and as we lead the congregation in worship today. Would You help us to worship you in spirit and in truth . . ."* (My mind wanders during this part of the prayer; I am wondering whether I remembered to add the third verse of one of our songs to the lyrics slides the congregation will be seeing on the screen.) *"In the mighty name of King Jesus we pray, Amen."*

"Okay, let's start with 'Holy Holy Holy.'"

"What's the order?" Jon asks.

"Oh, um, 'Holy Holy Holy,' then 'How Great Is Our God.'" He shuffles his stack of music while I pause to let him get them in order. "Then 'Lord, I Need You,' and then 'Before the Throne.' I'll do the closing song after the sermon on my own."

"Okay."

I start playing around with a *D* chord. "Everybody ready?"

As we begin Al plays with the knobs at the soundboard and flips through the slides of lyrics on the screen. We pause a few times to ask him to adjust what we are hearing. "Could I have a little more bass in this monitor? Jon, are you hearing your drums okay?"

At the end of the second song, Tia asks us to repeat a verse. "I'm just not sure my harmonies worked in that one spot."

"Sure. Let's pick up at verse two." I give a starting chord and count off, "two, three, four." We all start playing, and this time Tia looks over at me when it gets to the line she was worried about. Her harmony sounds beautiful.

"Okay. Yeah, I sang it differently that time. That will work."
We stop in the middle of the song and go to the next one. I start
the introduction. This is the one I couldn't remember in the car.
It's just simple quarter note chords, with a subdominant chord
on the third beat, while the bass note stays on the tonic.

Travis stops me midway through the verse. "Can you play
that third line? The bass note I'm playing sounds off."

"Sure. Are you talking about the B minor chord there?"

"Yeah. Oh, that's it. I was playing a B flat—Haha!" He plucks
the correct note repeatedly, as though marking it in his mind.

"Easy mistake. Let's pick it up from verse 2." I start those
quarter note chords again.

About ten minutes before the Sunday school hour other
people start to wander in. Eric comes in and meanders over
to the thermostat on the wall. A six-year old girl skips into
the church, followed by her grandmother carrying her baby
brother. They set a diaper bag in one of the front pews, and the
girl runs out to the nursery. A teenage girl comes in behind her
father and goes straight to the Keurig coffee maker, which is set
up on a table along the back wall. Her father gives us a nod as
he walks through the sanctuary to the fellowship hall where the
adults meet for their class.

"Is that last song in three-quarter time?" Jon asks. "Did that
drum pattern fit well, do you think?"

"Yeah, it was perfect!" I assure him. "Had you not ever
played that one before?" I look at him in disbelief.

"No, that's a new one to me."

"I would never have guessed that. You even dropped out at
the right time and came back in with a fill!"

"Well, that's how worship songs go," he chuckles as he stands up from the drum kit.

More people start coming in, including my husband, who is now clean shaven and sporting a crisp button-up shirt with his khakis. He saunters up to the piano carrying his Bible.

"You staying in here?"

I nod. Tia, Al, and Travis wander off to chat with people, and Rich joins the other adults as they migrate into the fellowship hall. There is laughter, the sound of chairs moving against the old wood floor, and muffled conversations: "Did you see the game last night?" "Hey, how's that new baby?" The old six-paneled, white-painted door between the sanctuary and the fellowship hall is pulled closed with a thud, and I am left alone at the piano. I sit back and breathe deeply.

The piano faces away from the sidewall of the sanctuary, close enough that I can lean my back against the wall if I scoot back on the bench. At this angle most of the congregation cannot see how awkward my hands look while I am playing, and I have a perfect view of the rest of the team and of the whole sanctuary. I look out at the empty old wooden pews that will soon be filled with worshipers. I glance up at the sunlight streaming in through the stained-glass windows. My eyes follow along the decorative crown molding to the front of the room, where the plain wooden cross hangs solemnly above the pulpit. I lean my elbows against the music rack above the keys and rest my chin in my hands. This is a golden hour.

I used to attend the adult class, which is going on now, and where my husband is probably sitting with his Bible open on the table in front of him. But I found I couldn't concentrate with all of those chords and lyrics rolling around in my head, and I was always worried about making it back to the piano in time to get settled in before the prelude. Indeed, I often got caught in a friendly conversation with someone and then realized that getting through a crowded doorway and across the front of the sanctuary in a timely fashion with my cane and lack of balance would be frustrating. By the time I started playing I would be rattled. Then one week, after a hectic rehearsal, I decided to stay at the piano and collect myself instead of going into the adult class. It was glorious. I was sold.

I rise from the bench, grab my cane, and walk back to the coffee table to brew myself a cup of tea. I am thankful someone has put lids out for the cups so that I won't slosh it as I limp back to the piano with my cane in one hand and the hot cup in the other. Setting it down on the piano, I settle back onto the bench and pull my coat around my shoulders.

"Lord, this is Your church. We are Your people. Help us to worship You today. Help my fingers to play the right notes. Help Travis and Jon to play well. Help Tia and me to sing well. Help the lyrics on the screen to all work smoothly. Bless Eric as he preaches. Bless the Sunday school teachers as they teach. Lord, help us all to learn more about You and grow closer to You."

I flip through the music in my black binder on the piano and choose a song to play for the prelude. I put all my music in order in my binder, and as I clip the metal rings closed the sound echoes through the empty sanctuary. I take a long sip of tea and look over each song. *Will I remember to go right to the chorus after the bridge?*

At about 10:15 people start coming in. Sweet Joann pushes open the door. She is in her eighties but still comes to collect the trash at the church every Wednesday. She gives me a high-pitched "Good Morning!" and I raise my cup of tea as though toasting her. In walks Barb, who has been coming to this church all seventy years of her life. She can tell you how she used to roller skate in the fellowship hall as a kid. She sits down in the pew behind Joann, and the two of them start to chat about the snow.

Travis's wife, Kiersten, comes in with her new baby boy in a carrier, covered with a blanket, and the ladies jump up to see this new treasure. Kiersten sets the carrier on a pew and lifts him out, flipping back her beautiful, long blonde hair to rest him on her shoulder.

More people come in. A new family that I don't recognize walks in timidly and fills one of the pews quietly with their four children. The adult class starts coming through the door from the fellowship hall, and I notice Eric walking right up to the new family and shaking hands. "Hey, I'm glad you're here!"

It's 10:25, so I need to start playing something. My fingers start finding the tune of "Blessed Assurance." The chords are underneath the melody line, my left hand doing its best to bring out the bass notes. It doesn't always have the strength to do what my mind tells it to do, but it is trying. My right pinky articulates the melody as the rest of my fingers fill in arpeggios and full chords, as the mood suggests. *"This is my story, this is my song, praising my Savior all the day long . . ."*

Travis straps on his bass and Jon sits down at the drum kit. Tia is still chatting with someone near the front pew, but she ends the conversation quickly when Travis speaks into his microphone: "Good morning! Stand with me as we worship the Lord!"

I begin the intro to "Holy, Holy, Holy," and everyone joins Tia and me as we sing out. The first verse of the first song is always a little weak, as people are still finding their seats and settling down, but by the second verse the sound is full and majestic. As we come to the end of the first song I try to segue into the second without much pause. Tia starts singing, and the congregation joins right in. They know this one really well. I can pick out individual voices from the pews, and there is a tug at my heart to think of the lives they represent. Kiersten's strong alto comes through, and I know she is praising God with that new baby in her arms. A familiar soprano fills the air with a high descant, and I think of her grief over losing her mother to cancer. A deep bass voice resonates through the crowd, and I recognize it as the father of a young man in a wheelchair.

We slow down reverently through the final lyrics, and Travis gives a hearty "Amen!" He tells everyone they can be seated while he goes through a few announcements from the bulletin. Then Rich comes forward to take up the offering.

"We have a chance to give back to the Lord as he has blessed us." Rich hands the baskets to the people seated near the aisle in the first pew and begins his slow walk down the middle aisle of the church. I am just having fun with some chords: D major, G major, E minor, A suspended to A major . . . and I peek up to see where Rich is now. He is almost at the last pew, so I work my way back to a D chord as he turns and makes eye contact with me. I arpeggio up the keyboard dramatically to end.

Travis gives us our next instructions: "Please rise for the Doxology." I play a strong *F* major chord to give us our starting note. The congregation sings this one a cappella, and the voices ring out strong with full harmonies.

> *Praise God from whom all blessings flow*
> *Praise Him all creatures here below*
> *Praise Him above, ye heavenly hosts*
> *Praise Father, Son, and Holy Ghost.*
> *A—men.*

We stretch out the "Amen," savoring the harmonies as they bounce off the white metal ceiling and around the plaster walls.

Rich walks forward with the baskets in hand as we sing and prays a short prayer: *"Lord, thank You for blessing us, and please accept these gifts for Your service."*

Travis dismisses the children for junior church, and they start coming out of the woodwork. I begin playing through the first verse of our next song while a dozen or more children tromp out through the door that leads to the fellowship hall. Annette and Corinne are close behind and will be herding them up the stairs to the children's room.

When the door closes behind them, it's my cue to start singing as soon as the right chord comes around again. The congregation joins me, and when we get to the chorus I can see out of the corner of my eye some hands being raised in praise. Some figures start swaying with each rhythmic phrase. As the drums kick in and drive the beat, I can feel the energy in the room. Then, as we bring down the volume for the final song, I can see hands holding onto the pews in front of them as the profound lyrics are sung from deep within healing and grateful souls.

As the last chord rings out, Travis prays into his microphone. *"Lord, we are so grateful for what You have done for us on the cross. That You gave Your life for us and that You stand, risen in glory, for all eternity. You are worthy. You are glorious. You are mighty. And it's in Your name that we worship You this morning. Amen."*

He looks up. "Please take a moment to greet those around you."

I play around with the chords from the final song as people mingle, pausing briefly to give Jon a high five. I have learned that if I play through a verse or two, when the music stops people will usually quiet down and take their seats. It's like musical chairs.

Eric stands up at the pulpit and looks out at the crowd, waiting for everyone to take their seats, and I lean back against the wall to take in his sermon. This will be good. Now I'm ready to listen. He reads a passage from 1 Peter and begins to expound on the price Jesus paid in order to purchase us. He is sincere. He is straightforward. Every once in a while he gets a little emotional when he talks about how much Jesus loves us. This brawny motorcyclist with a tattoo hidden under his dress shirt gets a little choked up sometimes when he preaches about the great sacrifice Jesus made.

When he closes his sermon in prayer, it's time for me to sit up on the piano bench and play our closing song. I've decided this morning to end our service with a worship song I wrote a few years ago. The congregation knows it pretty well, and I sometimes get requests for it. I start to finger the keys as Eric asks the congregation to rise. As soon as I finish the introduction, they sing right out with me.

My faithful Lord
Day after day
You are beside me
My faithful Lord
Night after night
You're watching over me.

My faithful Lord
Sin after sin
You still forgive me
My faithful Lord
Storm after storm
You come and hold my hand.

And when I'm afraid
I climb into your arms and you carry me
Never alone
Safe within your arms.

My faithful Lord
Day after day
You are beside me
My faithful Lord
Night after night
You're watching over me.

And when we're alone
I sing my song to You and You're listening
Longing to be
Looking in Your eyes.

My faithful Lord
Sin after sin
You still forgive me
My faithful Lord
Storm after storm
You come and hold my hand
Come now and hold my hand.

After the service, as I push myself up from the piano bench, Ligia approaches and reaches out to hug me over the piano. "How was your week?" We chat for a bit about her son, who was home for a visit. She flashes her winning smile at me and tells me I look glamorous in my scarf.

I wave to Annette from across the room, knowing that I'll talk to her later in the week. I make my way over to the new family and introduce myself to the mother of the brood. "Hi, I'm Suzanne." I hold out my hand and she takes it. We chat for a bit, and I find out that they have just moved into the area and that her husband has just started working where Rich works. I ask the children their names, and they each shyly answer me, except for the youngest, who is busy trying to get the zipper started on his coat. She answers for him and smiles. We talk about their recent move, and she comments that she is looking for a piano teacher for her older ones. We agree to find each other on Facebook, and as I turn to go I have a feeling we will be good friends.

The sanctuary is starting to clear out now. Rich comes to my side and asks if I am ready to go. I tuck my arm into his elbow, and we make our way around the empty pews, back to the piano to grab my binder. He takes it in his free hand and escorts me through the remaining people to the back door of the church.

As we walk outside, the bright sunlight surprises me, and I want to pause and soak it in. Most of the snow on the pavement has disappeared now. We walk across a few sparse puddles to the car. Rich opens the door for me, and I plop myself into the seat. He opens the back door and sets my music and his Bible on the backseat. Waving to other folks in the parking lot, he comes around to his door, and as he joins me in the car he leans over to kiss me on the cheek.

"Scenic route?" he asks.

I nod.

Just a half mile down the rural road from the church, there is a boat access where you can get a stunning view of the lake and the mountains. We drive in silence down the wet black road to the place where he slowly turns onto the snow-covered drive. The familiar crunch of gravel under the tires greets us as we face the peaceful, shining water. The mountains are pale blue and lavender against the white sky. Rich puts the car in park and takes my hand. We stare out at the beauty together.

I break the silence. "How did you think the music went?"

"It was great." He hums a line of the last song. "It was nice to have that new family today."

"Yes, that was really encouraging."

As we sit and gaze, it strikes me that this new family, this new friend I have made, will know me only as I am now. She will never know the spry person I used to be when I was younger, when I could run down the sidewalk or spring up a staircase. She will know only the malformed hands that just now shook hers and held onto a cane.

Rich reaches over and gently brushes my cheek with the back of his fingers. "I'm so glad you're my wife," he whispers. We sit for a half-minute more, and then he pulls the car around to head toward home.

AFTERWORD

In the three years it has taken me to finish writing my manuscript, secure a publisher, and get this book into your hands, time, like my determined steps, has limped onward. Sunflowers have bloomed, dropped seeds, and withered, and new seedlings have sprouted, bloomed, and dropped seeds again. Piano students have grown taller and learned to play more advanced pieces. Families have joined our church, while some dear friends have moved away.

Lois has graduated from Wheaton College and is now teaching high school choir and theater. In July of 2017 she and Mike were married in a splendorous ceremony with Travis officiating. Mike walked me down the aisle before taking his place at the altar, since Rich would be escorting the bride.

And, of course, the CMT has continued to progress. I use my cane inside my house more often. And at my doctor's suggestion I now own a wheelchair, which I occasionally use if I need to traverse a long distance, such as an airport or a museum, or if I'm going to be in a crowded place where I might get jostled and easily knocked over. The stairs in our home are increasingly more difficult. A lift is inevitable.

But some things have not changed. John is still writing software in downtown Chicago. My husband still walks to work every day. I am still directing the choir, and I am still playing the piano and singing with my worship team most Sundays.

And God is still faithful.

ACKNOWLEDGMENTS

It was my sister, Serena, who first asked me in the early 2000's to share my story at two different collegiate women's conferences, motivating me to organize my thoughts and begin writing them down. Then as my daughter grew into her teenage years and I would share pieces of my past with her and a few best friends around our kitchen table, she would often encourage me, "Mom, you should write a book."

I had only completed the first few chapters when Annette asked me to read from them at a women's retreat. Our guest speaker for the weekend, Abigail Carroll, author of *A Gathering of Larks*, heard my story and encouraged me to keep writing. Since then, Abigail has been a wonderfully supportive resource for the whole publishing process. Additionally, Vermont Christian author Matthew Dickerson has been a valuable reserve of practical advice.

I could not have completed this without my cheerleading squad: Annette, Corinne, Dinny, Joanie, Kiersten, Ligia, and the friend who finally appears in the last chapter, Ellie. God brought her into my life at just the right time. She has proven to be a perfectionist editor, spending late nights reading through my book proposal and kindly suggesting revisions.

Working with Tim Beals and his team at Credo House Publishers has been an absolute delight. I offer my heartfelt thanks to Tim for his expertise and patient replies to my endless novice questions; to Donna Huisjen for her precise editing and truly constructive comments; and to designer Frank Gutbrod for his perceptive ideas and impressive talent.

Finally, the dedication at the front of the book does not suffice to thank my gentle husband for the hours he has spent listening to me read aloud. You have not only provided a solid sounding-board for my story, you are my story. You are the concrete manifestation of the grace and faithfulness of God in my life, and I can't wait to run through the golden streets with you and Jesus, hand in hand.

Made in the USA
Middletown, DE
27 March 2019